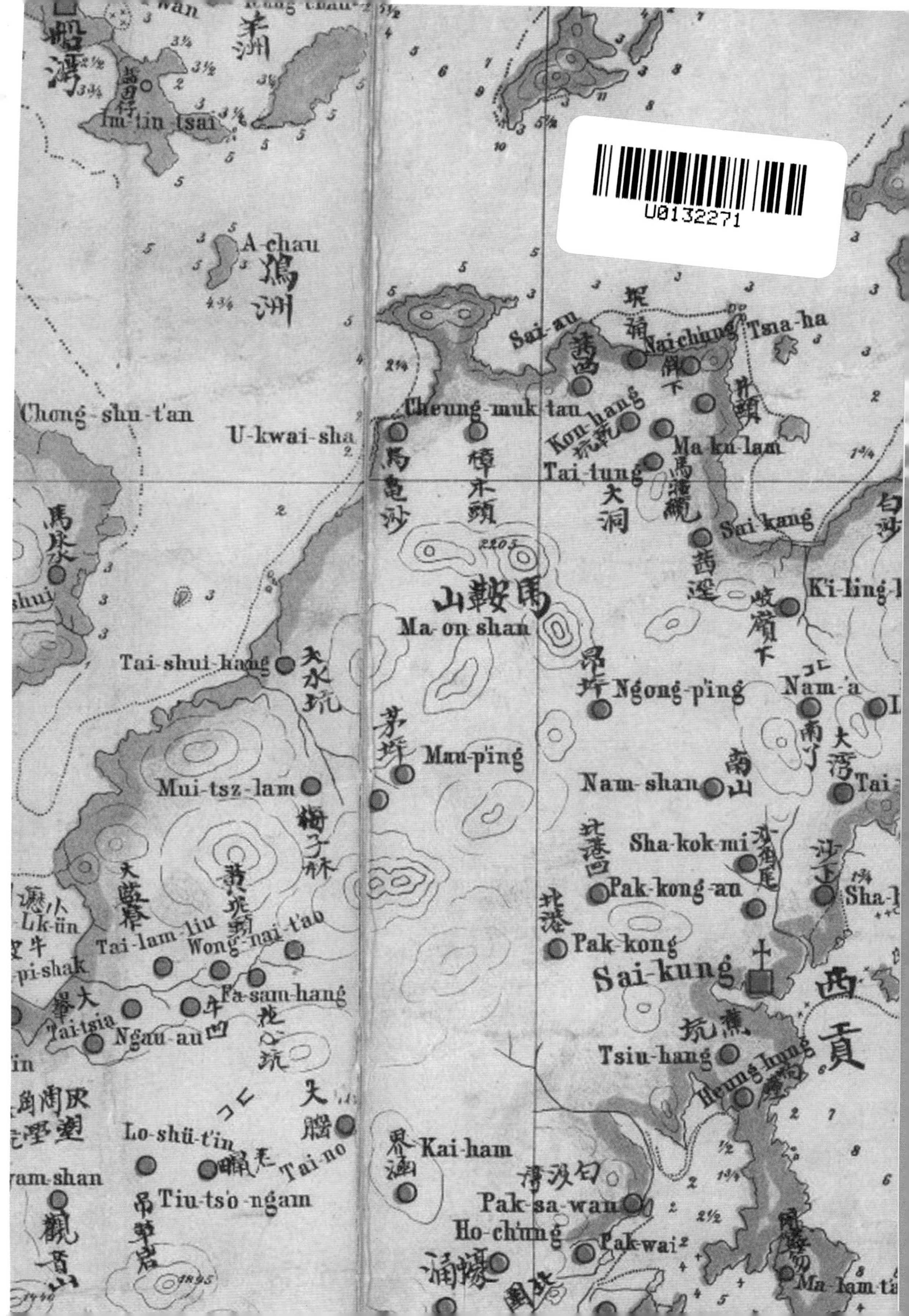

船灣

采洲

Im-tin-tsai

A-chau
鴉洲

Chong-shu-t'an

U-kwai-sha

馬尿
水

Tai-shui-hang
大水坑

Mui-tsz-lam
梅子林

大藍
蓬
Lk-ün

Tai-lam-liu
大
牛
pi-shak

Tai-tsia
Ngau-au
花心坑

Lo-shü-t'in
Tai-no
腦

ram-shan
觀音山
Tiu-ts'o-ngam
吊草岩

Sai-au
西澳

Cheung-muk-tau
馬龜沙
標木頭

昂坪
Mau-p'ing

黄泥涌
Wong-nai-t'au
Fa-sam-hang

Kai-ham
界涵

Pak-sa-wan
白沙灣
Ho-ch'ung
涌㙟

Pakwai

坭
涌
Nai-chung Tsa-ha
井頭

Kon-hang
汗坑
Tai-tung
大洞
Ma-ku-lam
馬過㰥
Sai-kang
白沙
西涇

Ki-ling

西
貢

山鞍馬
Ma-on-shan

2103

Ngong-p'ing
南山
Nam-shan

Nam-a
南丫 大
灣 Tai

北港口
Sha-kok-mi
Pak-kong-au
北港
Pak-kong
沙尾
沙上
Sha-

Sai-kung
西貢

Tsiu-hang
琼薄
Heung-hung
香港

Ma-lam-tai
涌㙟
國

Follow in the Missionary Footsteps

The Evolution of the Catholic Mission in Sai Kung

1841 — 2000

Editor-in-Chief and Translator ✛ YUEN Chi Wai, PhD, LLB

Co-authors ✛ YU Ka Ho, HUI Ka Long Aaron, NGO Tsz Leong

Catholic Diocese of Hong Kong Diocesan Working Committee for "Following Thy Way"

Table of contents

Preface 1

Diocesan Working Committee for "Following Thy Way" ("Following Thy Way"), under the Catholic Diocese of Hong Kong was officially established in January 2018 with the approval of the late Bishop Michael Yeung Ming-cheung. It is mainly responsible for the restoration, conservation and management of the historic chapels of the Hong Kong Diocese on the Sai Kung Peninsula.

Another important mission is to organize and study the missionary history of Catholic Mission in the villages of Sai Kung. Therefore, "Following Thy Way" has specially set up a historical research group, which is responsible for exploring the importance of Sai Kung chapels to the life of remote villages, the establishment of mission stations, and the connection between priests and villagers. "Heritage of Belief and Culture: "Following Thy Way" Historical Research on Catholic Church and Chapels in Sai Kung" led by the group is planned for this purpose. This research has also received sponsorship and support from the "Lord Wilson Heritage Trust", a major heritage conservation organisation in Hong Kong. Although the research work of this project has been postponed due to the COVID-19 epidemic, all project deliverables have been completed according to the revised timetable and targets by the end of 2021. The most important step of this project is to publish a book on the history of Catholicism in Hong Kong. The publication of the book *Follow in the Missionary Footsteps: The Evolution of the Catholic Mission in Sai Kung (1841-2000)* is the major achievement of this project. I am very delighted with this project outcome!

This project needs to organise the history of Catholicism in Sai Kung of more than 150 years. The project coordinator, Dr. Yuen Chi-wai, together with Dr. Lam Suet-pik from the Holy Spirit Seminary College of Theology & Philosophy and Mr. Anthony Yeung Kam-chuen, an expert in ecology and geography, are responsible for editing and supervising the research publication. They have also led a group of young scholars and researchers to read various diocesan documents of more than 100 years, and also visited more than 20 remote villages, over mountains and mountains, to find the routes of the missionaries of the past.

During the research process of more than two years, they sorted out and recorded the local historical events surrounding the chapels, and made monthly reports on historical investigation to the Executive Committee of "Following Thy Way". They were also responsible for liaising with the Antiquities and Monuments Office to carry out historical assessment for grading of the ten chapels together, in order to enhance the significance in historical and architectural merits. The research findings were also promulgated on our Facebook page, for parishioners and Non-catholics to learn more about the relevant information. During the epidemic, everyone could continue on their "virtual pilgrimage" to these chapels, and it was praiseworthy for being able to share this joy while staying at home!

Due to the considerable scale and geographical scope of the research, we were fortunate to have the full support of various diocesan organisations and parishes, including the Catholic Diocesan Archives, the Pontifical Institute for Foreign Missions (PIME) and the Sisters of the Precious Blood, and many brothers and sisters, including Mr. Paul Wong Yee-tin, the former Chairman of the Pastoral Council of the Immaculate Heart of Mary Church in Tai Po, and Mr. Ma Ka-wai, Chairman of the Pastoral Council of the Church of the Sacred Heart in Sai Kung. Both fully supported and helped connect the main informants, who have been the "human library of history" to tell their own stories. In order to let more Hong Kong people understand the deeds of the pioneering missionaries, genuinely an important part of the history of Hong Kong, we also invited and welcomed friends, scholars and villagers from all walks of life to explore together.

The historical research project depends on the support and encouragement of all parties. I wish the research projects of the historical research group could be pursued on this basis and have more fruitful results in future!

Rev. Peter Choy Wai-man
Vicar General, Catholic Diocese of Hong Kong
Chairperson of "Following Thy Way"

Preface 2

The History of Catholic Mission and Chapels in Sai Kung is not only a history of evangelisation in Hong Kong, but also a history of the regional and cultural landscape of the Sai Kung Peninsula. Since the inception of Hong Kong trading port in 1841, and after the British acquisition of the Kowloon Peninsula in 1860, Sai Kung was still under the jurisdiction of San On County under the Qing Dynasty. The missionary work in Sai Kung was actually Catholicism coming to China, which was a page in the history of Catholic Mission in China.

Since the departure from the Diocese of Macau in 1841, Hong Kong became the Prefecture Apostolic and was then upgraded to the Vicariate Apostolic in 1874. The pastoral area stretched from Hong Kong Island and Kowloon Peninsula, which were governed by the British, to San On, which was still under the jurisdiction of the Qing government, Guishan (Huiyang), Hoi Fung and other continental districts. It was not until 1898 that Sai Kung became part of Hong Kong's New Territories--north of Boundary Street and south of Shenzhen River. Due to its geographical location, Sai Kung was a district accessible to San On inland area through Mirs Bay and other places. Sai Kung had essentially become the "Mother's Cradle" of missionaries' evangelisation work. Many missionaries who came to China in those days were sent to Sai Kung for internship training, adaption to the new environment and learning of the local language and culture. Why did missionaries had to travel long distances across the ocean from the West to the East, and even preached the Gospels in remote villages like Sai Kung Peninsula, lived with local villagers, provided education, medical care and other livelihood benefits, and built homes with different local ethnic groups? There was only one reason, and that was to practice what Jesus said to His disciples after His ascension: "Go into all the world and proclaim the good news to the whole creation." (Mark 16:15). Therefore, missionaries, with the spirit of martyrdom, endured the sufferings and hardships, witnessed Christ's benevolence and perseverance, lived out the spirit of Christ, and became "Chinese" for the sake of Chinese.

There are not many scholars who have been studying the history of Catholicism in Sai Kung other than the church historians, in particular Rev. Sergio Ticozzi, Rev. Gianni Criveller, the priests of PIME, and Rev. Louis Ha Keloon of the Hong Kong Diocese. On the basis of their research outcomes, the "Following Thy Way" project team has conducted in-depth research for more than two years from the perspective of Catholics. The team leader, Dr. Yuen Chi-wai, edited and reviewed the first draft of the manuscripts, while two senior members, Dr. Lam Suet-pik and Mr. Anthony Yeung Kam-chuen, were responsible for supervising the research work conducted by young researcher Ivan Yu, writers Aaron Hui and John Ngo, and many other volunteers. The team earnestly collected information, conducted on-the-spot investigations in the mountains and seas, and conducted oral history records. Ms. Portia Lee also planned, organised and edited the "Walking with the Lord Series" to introduce four important chapels through publication of the booklets for free distribution to churches and religious organisations. This book *Following the Missionary Footsteps: The History of Catholic Mission in Sai Kung (1841-2000)* presents the encounter between the local Hakka people and Catholic faith in Sai Kung, as well as the transformation and development of Sai Kung district. While entering the chapels to explore the history with the research group, we admit the history of every chapel and village coincides with our life.

Rev. Deacon Faustus Lam Sair-ling
Conservation Architect

Preface 3

Sai Kung was a bridge between Hong Kong and Po On, Huiyang and other places of Guangdong from the Qing Dynasty to the post-war period. In fact, when the Catholic Mission was founded in Hong Kong during 1841, missionaries in the Central District mainly served missionaries in and out of the mainland and local Westerners. Nevertheless they wished to preach to the mainland, so they set off to Sai Kung, such as Yim Tin Tsai, for the first time by boat. At that time, Sai Kung was still under the jurisdiction of San On County of the Qing Dynasty, so it could be regarded as the first training place for Western missionaries at the onset of exposure to Oriental culture. They could also take boats via Sai Kung to San On County villages along the coast of Mirs Bay and continental districts.

Dr. Yuen Chi-wai, project coordinator and editor-in-chief of this book *Follow in the Missionary Footsteps: The Evolution of the Catholic Mission in Sai Kung (1841-2000)*, has been engaged in the research of lineages in the New Territories of Hong Kong for many years, especially the Hakka people in the border areas and major clans in the North-eastern part of the New Territories. When I served as a reviewer for his doctoral dissertation more than ten years ago, he took the Lin Ma Hang, a Hakka village as his research point of view on the border between Mainland China and Hong Kong, reflecting his desire to gradually shift the research perspective of Hong Kong history to the area that has always been ignored by scholars. In frontier history, he later published his doctoral dissertation as *A Hundred Years of Changes in the China-Hong Kong Boundary: Starting from Lin Ma Hang Village, Sha Tau Kok*, and then other publications on the China-Hong Kong border including *Entry Prohibition: History of Hong Kong Frontier Closed Areas and Restricted Areas: The Sha Tau Kok in the Gap*. After him, well-known Hong Kong historians have also developed a strong academic interest in the compilation of local chronicles in the border areas. In this regard, Dr. Yuen has made a great contribution to the establishment of a new perspective for the Hong Kong historians.

Sai Kung was a particularly densely populated area of Catholic villages, including Pak Sha O, Tai Long, and Chek Keng. There were Catholic missionaries in the villages as early as the 19th century, and chapels were built here. However, local scholars had little research on Sai Kung in the past and have rarely touched on the assistance and contribution of Catholicism to the life of the villagers in this area. For example, priests, sisters and the Catholic Social Welfare Bureau have made great achievements in social services in the Sai Kung Market and fishermen communities after the war. The Catholic communities in St. Peter's Village, Ming Shun Village and Tai Ping Village reflected the importance of the church's development in Sai Kung District. The connection between the Hakka villages in Sai Kung was not only the lineage organisations in South China focusing on the ancestral halls, but to a certain extent, they were organised by religious groups, such as those in Pak Sha O and Tai Long, as well as the Luk Yeuk and Shap Sze Heung, etc. In the past, scholars rarely studied the Sai Kung sub-districts of Tung Hoi District, such as Pak Tam Chung, Long Ke, and Wong Mo Ying. Different from the past research institutes that studied the history of Catholicism in Hong Kong in the 20th century from the perspective of the whole Hong Kong, and often less involved in the operation of faith groups in rural areas, this study, led by Dr. Yuen and supervised by other members of the "Following Thy Way" research group, focused on exploring in detail the connection between the Catholic Church and the countryside so that the gaps in the history of Sai Kung could be filled.

I wish that the historical research on Catholic History in Hong Kong can be further promoted by the scholars of the new generation in historical studies with more full-fledged support from the veteran professors and researchers. This could certainly render more comprehensive studies of Hong Kong history!

Frederick Cheung Hok-ming, PhD
Adjunct Associate Professor of Chinese University of Hong Kong and
Senior College Tutor of New Asia College

Introduction

Missionaries as a Medium of Cultural Exchange Between the East and the West

2021 was the 180th anniversary of the Hong Kong Catholic Mission. On 22 April 1841, the Roman Catholic Church established the Apostolic Prefecture of Hong Kong to shepherd the Irish soldiers of the British Army during the First Opium War.[1] Rev. Theodorus Joset was the first Pontifical Pastor. The Catholic Church began preaching in the Sai Kung area of San On County as early as in the 1860s during the Qing Dynasty. On 17 November 1874, the Apostolic Prefecture of Hong Kong was upgraded to Apostolic Vicariate of Hong Kong.[2] After this establishment, the founding of the Sacred Heart Church in Sai Kung Market in 1880 manifested the importance of the Sai Kung district in the development of Catholicism in Hong Kong. In 1890, St. Joseph's Chapel in Yim Tin Tsai was founded, followed by more than a dozen rural chapels built in other villages, such as Kei Ling Ha, Che Ha and even the easternmost Long Ke in the early 20th century. However, the Catholic mission stations established in Ting Kok, Ho Chung and Sha Kok Mei were obstructed by local people and had fewer congregants than in areas such as Pak Sha O, Tai Long and Chek Keng. In 1930s, the independent Tai Long District was established, and a new community different from the traditional rural society was adopted with the church as the centre of village life.

On 11 April 1946, the Holy See upgraded Hong Kong Catholic Mission from

---

1   An Apostolic Prefecture is generally the first step toward organisation of a church hierarchy in a determined territory. It is ordinarily headed by a priest, the Prefect Apostolic, a representative from Rome appointed simply by the decree of the Sacred Congregation of Propaganda Fide. See Hong Kong Catholic Diocesan Archives, "The Succession Line", https://www.archives1841.hk/Succession%20Line/SL-Index.htm, retrieved on 27 February 2022.

2   An Apostolic Vicariate is a local church governed by the Pope through the actual direction of the central missionary agency in Rome, the Sacred Congregation of Propaganda Fide, which assigned a titular bishop with apostolic letters to govern the vicariate. See Ibid.

Apostolic Vicariate of Hong Kong to Diocese of Hong Kong under the Episcopal Hierarchy.[3] Rev. Enrico Valtorta (PIME, 1883-1951) was appointed as the first Bishop of the Diocese of Hong Kong. In November 1949, he went to Sai Wan Village located at Tai Long Wan to serve the Introductory Sacrament for the first group of catechumens after the Second World War. Teachers and students of the Yuk Ying School in Tai Long Village also came to greet the Bishop under very lively atmosphere. Especially after the war, the Western missionaries changed the preaching methodology in the rural communities of Sai Kung. They no longer relied only on setting up mission stations to spread the gospel, but embraced the perspectives of Chinese in culture, language and customs when introducing this Western belief to the people, particularly those underprivileged and neglected ethnicities such as the boat people.

Further to the above general history, the Following Thy Way Historical Research Group would like to present the Catholic Mission of Sai Kung from a bottom-up historical perspective. As the beginning in the narration of this important part in the history of Hong Kong, the first chapter of this book briefly describes the history, people and ambit of Sai Kung before and after the British lease of the New Territories in 1898, including the settlement of mainly Hakka people in villages scattered over the Sai Kung Peninsula and their contribution to the development of Sai Kung market. This chapter will also illuminate the preaching journey of the missionaries in the remote and mountainous areas of Sai Kung.

Chapter 2 focuses on the early days of missionary work of the church. The first missionary from Milan Institute for the Foreign Missions (MEM) arrived in Hong Kong in 1858, whose footsteps were followed in by Rev. Simeone Volonteri (MEM, 1831-1904) and Rev. Andreas Leong Chi-hing (1837-1920) debuting their pastoral visits to Sai Kung. The chapter also reviews the missionary activities of Pontifical Institute for Foreign Missions (PIME, the then MEM) in Sai Kung by Rev. Richard Brooks and Rev. Emilio Teruzzi, also the Chinese priest Rev. Rectus Kwok King-wan, Rev. Francis Wong Chi-him and other clergys.

---

3   A Diocese is an ordinary territorial division of the church headed by a bishop, who governs it in his
    own name. The bishop, though he is subject to the Roman Pontiff, is not the vicar of the latter. A
    Diocese ordinarily takes its name from the see city, the community where the bishop resides, and his
    cathedral is located. See ibid.

Chapter 3 reviews the Catholic Mission in the Sai Kung Peninsula from the establishment of Apostolic Vicariate to the founding of Tai Long District. Most of the historic chapels in the area were built after the Vicariate's establishment in 1874. During this period, Sai Kung Catholic Mission, including Yim Tin Tsai St. Joseph's Chapel, Chek Keng Holy Family Chapel and Pak Sha O Immaculate Heart of Mary Chapel had become the internship training sites for Catholic missionaries. Before they started off their services, they had to first learn Hakka language and understand the Chinese customs, such as *feng shui* and popular beliefs. In particular, the Italian Rev. Emilio Teruzzi of PIME was still learning Chinese when he first came to Sai Kung in 1912, but soon he had to take over the Lung Shun Wan Chapel built in 1910 and dozens of chapels from the senior Rev. Angelo Ferrario.

Chapter 4 will be a retrospect of the martyrdom of missionaries and the establishment of Tai Long District. In 1931 when Tai Long became an independent mission district, and people living in Tai Long, Chek Keng and Pak Sha O had all converted to Catholicism along with the establishment of many chapels in rural Sai Kung, signifying the golden age of evangelism. However, the suffers faced by the clergy and murder of priests during the Japanese Occupation represents the "dark age" in the Sai Kung missionary history. Among them, Rev. Rectus Kwok was killed by gangsters when he was the acting director of the Sacred Heart Church in Sai Kung market from 1941 to 1942, and soon after, Rev. Francis Wong was also killed by gangsters while serving in Tai Long District. In 1942, Rev. Emilio Teruzzi was abducted by unknown armed soldiers during his mission in Tai Tung, the west of Three Fathoms Cove (Kei Ling Ha Hoi). He was carried in a sampan to Sham Chung offshore and got killed in the sea. The murder has remained as a mystery with identity and motive of the perpetuators yet to reveal. On the other hand, the guerrilla East River Column had once set up its headquarters with the use of the deserted Holy Family Chapel in Chek Keng during the war while the Hong Kong and Kowloon Battalion was also established earlier at the Wong Mo Ying Rosary Chapel in Sai Kung to fight against the Japanese army. They had successfully rescued and assisted many cultural celebrities to flee persecution.

Chapter 5 retraces the rebuilding of Sai Kung Catholic Mission in the aftermath of the Second World War. Although many priests returned to their villages to serve Masses, the church parishioners had been dropping continuously due to emigration overseas or resettled in the urbans. With the abandonment of the villages by the indigenous people, some of these chapels had been also dilapidated. Fortunately, some others were developed to serve other social purposes under the management of charitable organisations under the changing contexts with the consent of the Church. Regarding the way of evangelistic work and in view of the lack of resources after the war, daily necessities such as blankets, milk and bread were often brought along with the missionaries for the villagers, either taking boats to the coastal villages or strenuously walking up the hill to reach the sparsely populated Catholic villages. Their deep concerns about the needs of the villagers helped fortify much closer relationship or networks between the Church and the indigenous people. The Church had also established or expanded several primary schools in Sham Chung, Tan Ka Wan and Sha Tsui to provide elementary education for the children of both Catholics and pagans. These social services have reunited the church members under the same charitable cause in Sai Kung District and solicited the recognition from the town people or rural communities in general.

The church entered into the renewal cum localisation period since the late 1960s. Chapter 6 describes that, despite of the abandonment of many remote chapels, this period witnessed the Catholic Church's active interaction with Sai Kung villagers. In addition to preaching, missionaries provided charity and social services. Among other priests, Rev. Adelio Lambertoni and Rev. Valeriano Fraccaro focused especially on the less affluent ethnic groups surrounding Sai Kung Market. With the financial assistance of the National Catholic Welfare Conference (NCWC), USA, the two priests overseeing a charitable project aiming at provision of residential houses for the fishermen immersed in poor living conditions and relocation of the floating population from the shore to the land premises.

Chapter 7 begins with the celebration of the centenary of the Sacred Heart Church in Sai Kung in 1981. Despite priests from the Immaculate Heart of Mary Church, Tai Po had celebrated special Masses in several historic chapels in the Sai Kung Peninsula seasonally, like Lunar New Year, most of the chapels had been deserted for many years. Not till the end of the 1990s had enthusiastic church members, villagers and priests started to adapt the former sacred places for pilgrimages and spiritual gatherings. The restoration of Yim Tin Tsai St. Joseph's Chapel in the millennium aroused the interest of Catholics to be pilgrims to these historic chapels once again. Parishes began to organise tours for pilgrimages to follow in the footprints of the pioneering missionaries in the old rural Sai Kung.

The "Following Thy Way" Historical Research Group had not only spent more than two years in reading through the century-old archival documents of the related parishes and the government, but also tramping around the mountains to visit more than 20 villages in the Sai Kung Peninsula to trace the footprints of the missionaries. "Following Thy Way" aims to explore why the Catholic Church designated Sai Kung as the base to preach in Hong Kong. We hope the readers, both Catholics and non-Catholics, can know more about the history of Catholic missions in rural Hong Kong and how Catholicism had exerted influence in the development of Sai Kung as it is rarely discussed in the Hong Kong historical publications. Along with over one hundred meticulously selected precious photos, we hope to depict the routes the missionaries had taken during foundation of Catholic Mission in Sai Kung rural area with a view to probe into how they acted as a medium in cultural exchanges between the East and the West, especially the way these missionaries preached while meshing with traditional Chinese social structure, architecture, customs, and culture. This book adopts the perspective of historical anthropology instead of religious studies in examining the development and evolution of Hong Kong Catholicism in Sai Kung since the establishment of the Apostolic Prefecture in 1841. It focuses not only on the Catholic rituals or the belief itself, but also how Catholicism was practiced under the trend of localisation and the organic change of the lives of the followers in conjunction with their faith and relationship with the missionaries. The co-authors took a "History from Below" approach to study the perspectives of the Catholics towards the missionary work, instead of mere knowledge acquisition of the missionary activities. With a macro perspective in presenting Catholic development in Sai Kung since the inception of Hong Kong, the authors hope to heighten the authenticity and historical significance of Catholicism in Hong Kong. Owing to tight time constraints and limited capability, we admit that there will be inevitable omissions in the book. I sincerely hope that people from all walks of life will not hesitate to point them out and provide valuable advice. I also hope that this book is only a start, and a broader spectrum of books on Hong Kong Catholic history will be published successively.

In this book, we have adopted the traditional way of naming places and peoples according to their local Chinese dialects (Cantonese, Hakka or Hoklo). Therefore, the Romanisation is compatible with the sources and would be more familiar to most readers. For examples: Sai Kung, not Xigong; Po On, not Bao'an; Hoi Fung, not Haifeng, To Yeung, not Tuyang and so on.

Chinese who have Western names are presented in the following manner: Western first name in its English form, followed by the Chinese family name, in the most commonly established form. For instances, Andrew Leong, not Liang Zijing. Francis Wong, not Huang Ziqian.

Names of Western persons, including the names of PIME missionaries, are always kept in their original language. For example, Lorenzo Bianchi and not Lawrence Bianchi. The names of selected PIME missionaries who had worked continuously in Sai Kung (including Sai Kung North, Tai Po) are given in the appendix of the book together with their Chinese names, generally listed in order of arrival in Hong Kong. Owing to the limited space, some missionaries who just remained in Sai Kung for a short period are left out from list.

Yuen Chi-wai, PhD, LLB
Editor-in-Chief
History of Sai Kung Chapels Series
at the Chinese University of Hong Kong
in Early Autumn 2021

Chapter 1

Traditional Society of Sai Kung and the Encounter with Catholicism

1841

1874

1931

1945

1969

1981

2000

The Sai Kung District nowadays was originally part of San On County during the Qing Dynasty. After the First Opium War, China was forced to sign the unequal "Treaty of Nanking" with the United Kingdom (UK) on 29 August 1842, ceded Hong Kong Island to UK as a colony. Under this historic development, the Roman Catholic Church took the opportunity to formally enter South China, and Hong Kong became an important part of the missionary district in China established by the Holy See at that time, acting as a springboard for missionaries to set foot in Mainland China. Since the coast of Sai Kung was the hub of entry into the inland areas, the beginning process of Catholic missionaries in Sai Kung villages, including the establishment of mission stations and chapels, had become an important venue of demonstration for missionary activities stretching inland. The clergy who used to serve in this area had a very close relationship with the mainland. They toured between the coasts of Sai Kung and the mainland. The customs of social exchanges between the two places became the basis for maintaining an inseparable connection between Sai Kung and the mainland in the future.

The Geographical and Natural Environment of Sai Kung

Sai Kung is located at the southeastern part of the present-day Hong Kong New Territories. It is an administrative division under the jurisdiction of the present-day Hong Kong Special Administrative Region. It covers three administrative areas: Sai Kung, Hang Hau Rural and Tseung Kwan O New Town, with an area of 13,632 hectares, making it the fifth largest administrative region in Hong Kong.[1] There are currently 58 official villages in Sai Kung region, which are bordered by Tai Po in the north, Lei Yue Mun in Victoria Harbour in the south, Kowloon peak in the west, and Mirs Bay in the east.[2] Geographically, it comprises of the central area of Ma On Shan, the Sai Kung Peninsula and the Clear Water Bay Peninsula. Most areas of Sai Kung have been designated as country parks since the 1970s. The country parks now cover Ma On Shan, West Sai Kung, East Sai Kung and Clear Water Bay Peninsula. Therefore, Sai Kung also has the reputation of "back garden of Hong Kong" or "leisure garden of Hong Kong". Sai Kung area is well-known for its cliffy terrain abundant with river valleys, plentry of high mountains which are above 400 meters, and more than 70 various islands.

Sai Kung is relatively remote and inconvenient for transportation. In the past, it was isolated from the urban area, as well as the Kowloon Peninsula by mountains. Residents there mainly used two ancient mountain paths connecting Sha Tin and Kowloon. Before the 1970s, the branch from Hiram's Highway connecting Tai Mong Tsai from Sai Kung Market could only reach Tai Mong Tsai. Until the government started to build the High Island Reservoir and established a road system extending to the reservoir and its catchment tunnel and pumping station, road traffic could eventually reach Pak Tam Chung, but the section of Pak Tam Road between Hoi Ha and Pak Tam Chung was a vehicle-restricted road, and only allowed drivers with a license. On the whole, the main roads in Sai Kung include Clear Water Bay Road, Hiram's Highway, Sai Sha Road, Tai Mong Tsai Road, Pak Tam Road, Hoi Ha Road, etc. In addition, there are motor roads connecting the east and west dams on the north and south sides of High Island Reservoir. However, Sai Kung Man Yee Road is a vehicle-restricted road, under the jurisdiction of the Water Supplies Department, and non-local residents are not permitted to use the road directly.

History of Sai Kung

According to modern archaeological excavations, there are ancient traces of human activities in Sai Kung. For example, there are ancient depicting the image of a dragon stone carvings on Tung Lung Island, which are believed to be totems left by fishing people. Archaeological experts inferred that it may have a history of more than 3,000 years. Wong Tei Tung, located between Sham Chung and Yung Shue O villages, found a workshop where ancient humans made stone tools in the Paleolithic Age.[3] Cultural relics from the Eastern Han Dynasty were also unearthed in Kau Sai Chau in Sai Kung, whereas cultural relics including stone axes and pottery pieces were also unearthed in Tai Long Wan. There is a Song Dynasty stone carving near the Tin Hau Temple at the Fat Tong Mun to commemorate the salt official who visited the salt field at that time. Therefore, it is generally believed that the history of human settlement in the area can be traced back to the Song Dynasty (960-1279). In addition, in the 1970s, people discovered the remains of ancient shipwrecks, Ming Dynasty ceramics and Western glass beads in Sha Tsui, Sai Kung. In 2016, the Hong Kong Underwater Cultural Heritage Group discovered Song Dynasty shipwrecks in Leung Shuen Wan, Sai Kung, and two 18th century cannons and blue-and-white porcelain pieces in Town Island (also named as Fo Tau Fan Chau). These findings all reflected that Sai Kung was once an important transit point or supply post for ancient maritime trade.[4]

Checking out the coastal map of Guangdong in the "Grand record of Guangdong" (*Yue daji*) written by Guo Fei in the Ming Dynasty, the ancient villages and topography of Sai Kung was listed, including Lung Shuen Wan (literally means "Dragon Boat Bay", recently named Leung Shuen Wan), Kao Tong Village, Nam She Tsim, Kun Mun, Yung Shue O, Sha Kok Mei, Ho Chung, She Wan, etc.[5] During the Wanli period of the Ming Dynasty, Lung Shuen Wan became a military land. By mid 18th century, the area developed into a small port. Merchants began to open

The ancient villages of Sai Kung seen in the coastal map of Guangdong written by Guo Fei.
(Image source: *Grand Record of Guangdong*)

shops, trade with the fishing communities, and built the Tin Hau Temple in the early Qianlong period. Since the Ming Dynasty, Lung Shuen Wan has belonged to one of the six naval bases in Nam Tau Cai, and was an important coastal line of defense against Japanese pirates. According to the "Costal Defense Situation" recorded in the *San On County Chronicles*:

> Stockade of Nam Tau originally governed six places in the military land, namely, Fat Tong Mun, Lung Shuen Wan, Lok Kat, Tai O, Long To Wan, and Long Pak. In the 14th year of the Wanli period of the Ming Dynasty, Governor Wu and Yu Shi Wang recorded: Nam Tau is the "Gateway to Whole Guangdong", control the Japanese pirates, please move the general army to station in town.[6] Thus foreign ships can travel directly to Macau, but from Macau to the (Guangdong) province, the sea is too shallow for sailing. You must go straight from Lantau Island to Hutoumen via Nam Tau to reach the Pearl River. This is why Nam Tau is known as the "Gateway to Whole Guangdong".[7]

It is generally believed that the earliest establishment of a large-scale village in Sai Kung dates back to mid 16th century to late 17th century. At that time, there were at least three villages, including Ho Chung, Pak Kong and Sha Kok Mei.[8] Among them, Ho Chung and Pak Kong had been sold to the Mei Lin Wong clan in San On County. The Wongs family was an important and wealthy clan that owns most of the land in Sai Kung. Although the clan has never lived in Sai Kung, it used Sai Kung as the main source of land income and collected rent from the tenant farmers. Therefore, there was a dispute with tenant farmers in the 19th century.

During the Kangxi period of the Qing Dynasty, Ho Chung had become an independent as a village, and had been harassed by thieves. According to the *San On County Chronicles*:

> In September of the 11th year of the Kangxi period, the Taiwanese traitor Li Qi and others led the boats, looted places, wandered and landed in Ho Chung, and slaughtered the villagers. Li Ke-cheng, the county magistrate, and the guerrillas Cai Chang heard the news, that is, the rural officers and soldiers were gathered together to capture and suppress the traitors. When the traitors saw that the situation was difficult to resist the enemy, they had reached the point of no

return, and then hid into the mountains such as Lek Yuen. The soldiers did everything possible to sack and kill the traitors, and the area was finally free from riots again.

During the Qing Dynasty, Sai Kung was part of San On County, and the county official was located in Nam Tou, Shenzhen. According to the Jiaqing edition of *San On County Chronicles* compiled in 1819, there were about 26 Cantonese walled villages and 21 Hakka villages in Sai Kung at that time.[9] However, due to the mountainous terrain, there were no large villages such as Yuen Long, Tai Po or Sha Tin. In the early 20th century, most villages had a population of less than 100 people. Since the county office was located in Nam Tou, Shenzhen, which was far away from other areas in San On County, county government officials seldom patrol the villages. Therefore, in terms of tax revenue, the taxes were mainly from the large clans of Yuen Long and the north New Territories, such as the Tangs or the Lius and other powerful great clans representing the government to collect them. These great clans had long affected these smaller villages in Sai Kung for a long time. *San On County Chronicles* did not list the Sai Kung Market and Hang Hau Market, but Tai Po Market, Sheung Shui Shek Wu Market, Yuen Long Market and Shenzhen (Sham Chun) Market.

In ancient times, the external traffic of Sai Kung was basically separated from the Kowloon Peninsula. Residents generally relied on two ancient roads to travel back and forth between Shatin and Kowloon. The ancient roads are connected with the aforementioned ancient villages. One of them is from Ho Chung, and then out of Ngau Chi Wan or Kowloon City via the Tai Nam Wu (literally "Big Blue Lake"), Pak Fa Lam (literally "Hundred Flowers Forest") and Pak Kung Au. The second was from Pak Kong to Siu Lek Yuen via Mao Ping, Shek Long Tsai, Mui Tsz Lam, Fa Sum Hang, Wong Nai Tau, and Chap Wai Kon villages. The waterway went by sea, by passing the Clear Water Bay Peninsula, to Hang Hau in Tseung Kwan O as a midway stop, and then to Shau Kei Wan on the eastern coast of Hong Kong Island.

Since the villages in the southern part of the Sai Kung Peninsula were connected to Sai Kung by boats in the early days, therefore Pak Tam Chung, Sha Tsui, Lan Nai Wan, Yim Tin Tsai, Tsam Chuk Wan, Tso Wo Hang, etc., were all included in the jurisdiction of Sai Kung. However, since the villages along the northern part of the Sai Kung Peninsula, Tolo Harbour and the Tolo Strait, such as Sham Chung, Lai Chi Chong, Chek Keng, and even Ko Lau Wan, were mostly connected to the Tai Po Kau

Pier near Tai Po Market by boats, these villages were collectively referred to as "Sai Kung North" after the war and were included in the Tai Po District.[10] Therefore, the chapels in these areas were included in the jurisdiction of the Tai Po parish.

The theme of this book is based on the historical perspective of Catholic missions. Therefore, the Sai Kung district referred to in the book includes the original Sai Kung District (ie Sai Kung Market, Kei Ling Ha, Pak Tam Chung, Wong Mo Ying, Wo Mei and Yim Tin Tsai), Tai Long District and Sai Kung North (the villages on the south shore of Tolo Harbour) and does not include Hang Hau and Clear Water Bay Peninsula which belong to the present administrative region of Sai Kung.

The Population Distribution and Society of Sai Kung

Sai Kung was still a borderland in the 19th century. Most of the Puntis (in Cantonese, means "locals") and Hakkas did not gradually settle in Sai Kung until the 18th century. In such period, many fishing communities had possibly anchored near the Sai Kung Hoi. In the late 17th century, only three villages in San On County were included in the *San On County Chronicles*, including Ho Chung, Sha Kok Mei and Pak Kong where villagers mainly spoke Cantonese or local dialects. They were all located in valleys with abundant water resources in Sai Kung, and close to the footpaths leading to Sha Tin and Kowloon. Among them, the villagers in Sha Kok Mei had more than ten surnames such as Tse, Lau, Wai, Cheung and Tsang.[11]

In addition to the three villages mentioned in the *San On County Chronicles* of the Jiaqing edition of 1819, the villages under Guanfusi's management were also included in Tai Long Village and Pak Tam Village, while the Hakka villages under Guanfusi's management included Tseng Lan Shue, Sheung Yeung, Ma Yau Tong, Tai Lo, Mang Kung Uk, Sha Kok Mei, Pan Long Wan, Lan Nai Wan[12], Ko Tong, Wong Chuk Yeung, Cheung Sheung and Cho Wo Hang, etc. They reflected the trend of Hakkas migrating to San On County from the mid to late Qing Dynasty. They could only occupy some dry land or mountainous land, and mainly engaged in farming. The coastal Hakka people living on the shore would also rely on fishing as a sideline. In fact, the wealthier clans were mainly large clans residing close to the Sai Kung market, such as Ho Chung, Sha Kok Mei or Nam Wai villages. However, in the early 20th century, most of the villages had decreased to less than 100 people.[13]

The 1897 Guangdong Tongzhi (*A General Gazetteer of Guangdong*) also listed many villages, including Hoi Ha, Sheung Yeung, Ha Yeung, Tam Tsai, Pak Sha Au, Nam Shan, Sham Chung, Yung Shue Au, Ping Tun, Pak Tam, Ho Muk Tun, Uk Tau, To Ka Ping, Chek Keng, Tai Lau, Cheung Uk Wai, Tai Long, Chin Hang, Wong Nai Chau, Lan Nai Wan, Lung Kut, Pak A, Shue Wan, Pak Lap, etc.

The Lockhart Report written by the Great Britian during the lease of the New Territories in 1898, pointed out that villages in the New Territories had their own local government. If a person was arrested by the village's security guards, he would be sent to a special place in the village where squires and the elders would execute the punishment. This kind of village authority elected by the villagers to handle cases on behalf of the clan was called "Kuk" (Council in Cantonese). Usually such cases involved theft, land acquisition, family disputes or debts, and they were all handled by the "Kuk" in a simplified manner in accordance with local customs, and the "Kuk"'s decision was the final decision. If a party was dissatisfied with the decision, it could appeal to the "tung", or a larger "Kuk" represented by the "tung". The villages belonging to the Sai Kung District today were all included in the "Sheung U Tung" or "Kau Lung Tung" of the six sub-districts ("tungs"). However, the map of Hong Kong drawn by the British government in 1899 included part of the area originally belonging to Sheung U Tung and Kau Tung, including Sai Kung, Cheung Muk Tau, Ko Tong, Chek Keng, and Pak Lap Chau (Leung Shuen Wan) into the "Tung Hoi Tung".

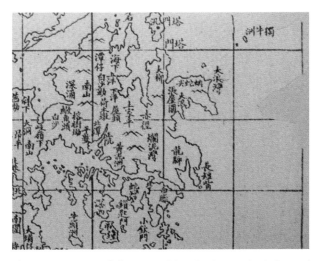

The Sai Kung part of the map of San On County in *A General Gazetteer of Guangdong* in 1897.

The villages, population and ethnic groups of the "Sheung U Tung" and "Kau Lung Tung" in the *Lockhart Report*.

Kau Lung Tung			Sheung U Tung		
Name of Village	Population	Ethnic Group	Name of Village	Population	Ethnic Group
Tai Po Tsai	100	Punti	Tai Wai	250	Punti
Po Toi O	60	Punti	Tap Mun	200	Hakka
Pak Lap	40	Punti	Pak Sha Au	150	Punti
Tai Long	80	Punti	Hoi Ha	50	Hakka
Sai Wan	40	Punti	Uk Tau	20	Hakka
Chik Kang	150	Hakka	Ko Tong	100	Punti
Lan Nai Wan	150	Hakka	Tan Ka Wan	80	Hakka
Wong Nai Chau	60	Hakka	Tai Lau	160	Hakka
Pak Tam Chung	30	Hakka	Im Tin Tsz	120	Hakka
Kau Sai	80	Punti/Hakka	Sai Kung	800	Hakka
Lai Chi Chong	60	Hakka	Tsiu Hang	20	Hakka
Nam Shan	30	Hakka	Heung Chung	20	Hakka
Ham Tin	50	Hakka	Sha Kok Mi	250	Punti
Sham Chung	50	Hakka	Pak Kong	100	Punti
Cheung Muk Tau	40	Punti	Ho Chung	600	Punti

Ethnic Group

Cantonese (also called "Punti" in Cantonese) were believed to have come from the southern provinces of the Yangtze River Basin. Their ancestors had settled in San On County as early as the Southern Song Dynasty, and they occupied on relatively fertile land. However, because the area was mountainous and there was no large plains, it was difficult to form large-scale villages. Most of the villages had fewer than 1,000 people in the early 20th century. In the *Lockhart Report*, the Punti mainly settled in the Ho Chung Valley, Sha Kok Mei and Pak Kong areas. In addition, the villages of Cheung Muk Tau, Wu Kai Sha, Tai Tung, Ma Kwu Lam, and Sai Keng along the "Sai Sha Highway" today also spoke local dialect. They occupied relatively flat river valleys and were mainly engaged in agriculture. They also engaged in commercial trade, shipping or other industries operating overseas. The Punti of Sai Kung included the Cheung clans in Ho Chung, the Lau and Wai clans in Sha Kok Mei, the Cheng and Lok clans in Pak

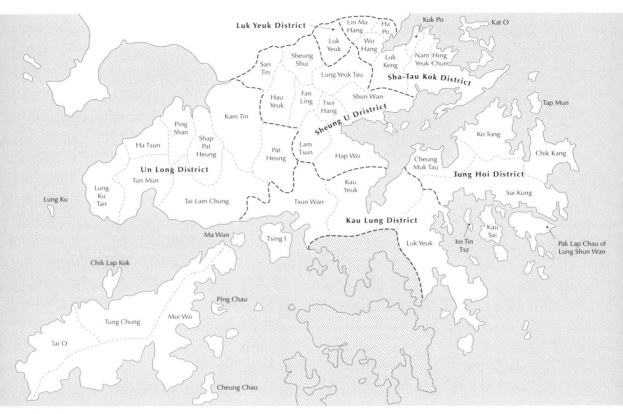

The Map of Hong Kong drawn by the British government in 1899 listed Sai Kung, Cheung Muk Tau, Ko Tong, Chek Keng and Leung Shuen Wan in Tung Hoi Tung. (modelled on the original)[14]

The villages within part of the "Tung Hoi Tung" when the British government compiled the Map of Hong Kong in 1899, including Tai Long, Sai Wan, Long Ke, Chek Keng, Pak Tam Chung, Wong Nai Chau, Wong Mo Ying and Yim Tin Tsai.

Kong, the Tsam, Cheung and Lam clans in Tai Long, the Lai family in Sai Wan, and the Wan's family in Cheung Muk Tau.[15]

Most of the Hakka people came to settled in this area in the 18th century and cultivated in the mountainous and relatively barren land. Regarding the theory of the origin of Hakka, Lo Hsiang-lin first proposed that the "ancestors of Hakka" were indigenous people (people of the Middle Kingdom) who originally lived in the north.[16] The Hakka moved in San On County was closely related to the policies of the imperial government. According to the *San On County Chronicles*, in the 18th year of Shunzhi (1661), the Qing imperial government with the excuse that "the worries over the sea were not yet settled" and the suspicion that Ming's survivor Zheng Chenggong was still assisted by coastal ordered the evacuation of people from the coastal areas to the inland. In the first year of Kangxi (1662), the imperial government issued an order to move people to the inland for fifty miles. During the relocation, the residents were displaced to live in the wild, or even lost their lives in the foreign land, and some migrated to Dongguan and Guishan counties. In the 7th year of Kangxi (1668), under the initiative of the viceroy of Guangdong and Guangxi Chau Yau Tak and the governor of Guangdong, Wong Loi Yam, and other officials, after repeated surveys of the border and the establishment of defensive frontier, the Qing government completely lifted the order in the 22nd year of Kangxi (1683). People of San On County could finally resume their lives only after the delimitation order was suspended.[17] The Qing government even encouraged the Hakka to move to San On to fill the emptiness along the coast. Driven by the Qing government's de-boundary policy, the people of Jiaying prefecture migrated to the Pearl River Delta region, including San On County (including Hong Kong), and settled. They were called "Hakka" people because of their dialects and living customs were different from those of the indigenous people. After moving to central and western Guangdong, compared with the local residents, they also had the consciousness of "visitors". Although the reference "Hakka" was first called by others, the term gradually became recognized by the ethnic group themselves and they also called themselves "Hakka".

In addition to farming in mountainous areas, Hakkas in coastal areas also had a sideline – lime kilns. Large lime kilns had been built in some Hakka villages, such as Hoi Ha and Pak Tam Chung. The Hakka people used the corals on the shore to burn lime to decorate the walls of the buildings in the villages or markets. 20th century, the brick industry also emerged in Pak Tam Chung. At the beginning, red bricks were the mainstay, and later they used to make grey bricks for the construction of rural houses. In addition, the livestock industry was mainly pig raising, and it was also a sideline for the villagers in Sai Kung and Hang Hau. In addition to food for the local area, pigs were also exported to the Kowloon area. Hakka people also operated ferry boats in Sai Kung Market and sold salted fish as agency for fishermen. The Sai Kung Hakkas includes the Ho family in Pak Sha O, the Yung family in Hoi Ha, the To family in Ko Tong, the Cheng family in Uk Tau, the Wong family in Wong Yi Chau, and the Lee family in Sham Chung.[18]

As for the floating people, they also accounted for a certain population of San On County. In the late Ming Dynasty, there were more local fishermen than in the early Qing Dynasty. After moving to the border in the early Qing Dynasty, the boat people continued to grow until 1900. They mostly anchored near Kau Sai Chau (because they lived within in the area of the British Army's artillery, they were relocated to Kau Sai New Village in Pak Sha Wan, Sai Kung in 1952), Leung Shuen Wan, Mun Channel (High Island Reservoir nowadays), Tap Mun, etc. Residents who lived in fishing villages and engaged in fishing in small islands and fishing ports included the Shek family of Ko Lau Wan (Kau Lau Wan), the four families of Lee, Ma, Cheng and Shek in Sam Mun Tsai, the families of Chan, Cheung, Lai, Shek, To, Ho and Fong in Tap Mun, and Chung in Yau Yue Wan, etc.[19] In addition, the indigenous inhabitants who gathered on the fishing boats of Sai Kung were mainly surnamed Ma, Ng, Kwok, Yuen and Lai. In Siu Sum Tsai which located between Pak Sha Chau, Sharp Island (Kiu Tsui Chau) and Cham Tau Chau, more than ten fishing boats operating with purse-seining (inshore fishing) docked at here several decades ago. This place was also a good place for repairing fishing gear and fishing nets. Fishermen of Siu Sum Tsai had built several mud huts commonly known as "fishing houses" to preserve their fishing gear, which were conserved nowadays. As for the Sai Kung Market, where fishermen from Leung Shuen Wan, Sam Mun Tsai and Kau Sai used as replenishment places. Fishermen would transport their catches to the main piers and other villages for bartering and in exchange for chicken, meat, grain, oil, tea and firewood, etc. The former manager of the Kaifong Welfare Association Chau Tin Sheng and the neighbor Mr. Choi operated a shipyard in the market to provide support services to fishermen. By the late 1970s, because of the construction of the High Island Reservoir, fisheries were reduced. Fishermen began to use fish cages to raise fish and develop fish rafts. Others also switched to operating yachts to transport people who went to Sai Kung for vacations to cruise or fishing in outlying islands.[20]

The other branch of Sai Kung's floating residents is the Hoklo fishermen. Among them, some of the fishermen sailed fishing boats from Hoklo Bay near Ha Chung in Guangdong to Chung Mei Tuk, Sai Kung as early as 1939. At first, there were only three fishing boats. Later, fishermen of Tsui, Shek and Lee families moved to Sai Kung, the number of fishing boats increased. In the old days, fishing boats were operated with wooden oars and sails. Fishermen originally lived on the boats. They did not build wooden houses in West Lane in Sai Kung until after 1947. The gods worshipped by the floating residents are mainly Tin Hau, and they also participate in the Tin Hau ritual activities in Sai Kung Market.[21]

According to a statistical survey in 1964, there were 4,482 fishermen in Sai Kung and 627 fishing boats.[22] Afterwards, the residents on the water increased their income and wealth due to the development of the fishing industry, because the market increased the demand for fresh food or salted fish, which contributed to the development of the fish market. Among them, Shau Kei Wan on Hong Kong Island has become a area of fishermen, and has enhanced associations with Hang Hau and the outlying islands of Sai Kung. The fish from Sai Kung were transported to Hong Kong Island through Hang Hau Market, which has become a fairly developed trade route. In addition, firewood produced in Sai Kung would also be shipped out to shops in Kowloon City for sale.

Market Development

The development of Sai Kung Market can be traced back to the middle of the 18th century.[23] About a hundred years ago, the Sai Kung market gradually became large, with 50 shops, four shipbuilding sheds, and a Tin Hau Temple. The Hang Hau Market also began to form at that time, with 18 shops and four shipbuilding sheds. In 1916, market merchants raised funds to rebuild the Tin Hau Temple, and moved the Heep Tin Kung from the barnyard to jointly build the Tin Hau and Hip Tin Temple in the market place. The merchants formed a neighbourhood organization called the "Sai Kung Kai Fong Association" to handle market affairs and act as arbitrator. In 1941, a group of young businessmen formed the Sai Kung Chamber of Commerce to contend with it, and also raised food to support the guerrillas during the Japanese Occupation. With the fall of Hong Kong in December 1941, Sai Kung fell into anarchy. The missionary Rev. Rectus Kwok was abducted and killed in the Sai Kung market. On 3 February 1942, the East River Column of the Chinese Communist Party also established the Hong Kong and Kowloon Brigade in Wong Mo Ying Rosary Chapel. The Hong Kong and Kowloon Brigade then founded the Sai Kung Squadron to conduct guerrilla warfare against Japan and led the Sai Kung villagers to conduct intelligence work. They escorted many cultural celebrities and international friends back to the mainland. In addition, the Sai Kung Tsung Tsin Church was conscripted by Japanese military police during the war. In 1945, Tang Chun Nam, the representative of the East River Column, negotiated with the Japanese here to force them to surrender. The villagers also had a meeting with British representatives to transfer Sai Kung to the British.

After the Second World War, the Sai Kung Market developed rapidly. At that time, it included several main streets: Main Street, Tai Street, Po Tung Road, Tak Lung Front and Back Streets, Yee Kuk Street, See Cheung Street, and Sai Kung Hoi Pong Street. The Main Street was the street where the Sai Kung Market originally developed with various shops. Villagers from various localities would go to the market to buy daily necessities, grain and oil groceries. Famous shops included Chinese medicine store "Yan Sheng Tong" and "Yan Sau Tong", Wah Sing Domestic Products, grocery store Tai Yik, Kam Lei Yuen and Hip Hing Lung, bakery Sam Yik Shing and Tse Hoi Kee, East River Restaurant, Ice-Cream Restaurant and Wo Cheung Iron Shop, etc.[24] Sai Kung Road was the outer street of the Market, with more residential buildings. In the 1940s and 1950s, there was a mountain product store run by Chaozhou people named "Lok Yau Sing". In addition, the Fong family in Yung Shue O built the "Fong Mansion", and a public school was opened in the house in 1942. Chung Mei Tuk was a haven for fishing boats and was reclaimed in the 1990s to build the Lakeside Garden under the management of the Housing Society.[25]

Village Alliance

The rural society in Sai Kung area was mostly multi-surnamed villages, and there was no strong lineage, such as the Liu's clan in Sheung Shui, the Tang's clan in Lung Yeuk Tau, or the Man's clan in San Tin.[26] Therefore, the community management was mainly in the form of sacrificial rites and rotation of tithings ("Kap" in Cantonese). For example, in Ho Chung Valley, the seven main villages including Ho Chung Village (including Nam Bin Village), Tai Po Tsai Village, Mo Tse Che Village, Sheung Sze Wan Village, Tai Lam Wu, Man Wo Village and Chuk Yuen Village scattered along the

Ho Chung River, formed the alliance with Che Kung Temple as the centre, to form a sacrificial rites committee and organized Ta Tsiu Festival every decade which lasts for a few days.[27] Formed by Pak Kong, Sheung Sze Wan and Tai Hang Hou, with the Tin Hau Temple in the village as the centre, Ta Tsiu Festival was also held every ten years. The main clans in Pak Kong Village include Lok, Leung, Cheng and Li.[28] The two alliances of Pak Kong and Ho Chung were originally belonged to the "Luk Yeuk" (Alliance of Six), but the reason for the subsequent split into two alliance was unclear.[29]

On the west bank of Three Fathoms Cove, the Sze Kap (Four communities) centered on the Tsat Shing Temple (refer to the table below). There were more than ten villages in Sze Kap, responsible for founding and managing the temple, and taking turns to organize Cantonese Operas for appeasing gods. Later, the original 11 villages that formed the Sze Kap, connected with Kei Ling Ha Lo Wai, Kei Ling Ha San Wai and Tin Liu (Tai Tung Wo Liu), collectively referred to as the "Shap Sze Heung".[30]

The Sze Kap members centered on the Kun Hang Tsat Shing Temple

Tung Ping She	Wu Kai Sha
Sai Ping She	Sai Keng, Nga Yiu Tau
Nam Hing She	Nai Chung, Sai O, Kwun Hang, Cheung Muk Tau
Pak Hing She	Ma Kwu Lam, Che Ha, Tai Tung, Tseng Tau

As for the Tsat Heung (Alliance of Seven) in the North of Sai Kung, it is composed of Cheung Sheung, To Kwa Ping, Pak Tam Au, Ko Tong, Tai Yeung and Tai Tan. Among them, the Wan's clan of Ko Tong Village came from Yung Shue O Village, Sha Tau Kok about two hundred years ago. They then moved to Ko Tong to settle down. In the early years, villagers made a living by farming, planting rice near the sea, planting sweet potatoes, peanuts, sugar cane etc. on mountainside terraces, and fishing as a sideline.

However, Sham Chung, Lai Chi Chong, Pak Sha O, She Shek Au, Nam Shan, Chek Keng, and Tai Long, which belong to the North of Sai Kung, do not belong to the Tsat Heung.[31] This might be related to their status as the early sites for Catholic missionaries. Pat Heung (Alliance of Eight) area is located in the southern part of Tsat Heung, but with a cluster of eight villages, including Tai Mong Tsai, Tai Po Tsai, Ping Tun, She Tau, Tit Kim Hang, Shek Hang, Wong Mo Ying and Tam Wat villages.[32] Although the cluster was centred on the altar of the Tai Wong God in Shek

The landscape of Sha Kok Mei, Sai Kung after the war. (Image source: PIME)

In 2020, Ho Chung Luen Heung Da Jiu Festival was held every ten years.

Hang Village to form a regional alliance, some of the villagers were also Catholics. For example, the Rosary Chapel in Wong Mo Ying was established in 1923, and the church members came from Wong Mo Ying Village and other villages in Pat Heung.[33]

Sai Kung (South) also had a Shap Heung (Alliance of Ten), including Tai Wan, Lam A, Shan Liu, Sha Ha, Cho Wo Hang, Wo Liu, Wong Chuk Wan, Ngong Wo, Long Keng and O Tau. The Wong Chuk Wan Public Tin Hau Temple was their centre in general. The temple was built by the Cheng's family in Wong Chuk Wan. According to the inscription on the reconstruction of the temple, the 17th ancestor of the Chengs branched from Mau Tso Ngam village of the Kowloon Peak to settle in Wong Chuk Wan, Fui Yiu Ha, Sai Kung. In 1905, 18th ancestor Cheng Cong paid land rent to District Office in Sai Kung and built the temple on the shore of Wong Chuk Wan, and he himself served as the manager. He named the temple "Wong Chuk Wan Public Tin Hau Temple", and registered it as a temple in the Land Office of District Office of Sai Kung. At that time, the villagers mostly relied on farming, fishing and burning ashes. The Tin Hau Temple was built in order to pray for wealthiness, health and peace. In the early stage, the old temple was enshrined by the Cheng's family. In the later period, other neighboring Shap Heung villages came to visit the temple, and the incense was flourishing. Later, the descendants of the 19th generation of the Cheng's family moved to San Yiu Village (named Cho Wo Hang nowadays) to settle down. Although the temple was not jointly managed by the Shap Heung, its reconstruction was supported by donations from the alliance.

Extending from the southern part of Ngau Yee Shek Shan to Sheung Yiu and Wong Yi Chau, this area belonged to Pak Tam Chung. Due to the geographical proximity and the need to take care of each other, the six villages in Pak Tam Chung form the Luk Heung (Alliance of Six), including Tsam Chuk Wan, Wong Keng Tei, Sheung Yiu, Tsak Yue Wu, Pak Tam and Wong Yi Chau. According to the memories of the elderly in Wong Keng Tei, Pak Tam Chung Luk Heung celebrated the birthday of the "Tai Wong" (a kind of humanized god functioning as the protector of certain territory) twice a year. Each village in Luk Heung would send a villager to preside over the birthday ceremony of the God. However, around the year 1,900, due to the conversion to Christianity, the village leaders in Pak Tam Chung and Pak Tam no longer participated in this celebration.[34]

The Pioneer of Rural Missions: the Encounter between PIME Fathers and Hakka

When Western missionaries arrived in China, Christianity had already been introduced to the Chinese for about a few centuries. The earliest missionary records in China today can be traced back to the "Nestorian Tele" (also known as "Xi'an Stele") with the heading "Memorial of the Propagation in China of the Luminous Religion from Daqin" established in the West Daqin Temple in the second year of Jianchung period, Tang Dynasty (781). This monument recorded the spread of Nestorianism (also known as "Nestorian Church"), the first Christian sect to enter China during the Tang Dynasty. During the Yuan Dynasty, the Pope sent an envoy to the east to preach. At that time, Nestorianism had 12 churches in China. In the 31st year of Zhiyuan period, Yuan Dynasty (1294), the missionary Giovanni da Montecorvino (1247-1328) arrived in Dadu (now Beijing) , and was welcomed by the emperor Chengzong. He was then invited to stay in China as a missionary. However, the European church was in a state of decline at that time, so there had not been much development until the end of the Yuan Dynasty.[35] It was not until the middle of the Ming Dynasty that missionaries represented by Matteo Ricci (1552-1610) began to go deep into the inland to preach, which became an important opportunity for cultural exchanges between China and the West.[36]

Matteo Ricci came to China by sailing from Rome, and arrived in the eighth year of Wanli period, Ming Dynasty (1580). He onboarded at Shan'ao (Macao) of the Xiangshan County, Guangdong, the only base of Westerners in China at that time. He entered Zhaoqing and Nanxiong in inland China the following year, and then via Jiangxi Province to both jurisdiction of Linjiang and Nanchang.[37] As Ruan Yuan said in *The Explanation of the Emperor Qing Jing – Chou Ren Biography*: "Matteo Ricci's voyage to Guangdong during the Wanli period was the beginning of Western Methodology's entry into China."[38] Matteo Ricci spent 28 years in China, and his mission was to spread Catholicism. His book *The True Meaning of the Lord of Heaven* successfully spreaded the content of the Gospel to the Chinese with the Six Classics (*Liujing*) attached to the saying of God; he also translated *Euclid's Elements, Qiankun tiyi* (Explication of the Structure of Heaven and Earth) and other Chinese classics, and was responsible in teaching astronomical arithmetic. The famous scholars of the imperial government such as Li Zhizao, Xu Guangqi, Li Tianjing, etc. were all students of him.[39]

Matteo Ricci introduced Catholicism to Guangdong Province and other areas, but afterwards, due to the imperial restriction on Catholicism, it could only be spread temporarily in Macau.[40] This was because during the Ming Dynasty, the Portuguese established power in Macau, and Macau was included under the Portuguese apologetic system. From the middle to the end of the Qing Dynasty, the Catholic Church was allowed to enter Guangdong again, and the pioneer at that time was the Missions étrangères de Paris (MEP). The Paris Foreign Missions was a missionary organization established in Paris, France in 1658. Its purpose was to supervise overseas missions, train local missionaries, and assist in the establishment of local churches.[41] Between 1825 and 1887, 964 missionaries were sent to the Far East to preach. Among them, 24 missionaries were sentenced to death and martyred by foreign courts, and seven were killed while preaching. At that time, it was reported that 600 missionaries were preaching in South Korea, Tibet, China, Japan, and the East Indies. An average of 10,000 adults and 100,000 babies were baptised each year. There were 700,000 Christians by then, reflecting the large scale of the Western missionary work in East Asia, especially in Mainland China.[42]

As for Hong Kong, before it was occupied by the British, it was attached to the Diocese of Macau under the apologetic power of Portugal. Although the Holy See was dissatisfied with Portugal's right in China, it did not want to directly conflict with it. Therefore, when the British landed on Hong Kong Island at Possession Point in January 1841 and occupied Hong Kong Island, the Holy See saw it as an opportunity to demarcate the missionary districts around Hong Kong Island and the surrounding six miles out of the jurisdiction of the Diocese of Macau on 22 April 1841, through the promulgation of *The Decree Establishing the Prefecture Apostolic of Hong Kong*, and the Prefecture Apostolic of Hong Kong was formally established.[43] At that time, Rev. Joset (1804-1842), who was the representative of Propaganda Fide (*Sacred Congregation for the Propagation of Faith*) in Macau and the Swiss priest, sent the Spanish Franciscan Rev. Michael Navarro (1809-1877) to Hong Kong, and started his missionary and pastoral work, and became the first Catholic missionary representing the Holy See in Hong Kong. Therefore, it can be said that since Hong Kong became a British colony in 1842, Western missionaries began to preach in villages outside of Victoria City on Hong Kong Island at that time, and there were many examples of all villagers being baptised.

Since the Roman Empire declared freedom of religion and recognized Catholicism as the state religion, most of the cities in the empire have believed in Christ. The bishop

Before the British occupation, Hong Kong was attached to the Diocese of Macau under the apologetic power of Portugal. (Image source: PIME)

of each city concentrated on spreading the gospel to the countryside outside the city and even other countries. What were the original Eastern religious beliefs of these rural residents in Sai Kung? How did Sai Kung establish a relationship with the Institute for Foreign Missions? How did the foreign priests guide the villages to convert to Catholicism and establish missionary points based on this?

It turned out that the "Pontifical Institute for Foreign Missions (also known as Pontifical Foreign Missions Institute)" of the Italian Missionary Order had obtained the religious jurisdiction of Hong Kong and the land of the south of Boundary Street in Kowloon from the Paris Foreign Missions in accordance with an agreement as early as 1860.[44] Pontifical Institute for Foreign Missions, the abbreviation "PIME" is the abbreviation of the Italian "Pontificio Istituto Missioni Estere". In 1850, its predecessor, the "Milan Foreign Missions" (or Foreign Missions of Milan) (in Italian : Missioni Estere di Milano, MEM) was established in Italy. It was composed of priests dedicated to evangelization and lay missionaries dedicated to sacrificial life. It has been more than 160 years since the congregation came to Hong Kong, and it was one of the first congregations to come to Hong Kong to preach. The mission has grown in sync with Hong Kong's Catholic activities and diocese, and is inseparable. It is a mission that must be known when studying the history of Hong Kong's Catholicism. In its heyday, the Diocese of Hong Kong covered the services in Hong Kong, which was a British colony at that time, and Po On, Wai Yeung and Hoi Fung in Guangdong. The missionaries from the PIME had used Hong Kong as a stepping stone to enter the Mainland for service.

The first Milan missionaries arrived in Hong Kong as early as 1858. The earliest was Fr. Paolo Reina (1825-1861) who arrived on 10 April, followed by Fr. Timoleone Raimondi, MEM (1827-1894) and his main companion, Fr. Giuseppe Burghignoli, MEM (1833-1892)[45]. In 1870, the MEM missionaries entered the mainland. After that, about 250 missionaries belonged to MEM began their missions in Guangdong, Henan and Shaanxi provinces. They preached the gospel in the Mainland from 1874 to 1949, including Fr. Alberico Crescitelli (1863-1900) who was martyred in July 1900. In the spring of 1888, Fr. Crescitelli set off from his hometown of Altavilla Irpina in the province of Alino, Italy, and finally came to the mission area in Hanzhong, Shaanxi after all kinds of hardships. Over the past 12 years, he has worked in different villages, cared for church members, and preached the gospel, and making the locals become believers. It is a pity that he was tragically martyred in 1900 when he was attacked by the boxers who were anti-Christian and expelled foreigners.[46] This incident was regarded as a microcosm of the problems and conflicts in the rural Catholic missions in the late Qing Dynasty, but it has not changed the Western missionaries' yearning and enthusiasm for preaching in China.

In 1926, the Pope merged the MEM with the Theological Seminary of St. Peter and St. Paul's Missionaries in Rome to form the "Pontifical Foreign Missions Institute". In 1934, Wai Chow had three Italian missionaries and two national priests serving there.[47] During the Japanese occupation (1941-1945), because Italy belonged to an enemy country, the bishop sent a Chinese priest to serve in the Sai Kung district of Hong Kong. In 1954, the last group of missionaries were evacuated from the mainland and sent to various parishes in Hong Kong. In 1968, Rev. Lorenzo Bianchi, the last bishop of Hong Kong affiliated with the PIME, handed over the management of the Hong Kong Diocese to Bishop Francis Hsu and other Chinese priests. At present, the missionary work of the PIME has spread to Asia, Africa, India, America and other places. Eighteen missionaries were martyred during their missions in China, Bangladesh, Myanmar, the Philippines and Oceania, including Rev. Emilio Teruzzi and

Rev. Valeriano Fraccaro who were killed in Sai Kung, Hong Kong.

According to the analysis of Catholic scholars Rev. Sergio Ticozzi and Rev. Louis Ha, the Hakka villagers were most willing to accept the gospel. Since the Hakka came from the north, they were still "guests" after they settled in Guangdong, so they felt like they were under the fence lonely and weak. During the Qing Dynasty, they were controlled by the local clans who had many fields in the area of Sheung U Tung. As tenant farmers, they had to pay land tax. Therefore, they tended to rely on the power of missionaries to resist the clans. In other words, without the close social organization of local clans, such as a core organization centred on temples or ancestral halls, it is easier for missionaries to enter these Hakka villages to preach. As a result, as early as the 1860s, Catholics began to preach in Sai Kung, including the establishment of churches in Yim Tin Tsai and Wo Mei Village.

Rev. Louis Ha also pointed out that the Catholic missionary work in the Hakka region of Guangdong began during the Daoguang period. At that time, some Hakkas who had accepted Catholicism in Southeast Asia brought their faith back to their hometowns, such as Hakka migrant Wu Dong. While making a living in Thailand and Penang, Malaysia, he was baptised in 1844, and when he returned to his hometown in Ka Ying (now Meixian), he led the villagers to the belief of Catholicism. Later, there were more and more people around Wu Dong expressed their will to believe in this religion. In 1850, he invited Fr. Pierre Le Turdu (1821-1861) who had been preaching in Hong Kong for more than three years to baptise them.[48] In addition, the Hakka people attached great importance to education, and often established voluntary schools in the villages, so that missionaries who focused on educational services could integrate easily into the Hakka community. In the Catholic villages of Sai Kung, such as Pak Sha O, the missionaries used to establish village schools, allowed Hakka children to receive education, and at the same time spread the Catholic faith to them. In 1858, foreign missionaries from Paris began to administer the Apostolic Prefecture of Guangzhou, which was separated from the Diocese of Macau, and preached to the Hakkas in the district. In 1914, Swatow was seperated from the Apostolic Prefecture of Guangzhou and became the Apostolic Prefecture of Swatow to manage the Hakka settlements. The Apostolic Prefecture of Ka Ying was also specially set up for the Hakka people includes Meixian, Dapu, Pingyuan, Xingning, Longchuan, Jiaoling, Heping, Lianping, Wuhua and other counties.

Generally speaking, the format of preaching of the Foreign Mission Society of

Paris (Société des Missions Etrangères de Paris, MEP), were in the form of buying the land to build a church, building houses around the land, and hiring local people to farm, which they could live near the church for generations, and farming on the fields bought by the church. Later, after the PIME took over the Apostolic Prefecture of Hong Kong from MEP, it also operated in a similar way. Therefore, in the records of the Hong Kong Government Records Office, it is common for the Roman Catholic Church to use "Cathedral", "Roman Church" or "Roman Temple" as the name of the land registrant. The land record made when the British leased the New Territories in 1898, showed that the villages in Sham Chung, Pak Tam Chung and Pak Sha O, etc., were registered under one of the above-mentioned registered names. In addition, in the 1910, the Catholic Church also purchased land for farming in Kei Ling Ha and Che Ha of Shap Sze Heung, and built chapels near the areas. Although these chapels no longer exist, the registration of the land can directly prove how the missionaries used the purchase of land as the first step, assisting the Hakka people to improve their lives by farming. Moreover, in the area of Sham Chung, the long embankment and dam built by Rev. Piazzoli, Luigi Maria, MEM (1845-1904) assisted by the villagers, and the agricultural land covered and irrigated by the dam can still be seen nowadays.[49] The

In 1917, the Roman Catholic Church applied to the Hong Kong Government for agricultural land in Kei Ling Ha. (Image source: Government Records Office)

church would also sold land to farmers at low prices, and implemented the advanced land reform of "land-to-the-tiller". This was an important step for missionaries to preach in the countryside at that time.

When preaching between Hakka villages, the priest would travel around various stations, staying in each place for no more than eight days. In addition to learning the Hakka language, missionaries also needed to understand the customs of the villagers in order to successfully preach in the villages and build chapels. Therefore, besides preaching, the priests would also provide a lot of alms and helped the Hakkas to solve their difficulties. He also applied for the construction of educational places such as schools or private schools, usually attached to or next to the chapels. After the war, missionaries also helped refugees, especially those who escaped from the mainland to Hong Kong, or the lower classes of society such as floating people (or "Tanka"). In the next few chapters, we will review the development of the chapels established by the missionaries after their encounter with the Hakkas in Sai Kung area and how they coped with the various predicaments and consolidated the foundation of Church in this district.

The terraced fields in Sai Kung in the past. (Image source: PIME)

Notes

1   Sai Kung District Council, "District Highlights – Local Characteristics of Sai Kung District", District Information, 31 March 2017, http://www.districtcouncils.gov.hk/sk/english/welcome.htm, retrieved on 1 August 2021.

2   Planning Department, "NT Pamphlet", Planning Department, 18 August 2021, www.pland.gov.hk/pland_tc/press/publication/nt_pamphlet02/sk_html/, retrieved on 1 August 2021.

3   Hong Kong Archaeological Society, "The Second Excavation on Wong Tei Tung Site"(〈香港西貢黃地峒遺址二零零五年度考古發掘工作報告〉), *Journal of the Hong Kong Archaeological Society* (Hong Kong: Hong Kong Archaeological Society, 2003-2008, Vol. 16), pp. 50–68.

4   According to the exhibits of the Antiquities and Monuments Office, this anchor stone is a device used to fix the position of ships. The anchor stone found at Leung Shuen Wan Chau is one of the stone components of the wooden stone anchor. The shape of the stone Leung Shuen Wan Chau anchor is similar to that of the shipwreck of Hakata Bay in Japan, Quanzhou in Fujian, and Nanhai No.1. It is smaller in size, and it is preliminarily inferred to be from a foreign trade vessel. See Hong Kong Maritime Museum Limited, "Activating Local Records – the Story of High Island (Leung Shuen Wan)".

5   [Ming] Compiled by Guo Fei, Huang Guosheng, and Deng Guizhong, *Grand Record of Guang dong* (粵大記)(Guangzhou: Zhongshan University Press, 1998), p. 918.

6   Sai Kung now has a village called "Man Wo", which has the same pronunciation as "Japanese Pirates". Some people speculate that it may be related to the invasion of this place by Japanese pirates.

7   Sai Kung District Council, *Sai Kung Scenery* (《西貢風貌》) (Hong Kong: Sai Kung District Council, 1994), p. 73.

8   P. H. Hase, *The Historical Heritage of Ho Chung, Pak Kong, and Sha Kok Mei, Sai Kung* (Hong Kong: S.Y. Consultancy Services Co. Ltd, 2003).

9   The first compilation of *San On County Chronicles* was completed in the 14th year of the Wanli period of the Ming Dynasty (1586). It was revised and supplemented many times in the early years of the Republic of China. Unfortunately, there are only two remaining editions, namely the Kangxi edition (1688) and Jiaqing Edition (1819).

10   Sai Kung North Rural Committee is comprised of villages including Che Ha, Chek Keng, Cheung Muk Tau, Cheung Sheung, Ha Yeung, Hoi Ha, Kei Ling Ha Lo Wai, Kei Ling Ha San Wai, Ko Lau Wan, Ko Tong, Kwun Hang, Lai Chi Chong, Ma Kwu Lam, Nai Chung, Nam Shan Tung, Nga Iu Tau Tsun, Ngong Ping, Pak Sha O, Pak Tam Au, Ping Chau Chau Mei, Ping Chau Chau Tau, Ping Chau Nai Tau, Ping Chau Sha Tau, Ping Chau Tai Tong, Sai Keng, Sai O, Sham Chung, Tai Tan, Tai Tung, Tan Ka Wan, Tap Mun, Tap Mun Fishermen Village, Tin Liu, To Kwa Peng, Tseng Tau, Tung Sam Kei, Uk Tau, Wong Chuk Yeung and Yung Shue O. See Home Affairs Bureau, "List of Village Representatives in Sai Kung North Rural Committee", Home Affairs Bureau, https://www.had.gov.hk/rre/chi/images/elections_1519/saikungnorth.pdf, retrieved on 30 April 2021.

11   Sai Kung District Council, *Sai Kung* (Hong Kong: Sai Kung District Council, 1983), p. 8.

12   Lan Nai Wan, later known as Man Yee Wan. In the 1970s, because the government had to build the High Island Reservoir on the Kwun Mun Channel where the village was located, the entire village had to be relocated to Sai Kung Market.

13   Johnston, Elizabeth, *Recording a Rich Heritage :Research on Hong Kong's "New Territories"* (Hong Kong: Leisure and Cultural Services Department, 2000), pp. 61-76.

14 Map of Hong Kong and of the Territory Leased to Great Britain under the Convention between Great Britain and China signed at Peking on the 9th June, 1898. Based on the 1866 Map of Sun On District (Source: Hong Kong Public Records Office; ref. HKRS208-12-51).

15 *A Gazetteer of Place Names in Hong Kong Kowloon and the New Territories* (Hong Kong: S. Young, Government Printer, 1960), pp. 128-141, 182-192.

16 Luo Xianglin, "A Study on the Origin of Hakka" (Beijing: China Huaqiao Publishing House, 1989). In addition to Luo's "northern aboriginal theory", there is also an aboriginal theory proposed by Fang Xuejia's "*Exploring the Origins of Hakka*" (《客家源流探奧》) in 1994, which points to the fact that Hakkas are actually a community. The community after the mixture of the remnants of the ancient Yue nationality in the triangle area. For the main debates in the current academic circles about the origin of Hakka, see Xie Chongguang, *A Review of Hakka Culture*《客家文化述論》) (Beijing: China Social Sciences Press, 2008), pp. 13-21.

17 Li Limei, "The Origin of Baode Temple", in Chou and Wong Temple Co., Ltd., *The Memorial Album of Zhou Wangergong's Historical Relics* (《周王二公史蹟紀念專輯》) (Hong Kong: Chou and Wong Temple Co., Ltd., 1982), pp. 2-7.

18 *A Gazetteer of Place Names in Hong Kong Kowloon and the New Territories* (Hong Kong: S. Young, Government Printer, 1960), pp. 128-141, 182-192.

19 *A Gazetteer of Place Names in Hong Kong Kowloon and the New Territories* (Hong Kong: S. Young, Government Printer, 1960), pp.128-141, 182-192; "Introduction to Establishment of Tap Mun Fishermen Village" (〈塔門漁民村建村簡介〉), *Jubilee Publication of Tap Mun Fishermen Village* (《塔門漁民村五十週年金禧特刊》) (Hong Kong: Tap Mun Fishermen Village Management Committee, 2014), p. 22.

20 Sai Kung Kaifong Association, *Special Issue on the Reconstruction of Sai Kung Tin Hau Guan Di Ancient Temple in Wu Zi Year* (Hong Kong: Sai Kung Kaifong Association, 2009), pp. 29-34.

21 Ibid.

22 Kani Hiroaki, *A Study of Hong Kong Boat People* (Hong Kong: Southeast Asia Research Office, New Asia Research Institute, 1967), p. 6.

23 David Faure, "The Making of the District and its Experience in World War II", *Journal of the Hong Kong Branch of the Royal Asiatic Society*, Vol. 22 (1982), pp. 161-216.

24 Sai Kung Kaifong Association, *Special Issue on the Reconstruction of Sai Kung Tin Hau Guan Di Ancient Temple in Wu Zi Year*, p. 29.

25 Ibid.

26 According to Faure's research, the New Territories villages are organized on the basis of two principles: clan and region. See David Faure, "Sai Kung, The Making of the District and Its Experience During World War II", *Journal of the Hong Kong Branch of the Royal Asiatic Society*, Vol. 22 (1982), p. 174. Quoted from: Ma Muk Chi et al., *History and Scenery of Sai Kung* (《西貢歷史與風物》) (Hong Kong: Sai Kung District Council, 2003), p. 103.

27 The last Da Jiu Festival in Ho Chung Village Alliance was held from 24 - 28 December 2020.

28   "Jiao" is a festival with multiple purposes, including the four realms of heaven, earth, water, and yang, people, ghosts, and gods. For the villagers, "jiao" is a festival for offering sacrifices to yin and yang, and repaying wishes. Therefore, during the pilgrimage process, we can see the sacrifice ceremony during the Yulan Festival, the rewarding activities during the birthday of the gods, and the monitoring of lonely ghosts during the Yulan Festiva by the Ghosts King who distributes clothing and food. One can also enjoy lion dances and qilin dances during the birth of the gods. For the integration of local communities in Sai Kung, see Ma Muk Chi et al., *History and Scenery of Sai Kung* (Hong Kong: Sai Kung District Council, 2003), pp. 34-35.

29   Government Records Service, HKSAR, *Map of Hong Kong and of the Territory leased to Great Britain under the Convention between Great Britain and China signed at Peking on the 9th June, 1898, (1899)*. This Map has the footnote: "This map has been compiled from existing intelligence Division maps of Hong Kong Admiralty Charts and a map of the Sun on District compiled in 1866 from the observations of an Italian Missionary".

30   The other said that instead of Wu Kai Sha, Tseng Kwan Li ("General Lane") (Cheung Muk Tau branch) should be one of the members.

31   The District Office North, New Territories was established in 1907. After the war, it was divided into Tai Po District Office and Yuen Long District Office. As the villages on the northern shore of the Sai Kung Peninsula maintained historical connection with Tai Po, they belonged to the scope of District Office North.

32   Yuen Chi Wai, Herman Tsang and Susan Chung, *Walking with God Series- Wong Mo Ying and Rosary Chapel* (Hong Kong: Catholic Diocese of Hong Kong Working Committee for "Following Thy Way", 2020), p. 7.

33   Ma Muk Chi, "Economic Development and Regional Social Changes in the Eastern Coast of Hong Kong in the Nineteenth Century", Zhu Delan (ed.) *Essays on the History of China's Ocean Development*, Vol. 8 (Taipei: Zhongshan Institute of Humanities and Social Sciences, Academia Sinica, 2002), pp. 73-103.

34   Historical Building Appraisal, *The Chapel of Our Lady of the Seven Sorrows at Pak Tam Chung Sheung Yiu* (Hong Kong: Historical Research Group of Catholic Diocese of Hong Kong Working Committee for "Following Thy Way", 2020) (unpublished).

35   Luo Xianglin, *The History of the Chinese Ethnicities* (Taipei: Chinese Culture Publishing Company, 1966), p. 217.

36   Li Ji, "The Arrangement and Research of the Archives of the Manchukuo Pastoral Areas in the Foreign Missions of Paris", *Journal of Catholic Studies: Historiography of the Chinese Catholic Church: Historical Resources and Methodology*", 10th Issue, 2019 (Hong Kong: Centre for Catholic Studies, Chinese University of Hong Kong, 2019), pp. 131-152.

37   Hisashi Nakamura, translated by Zhou Yiliang, "The Story of Matteo Ricci", in Zhou Kangqiu (ed.), *Cun Cui Society Edited: Matteo Ricci Research Collection* (Hong Kong: Chong Wen Bookstore, 1971), pp. 5-28.

38   [Qing] Ruan Yuan, "Matteo Ricci", in Zhou Kangqiu (ed.), *Cun Cui Xue She Compilation: Collection of Matteo Ricci Studies* (Hong Kong: Chong Wen Bookshop, 1971), pp. 1-4.

39   Zhou Kangqiu (ed.), *Cun Cui Xue She Compilation: Collection of Matteo Ricci Studies* (Hong Kong: Chong Wen Bookshop, 1971).

40   Fang Zhiqin and Jiang Zuyuan (eds.), *Guangdong General History: Modern Part 2* (Guangzhou: Guangdong Higher Education Press, 2010), pp. 1148-1157.

41   "Catholic Missionaries in the East", *The China Review*, 1887; Li Ji, "Collation and Research on the Archives of the Manchukuo Pastoral Area in the Paris Foreign Mission Church", *Journal of Catholic Studies: Historiography of the Catholic Church in China: Historical Resources and Methodology*, 10th Issue, 2019 (Hong Kong: Centre for Catholic Studies, Chinese University of Hong Kong, 2019), pp. 131-152.

42   "Progress", *The China Review* or notes and queries on the Far East, Vol. 9, No. 5, 1881.

43   The decree reads: "After careful consideration of the opinions of the Sacred Congregation for the Propagation of Faith, Pope Gregory XVI, for the spiritual needs of Catholic soldiers and congregants, and for the purpose of preaching, temporarily appoints the Procurator of the S. C. for the Propagation of Faith stationed in Macau as the Prefect Apostolic to deal with the pastoral and administrative work of the above-mentioned islands and the surrounding six miles". See "The Order of the Propaganda Fide of Rome to Establish the Apostolic Prefecture of Hong Kong", Hong Kong Diocesan Archives, https://archives.catholic.org.hk/, retrieved on 31 March 2021.

44   Ha Keloon, *The Foundation of the Catholic Mision in Hong Kong, 1841-1894* (Hong Kong: Joint Publishing H.K. Co., Ltd., 2018), p. 78.

45   Sunday Examiner, "Another China: PIME Missionaries between China and Hong Kong", *Sunday Examiner*, 8 November 2020, p. 12.

46   In 1951, Pope Pius XII announced that Rev. Alberico Crescitelli, 1863-1900 was listed as Beatitude and set February 18th every year as the anniversary of St. Alberico Crescitelli. See Gianni Criveller, translated by Aijie Chen, *The Martyrdom of Alberico Crescitelli: Its Context and Controversy* (Hong Kong: Catholic Truth Society, 2014), p. 21.

47   The priest by nationality means a Chinese priest appointed by the Vicariate Apostolic of Hong Kong.

48   Ha Keloon Louis, "The Encounter of the Hakka and the Catholic Church", *God is a Guest at Yim Tin Tsai: A Century Story of Yim Tin Tsai, Sai Kung, Hong Kong* (Hong Kong: Centre for Catholic Studies, CUHK, 2010), pp. 223-235.

49   Rev. Luigi Maria Piazzoli (1845-1904) arrived in Hong Kong in 1869 and preached in Sai Kung in 1870. On 11 January 1895, he was succeeded as the second Vicar Apostolic of Hong Kong and he was renamed the Bishop of Hong Kong after his death.

Chapter 2

The Period of Apostolic Prefecture: the Foundation of Catholic Mission in Sai Kung (1841-1874)

1841

1874

1931

1945

1969

1981

2000

Since the first priest of the Milan Institute for the Foreign Missions (later called the "PIME") came to Hong Kong in 1858, Sai Kung has become an important place for missionaries for learning Chinese culture and language, whereas spreading the Western culture. Missionaries touring Sai Kung area included Rev. Simeone Volonteri (MEM, 1831-1904)[1] and Rev. Andrew Leong Chi-hing (1837-1920). They went to different villages for preaching. After their serving in Sai Kung, other priests such as Rev. Riccardo Brookes (PIME, 1892-1980) and Rev. Angelo Ferrario (PIME, 1876-1933) successively took over the missionary work in Sai Kung. The reason why Sai Kung was chosen as the training place for Catholic missionaries, was the geographical convenience for them to enter the mainland China via Mirs Bay, and there were also many scattered villages and Hakka groups in Sai Kung who were in need of help, such as fighting against the control of the big clans. Most of the historic chapels on the Sai Kung Peninsula were established during this period, including St. Joseph's Chapel in Yim Tin Tsai, the Holy Family Chapel in Chek Keng, and the Immaculate Heart of Mary Chapel in Pak Sha O. In 1866, there was the first batch of Catholics from Yim Tin Tsai.

After the New Territories was leased to the United Kingdom in 1898, the PIME members treated Sai Kung as a stepping stone and successively moved to the mainland areas to preach. However, religious persecutions occurred in the inland areas afterwards and the lives of the missionaries were threatened. As a result, many missionaries stayed more frequently in Sai Kung chapels.

Sai Kung under the Management of the Apostolic Prefecture of Hong Kong

As early as 1860, the San On County area under the jurisdiction of the Qing

Dynasty was part of the "Apostolic Prefecture of Hong Kong" (Apostolic Prefecture), while MEP, which was responsible for preaching in the Guangzhou area, handed over Tai Po, Sai Kung and other places under its jurisdiction to MEM, who were already in Hong Kong.[2] Rev. Timoleone Raimondi (MEM, 1827-1894) was the first to explore the area. He started his journey from Tsuen Wan, traversed through Tai Mo Shan, and arrived at Sap Pat Heung, Lam Tsuen, Tai Po Market and even Wun Yiu (formerly named Wun Tou) before returning to Tsuen Wan. Later, Rev. Giuseppe Burghignoli continued to live in his residence in Tsuen Wan in early 1861, until the Prefect Apostolic, Rev. Timoleone Raimondi, settled in Wun Yiu.

Tai Wo Village Mission Station which was closer to Wang Gong, Guangdong Province was established in 1862. Rev. Volonteri established a school in Tai Wo in 1861 with a male villager from Aberdeen. Unfortunately, in 1864, due to *feng shui* problems, the priest was forced to leave this place and moved to Ting Kok, not far from Tai Po Market[3]. In Ting Kok Village, with the assistance of Rev. Leong, Rev. Burghignoli and

The scope of the Apostolic Prefecture in Hong Kong from 1861 to 1874.

Rev. Gaetano Origo (MEM, 1835-1868), they built a school, a small chapel and a residence for themselves.[4] During this period, the priests travelled around the villages to get to know new villagers and spread the gospel; and they later also began to visit Sai Kung to get to know the local Hakkas, and then they decided to start missionary work in the local Catholic Church.

In the early 20th century, the population of the parishioners in Sai Kung continued to increased, and became a Catholic-Hakka community in the New Territories. On 16 August 1867, Rev. Raimondi (later the Vicar Apostolic) stated in a report to the Sacred Congregation for the Propagation of the Faith (abbrev. Propaganda Fide):

> There are other chapels in the mission area in Aberdeen, Ting Kok, Sai Kung, Yim Tin Tsai, Tai Long, Shui Mun Tau and other places. Each convent also has a chapel where the Eucharist is preserved...[5]

Later, due to lack of perseverance and progress in the Ting Kok district, Sai Kung became the main residence of missionaries throughout the region.

The Arrival of the First Priest of Pontifical Institute for Foreign Missions in Hong Kong

At that time, Hong Kong Island had been a British colony for many years. The Victoria City on the island was still an European-dominated community, with people of various nationalities living. In 1858, Fr. Rudolf Krone from the Lutheran Missionary settled in Fuyong. He wrote a notice for San On County and described his missionary work in Tsuen Wan:

> Christianity has been spread to this province for several years. Some people in the district have been baptized, but the number is unknown. There is a Catholic church in Tsin Wan (Tsuen Wan), but no European missionaries live there.

Since the first batch of Italian priests arrived in Hong Kong in 1858, besides preaching for the local European Catholics, they were also eager to spread the gospel to the Chinese. At that time there were some local priests, such as Rev.

Francis Leong (1818-1884), who preached and baptised in villages on the Hong Kong Island, including Stanley and Shek Pai Wan; while Rev. Volonteri and Rev. Giuseppe Burghignoli left the Victoria City after learning Chinese, and started to preach in remote villages. Rev. Volonteri arrived Aberdeen in 1860, followed by Rev. Burghignoli.[6] In fact, they were not satisfied with preaching in only a few villages on the island. Instead, they were more keen on exploring new paths to the mainland, so that their successors would continue their work and relay missions to the mainland.[7]

Integration into the Hakka Island: St. Joseph Freinademetz in Yim Tin Tsai

The missionaries' first contact with rural people began in the middle of the 19th century. At that time, Hong Kong had two working branches to support missions in mainland China. One belonged to the MEP and the other belonged to the Dominicans (Ordo Praedicatorum, OP). Since MEP handed over the mission area to the PIME, many priests from the PIME have gone to Tai Po and Sai Kung to carry out missionary work. Some missionaries began to preach to Yim Tin Tsai, a small island in Sai Kung.

Yim Tin Tsai, also known as "Yim Tin Tsz", was established by the Chan's family of Wuhua, Guangdong. Their ancestor Chan De moved to Guanlan Songyuansha, San On County in the 18th century, and his descendants divided in three branches in the 19th century, scattering in Sai Kung Yim Tin Tsai, Tai Po Yim Tin Tsai (near Shuen Wan Typhoon Shelter) and Ta Kwu Ling Ping Yeung. They originally had five acres of salt fields in Yim Tin Tsai, and engaged in fishing and farming for their livelihoods. Later, there were more than 200 people in its heyday. The salt produced from the island was then transported to Sai Kung Market and nearby areas for sale.[8] In 1864, Rev. Volonteri went to preach in Yim Tin Tsai, and in 1866, Rev. Origo, who was appointed to assist Rev. Volonteri, built a chapel and a school in Sai Kung. He baptised 19 villagers in Yim Tin Tsai on Pentecost Sunday, who were the first batch of parishioners from the Mainland in Hong Kong.[9] During the Christmas time of the same year, Rev. Volonteri were invited to baptise the other 33 villagers of the Chan's family on the island. This group of villagers included three generations of the Chan's family, namely Chan Yuen-cheung (80 years old) of the Yuen generation; Lung-kei (43 years old), Sing-kei (41 years old), Kwong-kei (27 years old) and Chuen-kei (19 years old) of the Kei generation; Ting-wo (3 years old) and Ting-hing (9 years old) of the Ting generation. According to scholars' research, this baptism of villagers of three generations, was the first of its kind in Hong Kong's missionary history.[10] In 1867, villagers on the island reclaimed land and rented out thatched cottage houses, in order to build a chapel and a school, and their patron saint was Saint Joseph. It was one of the first places where a Catholic church was established in Hong Kong.

According to Bishop Pozzoni, Domenico (MEM, 1861-1924), when he was preaching in Sai Kung: "In addition to performing herdsman duties, we must also solve problems for believers or non-believers."[11] Villagers were often bullied by local tyrants and gentry. Therefore Rev. Volonteri formed a self-defense organisation for the church members.[12] Thanks to the hard work of the priest, Yim Tin Tsai Village became a "Catholic Village" in 1875. In the same year, during his second pastoral visit, Bishop Raimondi witnessed that all villagers of the whole island were baptised, and often held parades and feasts. This reminded him of the churches in his hometown of Italy. He believed that faith and simplicity can be found here.[13]

Rev. Josef Freinademetz (SVD, 1852-1908, canonized in 2003 as St. Joseph Freinademetz), had also preached in Sai Kung during the early days of Hong Kong's opening.[14] He was born in Italy (then Tirol of Austria) in 1852, and raised in a devout Catholic family. He was ordained as a priest at the age of 23 and joined the newly established Society of the Divine Word (SVD) two years later.[15] He arrived in Sai Kung in 1879 and served in Yim Tin Tsai. In 1890, a new church was built in the area, replacing the original chapel. He served in the village for two years, and had baptized two baby girls. (Please refer to Chapter 7 for more about St. Joseph Freinademetz).

Travelling Missionaries: Drawing of the first "Map of the San-On District, Kwangtung Province" by Rev. Volonteri and others

As said in Chapter 1, the Pontifical Foreign Missions Institute (PIME) was established in Italy in 1850. It is composed of priests dedicated to evangelization and lay missionaries.

As early as the 1850s, these missionaries paid much attention to the villages closer to the mainland, such as Tai Po and Sai Kung, and set up mission stations there so that they could easily enter the mainland, such as Po On and Wai Chow, to set up more mission points. At that time, bishops, priests or missionaries often carried out mission journeys or visits the country missions in this area. In 1865, Rev. Origo and Rev. Volonteri began to preach in Ting Kok, Tai Po. They often travelled by small boats or on foot between villages, and were known as the "travelling missionaries". After Easter that year, they went to Tamsui, Guangdong. On 1 July, Rev. Origo went to Kei Ling Ha in Sai Kung to baptise an adult, and then went to other villages in Sai Kung. If missionaries considered that Catholicism was unlikely to spread in that village, they would not stay long and would move to another village. Therefore, they often targeted remote and scattered Hakka villages which were more open to foreign religion instead of areas resided by big clans.[16]

Rev. Volonteri and Rev. Leong continued to preach in Ting Kok. They visited the surrounding villages from time to time, which they had to cross mountains and ridges to get there. Rev. Volonteri would record the villages they passed each time, and later completed the famous "Map of the San-On District, Kwangtung Province" in May 1866. It is regarded as the first map depicting the early conditions of Hong Kong in detail. It recorded countless villages in San On County, including the villages they have visited or were familiar with, in both Chinese and English.[17] It is believed that the place names in Chinese of the map were handwritten by Rev. Leong.[18] Some scholars pointed out that although the map was bilingual, but apparently the map was mainly for English readers. Not only serving as a map, it was also a local chronicle of the area, which could be used for local travel or business purposes.

In fact, when the United Kingdom leased the New Territories, its diplomats and administrators used this map as a reference. On 10 February 1899, when Sir Henry Arthur Blake (1840-1918) sent a telegram to Sir Claude Macdonald (1855-1915), the British ambassador to China and urged him to acquire important towns in Shenzhen, and indicated that he could refer to "the Missionary Map of 1866", which obviously referred to the map of Rev. Volonteri.[19] When leasing the New Territories, James Stewart Lockhart, Colonial Secretary, was sent to write a report on the Hong Kong Colony (named the *Lockhart Report*) which served as a reference for future governance of the area. The villages listed in the report are also based on the villages included in the "Map of the San-On District, Kwangtung Province" by Rev. Volonteri. Rev. Volonteri published a notice in the *Hong Kong Government Gazette* on 10 May 1866, suggesting that each map was to be sold for $5, which the amount of subscription should be over 120 in order to cover the cost of printing, and if there were any revenue, it would be allocated for missionary purposes. The content of the notice is as follows:

The scope of this Map embraces an area of about Forty Five miles from North to South, and of about Sixty miles from East to West – that is to say the District of Sun-on whereof Nam-tao, is the departmental town. It is within the district of Sun-on that Hongkong and its dependencies stood prior to their cession, and the whole Coast line for many miles adjacent is under the jurisdiction of the Mandarin at Nam-tao.

The Map is the result of four years' labor, and is made entirely from the personal observations of the author. The dangers, the difficulties, and the hardships which the work has involved, have been very great. The district is excessively mountainous and as occular demonstration had exclusively in all cases to be relied on, by reason of the worthlessness of native information, the fatigue attending travel has been no light matter. The villagers entertain the idea that their mountains contain auriferous deposits, and are very jealous of foreigners examining them. The consequence is that there is much difficulty in procuring the services of guides and still more difficulty in obtaining correct information on any point. In fact the idea above alluded to proves a strong incentive to the conveyance of false information, and excites resistance to the progress of the traveller, besides creating great personal danger.

Under these circumstances this Map has been produced, and it has been suggested to the author that it is a pity the result of so much labor, danger, and difficulty, should in these days of progress, be concealed from the world. Science, Religion and Commerce are now allied in the vast work of the dissemination of knowledge and of Western Civilisation, and it cannot be doubted that Geography is the pioneer of the movement.

But in a local and a directly utilitarian point of view, the author is encouraged to believe that his work should not be placed as a candle under a bushel. This wealthy and most important Colony stands in the midst of the Sun-on District, and it seems to betoken a feeling in rear of the age, that the topography of the immediate neighbourhood should be a matter of perfect indifference. To the naturalist, the traveller, the sportsman, and the Missionary, the information should be acceptable, to say nothing of its political value. Besides, for police purposes in dealing with the all prevailing evil of piracy, when the subtlety of the Mandarin is considered, the author cannot doubt the value of his work to the British authorities.

He therefore calls attention to his Map, and solicits the favor of subscriptions to enable him to publish it.

REVD. S. VOLONTERI, Mission, Apost.

Hongkong, 10 May, 1866[20]

At that time, there were more than a dozen villages on the Sai Kung Peninsula, namely Sai Kung, Yim Tin Tsai, Chek Keng, Tai Long, Kei Ling Ha, Che Ha, Wu Kai Sha, Tai Mong Tsai, Tsam Chuk Wan, Wong Mo Ying, Pak Sha O, Nam Shan, Leung Shuen Wan, etc. They were the working areas of the priests of PIME. It could be seen from the New Territories report written by Lockhart that, these villages in Sai Kung were mainly inhabited by Hakka and local people.[21]

Villages and population in Sai Kung in the *Lockhart Report*

Village	Population	Ethnic Group
Cheung Uk Wai	40	Punti
Tai Long	80	Punti
Sai Wan	40	Punti
Chik Kang	150	Hakka
To Ka Ping	20	Punti
Lung Keuk	50	Punti
Lan Nai Wan	150	Hakka
Wong Nai Chau	60	Hakka
Pak Tam Chung	30	Hakka
Ching Hang	20	Hakka
Pak Tam	10	Punti
Ping Tan	10	Hakka
Ngong Wo	80	Hakka
Wong Mo In	40	Hakka
She Tan	20	Hakka
Chap Chuk Wan	60	Hakka
Pai Au	10	Hakka
Tai Mong Tsai	100	Hakka
Pak A	80	Hakka

(cont.)

Village	Population	Ethnic Group
Tung Wan	—	—
Pak Lap	40	Punti
She Wau	10	Hakka
Kan Sai	80	Punti/Hakka
Lai Chi Chong	60	Hakka
Nam Shan	30	Hakka
Ham Tin	50	Hakka
Sham Chung	50	Hakka
Tap Mun	200	Hakka
Hoi Ha	50	Hakka
Tam Tsai	10	Hakka
Pak Sha Au	150	Punti
Sheung Yeung	120	Hakka
Ha Yeung	220	Hakka
Ko Tong	100	Hakka
Ho Muk Tun[22]	50	Hakka
Uk Tau	20	Hakka
Cheung Sheung Au[23]	10	Punti
Tan Ka Wan	80	Hakka
Wo Li Kiu[24]	60	Hakka
Tai Lau[25]	160	Hakka
Nam Tsai[26]	60	Punti
Lam Uk Wai	60	Punti

In addition to preaching in Sai Kung, the touring priests also helped the parishioners in Sai Kung and Yim Tin Tsai to oppose to the intrusion of the large clans in Sheung Shui. As Sai Kung belonged to the area of Sheung U Tung owned by the Liu clan of Sheung Shui, local villagers needed to pay tax to the Liu's, and become tenant farmers. Under long-term oppression and exploitation, these villagers could only rely on the help of priests to organise self-defense armed groups to resist the big clans. However, during the crusade against the Sheung Shui tribe, some villagers were killed. After the incident, Rev. Volonteri was transferred to Henan Province on 8 February 1870.[27]

In addition, *A Ramble round the World* (1871) by Baron Hübner (1811-1892) had depicted the deeds of Bishop Raimondi and another priest, as well as the author's own observations in Hong Kong. Hübner was an official and diplomat of the Austrian Empire. He visited different countries including France, Portugal, Italy, and Germany. When he was sent to Milan in 1848, he was imprisoned for three months because of his involvement in revolutionary activities, and was later released.[28] He began to travel around the world starting from 1867, and visited Hong Kong in 1871, where he wrote *A Ramble round the World* in the same year. In his book, he described Kowloon City and several Hakka villages at that time:

> The countryside here was inhabited by either farmers or gangsters. What they need for their livelihood is a shovel, an oar and a gun. Those hawkers and small businessmen travelling along the mountain trails are often robbed. "So, let's dispel the idea of going to San On County." Rev. Raimondi happened to be there, and he smiled and said to us when he heard our words: "I will take you there personally and ensure that you are safe."[29]

The travel memoir recorded that Bishop Raimondi and another Latin-speaking priest had once set-off with Baron Hübner to San On County. They crossed the sea between Hong Kong and China (believed to be Victoria Harbour) within 50 minutes, and climbed up a wall, where the scenery of Hong Kong was unobstructed. From his description, it was obvious that they were on the wall of the Kowloon Walled City while watching the scenery:[30]

> During these three days, we stayed in and travelled along these huge areas and places where pirates gather. Some of the pirates there have been willing to convert to Catholicism. We spent the first night in Sai Kung Village; the next morning we visited Yantian Tsai, all the residents on this small island were baptized; in the evening we came to Ting Kok, the centre of San On Missionary, where there is a spacious house, owned by the priest and hidden in the shade of the trees, because non-believers were superstitious and refused to cut down those trees.

Since mid 19th century, the political turmoil in China, such as the emergence of the Boxer Rebellion and the Eight-Power Allied Forces, has made missionary work in the mainland difficult. Hong Kong, as a colony, had a relatively stable political situation. Missionaries could preach in the New Territories and establish multiple mission stations in Tai Po, Pun Chung, Ting Kok, Sai Kung, Yuen Long etc. Despite conflicts arose during the establishment of some chapels, the mission area in Hong Kong was still a relatively safe place, and as a whole there had been no serious violent incident. Although the piracy problem in Sai Kung was relatively rampant, it was not a major threat to missionaries. According to the records of PIME, although the incidents of persecuting Catholic missionaries and believers occurred in the mission areas in the Mainland at that time, such incidents rarely happened in the New Territories of Hong Kong. Instead, Catholics in Hong Kong were still able to use the opportunity to rescue people in need from the Mainland.

At the same time, the transportation to the Eastern New Territories became more convenient. For example, they could take small boats to coastal villages, avoiding the need to travel long distances on mountain trails; in the past they had to travel by sampan, but motor boats were available at that time.[31] Therefore, missionaries built up relationship with the Hakka settlements during the period of Apostolic Prefecture, laying foundation for further development of the Apostolic Vicariate.

Notes

1   Rev. Volonteri, Simeone MEM (1831-1904) arrived in Hong Kong in 1860 and served in Sai Kung Chek Keng, Tai Long, Yan Tin Tsai, Tai Po Ting Kok and other places. Later, he transferred to Henan as a missionary and was promoted to bishop in 1874.

2   Ha Keloon Louis, *The History of Evangelization in Hong Kong-Wun Yiu, Yim Tin Tsai, Ting Kok* (Hong Kong: The Diocesan Ad Hoc Committee for The Year of Evangelization, 2005), p. 3.

3   It is said that the priest and the priest ordered someone to open a window in the residence, but on the day of the excavation, a baby in the village died and the other woman felt unwell. The villagers believed that it was because the god was disturbed and the priest had to leave. Ibid., p. 13.

4   According to Rev. Ha's speculation, the original site of this school should be in an open space next to the Wu Di Temple in Ting Kok Village, which has now been demolished. Ibid.

5   Gianni Criveller, *Piccola Storia Missionaria di Yim Tin Tsai, Saigon, Hong Kong* (Hong Kong: Publisher Unknown, 2004), p. 3.

6   The missionary and priest of PIME (Monsigneur Simeone Volonteri) drew the "Map of the San-On District, Kwangtung Province" when preaching in the villages of the New Territories in San On County (i.e., Po On County). This map became an important reference blueprint for the British government when Britain leased the New Territories in 1898.

7   For the deeds of Rev. Simeone Volonteri, See Sergio Ticozzi, *IL PIME e La Perla Dell'Oriente* (Hong Kong: Caritas Printing Centre, 2008), http://www.atma-o-jibon.org/italiano8/ticozzi_pimehk12.htm, retrieved on 13 August 2021.

8   Anthony Siu, *The History and Nostalgia of Hong Kong's New Territories* (Hong Kong: Chinese Culture and Education Exchange Service Centre, 2008), pp. 76-77.

9   Gianni Criveller, *From Milan to Hong Kong: 150 Years of Mission: Pontifical Institute for Foreign Missions 1858 – 2008* (Hong Kong: Vox Amica Press, 2008), p. 14. Rev. Origo died on 26 March 1868, at the age of 33.

10   Ha Keloon, "Catholic Missionary Work in Hong Kong Hakka Villages", http://www.cultus.hk/writings/hakka.htm#_ftn96, retrieved on 28 March 2021. The Chan clan was originally named Mang, Ho, Yuen, Ting, Kok, Wing, Wah, Fu and Kui. In recent years, ten generations of characters have been completed. Therefore, the village committee decided that the descendants should be based on Pak, Nin, Shue, Tai, Yip, Sai, Chin, San and You generations are combined, in order of positive growth and youth. See Anthony Siu, *The History and Nostalgia of Hong Kong's New Territories* (Hong Kong: Chinese Culture and Education Exchange Service Centre, 2008), pp. 76-77.

11   Ha Keloon, "Catholic Missionary Work in Hong Kong Hakka Villages", http://www.cultus.hk/writings/hakka.htm#_ftn96.

12   Anthony Siu, *The History and Nostalgia of Hong Kong's New Territories*, pp. 76-77

13   Gianni Criveller, *From Milan to Hong Kong: 150 Years of Mission: Pontifical Institute for Foreign Missions 1858-2008* (Hong Kong: Vox Amica Press, 2008), p. 14.

14   Records of the baptism of Yim Tin Tsai; Catholic Hong Kong Diocese Archives, IV-14-04; Rev. Josef Freinademetz (1852-1908) was declared a saint by the church on 5 October 2002. See Ha Keloon, "Catholic Missionary Work in Hong Kong Hakka Villages". Rev. Josef Freinademetz of the Society of the Divine Word was canonized by the Pope in 2003.

15   Gianni Criveller, *Piccola Storia Missionaria di Yim Tin Tsai Sai Kung, Hong Kong*, p. 2.

16   Sergio Ticozzi, translated by Yau Lai Ching, *The Story of the Catholic Church in Hong Kong* (Hong Kong: Holy Spirit Research Centre, Extracurricular Curriculum of Holy Spirit Seminary, 1983), p. 76.

17   The "Map of the San-On District, Kwangtung Province" drawn by Italian missionaries and priests in 1866 is collected by the National Library of Australia (Canberra), https://nla.gov.au/nla.obj-231220841/view, retrieved on 13 August 2021.

18   Ha Keloon, *The History of Evangelisation in Hong Kong: Wun Yiu, Ting Kok, Yim Tin Tsai*, p. 16.

19   James Hayes, "The San-On Map of Mgr. Volonteri", *Journal of the Royal Asiatic Society Hong Kong Branch*, Vol. 10 (1970), pp. 193-196.

20   Ibid.

21   Report by Mr. Steward Lockhart on the Extension of the Colony of Hong Kong October 8, 1898, Eastern, No. 66, Colonial Office, 1900; Editor-in-Chief Lau Chi-pang: *Extension of Boundary Site: Early Historical Exploration of the British New Territories* (Hong Kong: Chung Hua Publishing Co. Ltd., 2010), pp. 225-226.

22   "Ho Muk Tun" is believed to refer to today's "Ngau Wu Tun".

23   "Cheung Sheung Au" is today's "Cheung Sheung" on the plateau of the Sai Kung Peninsula.

24   "Wo Lei Giu" means today's "Fox squawk" in the northeast of Chek Keng, Sai Kung. Its population was later included in Ko Lau Wan, see *A Gazetteer of Place Names in Hong Kong Kowloon and The New Territories* (Hong Kong; S. Young, Government Printer, 1960), p. 190.

25   "Ta Lou" is the place where the Wo Lei Giu is called today.

26   "Nam Che" is today's "Nam She Tsim".

27   Gianni Criveller, *Piccola Storia Missionaria di Yim Tin Tsai Sai Kung, Hong Kong*, p. 4.

28   Count Alexander Hübner, Catholic Encyclopedia, New Advent, https://www.newadvent.org/cathen/07509a.htm

29   Ibid, p. 77.

30   Ibid, p. 78.

31   Thomas F. Ryan, S. J., *The Story of a Hundred Years, The Pontifical Institute of Foreign Missions (PIME) in Hong Kong,1858-1958* (Hong Kong: Catholic Truth Society, 1959), pp. 113-120.

Chapter 3

The Period of Apostolic Vicariate: Hardship and Harvest (1874-1931)

1841

1874

1931

1945

1969

1981

2000

Bishop Raimondi was a member of the Milan Institute for Foreign Missions (later known as The Pontifical Institute for Foreign Missions, PIME) and was described as "a staunch, authoritative, wise and determined person". Based on various reasons, he opined that the then Apostolic Prefecture of Hong Kong led by a priest should be raised to an Apostolic Vicariate under the management of a Bishop. He came to Hong Kong in 1858 and was formally appointed by the Holy See as the Apostolic Prefect in 1868, responsible for the management of the Hong Kong Catholic Church.

The Hong Kong Catholic Church made great progress during the time Bishop Raimondi was the Apostolic Prefect. The number of Catholics tripled from 1,500 in 1867 to approximately 5,000 in 1872. The Milan Institute for Foreign Missions, to which Bishop Raimondi belonged, was eager to set up a mission of its own at the gateway to China, and found Hong Kong suitable. Compared with other missionary groups such as the Jesuits, the Franciscans and the Paris Foreign Mission, the Milan Institute for Foreign Missions was relatively small-scale and powerless, and Hong Kong became the foundation for the development of the Mission in the Mainland.[1] On the other hand, the Mission considered that promoting the local church to Apostolic Vicariate would bring benefits in terms of diplomatic hierarchy—while a foreign bishop would be officially received and treated well by a Provincial Governor of the Manchu government, a priest would only be received by a County Magistrate. Obviously, the title of the leader of Hong Kong Catholic church affected the way he dealt with Chinese officials. At the same time, Hong Kong Sheng Kung Hui was about to welcome a new Anglican bishop, and there was already a bishop in Guangzhou's Apostolic Prefecture. Therefore, Bishop Raimondi believed that it is inappropriate for a priest to serve as the head of the local church. Furthermore, the vacancy of Bishop of the Diocese of Macau would be filled after remaining vacant more than ten years. Bishop Raimondi was worried that Portuguese Catholics in Hong Kong would be inclined to follow the

Bishop of Macau due to different hierarchical positions of the Catholic leaders in the two places.

Based on the above considerations, Bishop Raimondi persuaded the Holy See to upgrade Hong Kong to an Apostolic Vicariate led by a bishop. He hinted that he intended to resign as the head of the Catholic Church in Hong Kong to show that he would not benefit from this proposal. After intense lobbying, the Holy See accepted and gave the Milan Institute for Foreign Missions permission to manage the Catholic Church in Hong Kong, upgrading it to a vicariate on 17 November 1874. Its jurisdiction was expanded to include the Guishan region in Guangdong (hereafter "Wai Yeung") and Hoi Fung County—a total area five times larger than its original purview. Bishop Raimondi was also ordained as the first Apostolic Vicar of Hong Kong.

This period also saw the Holy See changed its views and policies towards Hong Kong. It no longer regarded Hong Kong as the representative of the Holy See and let the Procura in China base in Hong Kong. The Convention of Peking signed by the Qing government between 1858 and 1860 granted missionaries the legal right to live and preach in China. It was stipulated: "It must be announced to the entire land that missionaries can preach and carry out the teachings of Catholicism for all persons in all places in China."[2] The Holy See therefore noticed that a large number of missionaries could enter China without the assistance of the Procura in China. The improvement of transportation and communication channels also made the missionaries in China less reliable on the Procura in China when communicating with the Holy See. Recognising the lowered importance of the Procura, the head of the Catholic Church in Hong Kong did not need to juggle the Procurator. Therefore, he no longer had to deal with the financial affairs of missions in mainland China as his predecessor had done, instead focusing solely on local missionary work in Hong Kong.

With its promotion to a vicariate, the Catholic Church of Hong Kong had a larger area of jurisdiction to carry out missionary activities. After unlinking with the Procura in China, Hong Kong was officially taken over by the Milan Institute for Foreign Missions and enjoyed greater autonomy. Under the leadership of the Bishop Raimondi, the development of the Catholic Church in Hong Kong had entered a mature stage, rapidly developing its pastoral service, mission, charitable welfare and education work.[3]

Bishop Raimondi's Visit to Sai Kung after a Typhoon

On 22 September 1874, a powerful typhoon struck Hong Kong and its neighboring areas, causing huge damage, killing 2,000 people and wrecking 350 ships. The typhoon destroyed much of Sai Kung, and the community worked hard to rebuild after the disaster.[4] After Bishop Raimondi was ordained as a bishop in Italy, he returned to Hong Kong and immediately went to various mission stations in the continent district for pastoral visits. In February 1875, Bishop Raimondi made his first visits to Yim Tin Tsai, Wong Nai Chau, Chek Keng, Tai Long, Tan Ka Wan and Sham Chung, all in Sai Kung area, and then went to Wu Kai Sha and Kowloon City before returning to Hong Kong Island.[5] When he arrived at Sai Kung market, he was warmly received by the villagers who welcomed him with a musical performance—they had never seen the bishop in person. From there Bishop Raimondi travelled to Yim Tin Tsai by boat. The residents on the island were all church members and they were very hospitable. The Bishop then took a small boat to Wong Nai Chau in the northern part of the bay. The village had initially had only one believer, but by the time of the Raimondi's visit the number had increased to 25, with the same number of catechumens. Bishop Raimondi then walked two hours to reach Chek Keng, which had been established as a mission station for eight years. The original chapel was very small and had been destroyed by strong winds. After visiting Chek Keng, the Bishop crossed the mountains to revisit Tai Long, where he was greeted by the village elders. Almost all the villagers in the area believed in Catholicism, and the Bishop also spent time celebrating the Lunar New Year, an important Chinese festival, with them, but in a Catholic way.

After Chek Keng, Bishop Raimondi travelled to Tan Ka Wan, where a chapel was already constructed before the Bishop's visit to Europe. Although its roof had been destroyed by strong winds, the chapel was still in use. Raimondi then boarded the mission boat "Stella Maris" ("Star of the Sea"), a sampan, and traveled along the coast to Sham Chung where an intrepid missionary was doing as much for the lives of the people as for their souls. This village was located at the tip of an inle and covered a wide area of flat land. Rev. Luigi Maria Piazzoli (MEM, 1845-1904) once encouraged villagers there to build an embankment, which allowed the village's land to expand to accommodate more than half of the population. When Bishop Raimondi arrived there, he saw that the villagers were distressed by the wind-blown dike, so he gathered all the Catholics to rebuild and strengthen it. The village itself remained damaged, but Bishop

Raimondi encouraged them not to give up. His words inspired the villagers, and soon after, even the pirates and bandits problems happened in the area disappeared.

After completing this route, Bishop Raimondi walked from Sham Chung to the Sha Tin Peninsula, and then returned to Kowloon.[6] He passed Wu Kai Sha on his way, where a chapel was built a few years ago and where there were 30 Catholics. Bishop Raimondi's trip to Sai Kung ended in Wu Kai Sha and returned to Victoria City, Hong Kong Island on Ash Wednesday.[7]

Raimondi did not have sufficient time to travel to Wai Yeung and Hoi Fung, which had just been incorporated into the Apostolic Vicariate of Hong Kong. Instead, they were visited by Rev. Piazzoli and Rev. Andrew Leong,[8] who had preached at Hoi Fung from 1877 to 1892.[9] In response to the expansion of the mission area, the local church felt the need to promote its services more systematically, so on 9 May 1875, Bishop Raimondi convened a local religious conference (a Vicariate Synod), the purpose of which was to review missionary work and methods. All missionaries participated in the meeting. At the meeting it was decided that Catholic Church in Hong Kong would be divided into four Districts:

(1) The area of Hong Kong Island from the east of Murray Barracks[10], including Stanley, would become the "Eastern District";

(2) The area of Hong Kong Island from the west of Murray Barracks to Queen's Road West would become the "Central District";

(3) Queen's Road West and the rest of Hong Kong Island including Aberdeen, British Kowloon, Tsuen Wan, Lantau Island and outlying islands would become the "Western District";

(4) Nortern part of the Kowloon Peninsula and the north of Kowloon Mountains would become the "Continental District". This inland area was to include all of Wai Yeung and Hoi Fung County, as well as San On County, with the exception of the outlying islands and Tsuen Wan.

The fourth District was led by four priests, including: Rev. Piazzoli, Rev. Leong, Rev. Stephen Chu (?-1882) and Rev. Antonius Tam (1850-1875, see Chapter 5). The area encompassed the Sai Kung Peninsula, including the Sacred Heart Church in Sai Kung, St. Francis Church in Kowloon, St. Joseph's Chapel in Yim Tin Tsai, St. Peter's Church in Wunyiu, Taipo, and Church of St. Andrew in Ting Kok. Rev. Tam was

The Apostolic Vicariate of Hong Kong established in 1874 included Hong Kong, Kowloon, Hoi Fung, Po On and Wai Yeung.

drowned in Ting Kok Hoi, and in 1877, Rev. Fu took over his duties.[11] Also active in this priesthood district were three Lay Sisters and two nuns from the Daughters of Mary.[12] According to the *Catholic Directory* of 1877, a chapel named Our Lady of the Immaculate Conception had been established in Tai Long Village, as well as a chapel in Chek Keng, called the "Holy Mother of God" chapel (a predecessor of the Holy Family Chapel). Priest's residence in the east of this District located in Tai Long while that in the middle part of this District located in Sai Kung. The district had about 15 missionary stations, serving 700 Catholics in about 40 villages.[13] Several schools had also been established in Sai Kung by this time.[14]

The Vicariate Synod held in 1877 made Sai Kung the centre of Continental District, and the priests responsible for this district continued to use such location as priests' residence. From then onwards, Sai Kung became the "Mother and Cradle" of evangelisation in the region. All newly arrived PIME Missionaries first settled in

Sai Kung, where they received training and adapted to the new environment. In this way, Catholicism spread from Sai Kung to other places in Po On, Wai Yeung and Hoi Fung. This continued until part of San On County was leased by the British in 1898 for a period of 99 years and became the New Territories; while another part of San On County became an autonomous region.[15]

When missionaries proposed candidates for the Bishop of Hong Kong to the Holy See, experiences of working in the mainland was one of the main considerations. In addition to the first Apostolic Vicar, Bishop Raimondi, all the four successors, Bishop Piazzoli, Bishop Dominic Pozzoni (PIME, 1861-1924), Bishop Enrico Valtorta (PIME, 1883-1951) and Bishop Lorenzo Bianchi (PIME, 1899-1983), have worked in rural areas within the mainland area.

The upgrade of the Catholic Church of Hong Kong to the Apostolic Vicariate in 1874 was closely related to the missionary activities of Sai Kung: Kwai Shin and Hoi

—25—

WESTERN DISTRICT.

This district comprises that part of Hong-kong lying between Gap Street, and Queen Road West, and Aberdeen inclusive; and on the Mainland, British Kowloon, Chinwan and the Island of Lan-tao.

RESIDENT PRIESTS:

REV. A. TAGLIABUE, ...Miss. Ap.

CHAPELS:

THE SACRED HEART, ...West Point Reformatory.
ST. PETER'S,... ... ... Chinwan.
ST. JOSEPH'S, ...Aberdeen.

EDUCATIONAL AND CHARITABLE INSTITUTIONS:

REFORMATORY
FOR CHINESE BOYS.

Under the direction of the Christian Brothers, one school for boys, shops for Carpenters, Tailoring and Shoemaking.

Director:
BROTHER ISFRID.

Assistants;

BR. IBONDIUS. | BR. PETER.

—26—

ON THE MAINLAND.

CONTINENTAL DISTRICT.

REV. A. PIAZZOLI, ...Superior
REV. A. LEANG,
REV. S. CHU AND REV. MATHEUS FU.

Sisterhood:

Three lay Sisters and two Daughters of Mary.

SUNON.

EASTERN RESIDENTIAL PLACE AT TAILONG.

CHAPELS:

OUR LADY OF THE
IMMACULATE CONCEPTION,
At Tailong.

HOLY MOTHER OF GOD,
At Chukau.

CENTRAL RESIDENTIAL PLACE OF SI-KUN.

Chapels:

THE SACRED HEART, ...At Si-kun.
ST. FRANCIS XAVIER, ... At Kowloon.
ST. JOSEPH, ...At Yan-tin-sei.
ST. PETER, ... At Wan-yau.
ST. ANDREW, ...At Tankok.

Schools:

BOARDING SCHOOL, ...At Si-kun.
DAY SCHOOL, ... At Wong-nei-chong.

The Western District decided in Vicariate Synod included West Point, Aberdeen, British Kowloon, Chin Wan (now Tsuen Wan) and Lantau Island. (Image source: Catholic Diocesan Archives)

Information about the clergy and churches of the mainland districts published in the Catholic Handbook of 1877. (Image source: Catholic Diocesan Archives)

Fung were included in the Apostolic Vicariate of Hong Kong. Due to the enlargement of the jurisdiction, the Hong Kong Catholic Mission was divided into four districts owing to the review of missionary activities. Sai Kung became the centre of the Continental District, which laid the foundation for its uniqueness in spreading the Catholic faith in Hong Kong at that time. Since then, Sai Kung has become a training place for all newly arrived foreign missionaries in Hong Kong. Hereafter, the successive foreign bishops of Hong Kong have preached in the Continental District, which showed the important position of Sai Kung.

From 1878 to 1879, posters, leaflets and pamphlets that satirized and criticized Europeans created a feeling of hatred for Europeans and their beliefs in mainland areas. In Taoyuan, Kwai Shin County, this engendered a sense of hostility towards Catholicism that lasted for almost ten years. According to the records of Bishop Piazzoli in early 1879, the villagers printed posters against missionaries and Catholicism and posted slanderous notices everywhere. Five Catholics were killed because of their religion, there were other Catholics who were injured, and two missionaries were robbed. The villagers forced the Catholic community to abandon and disband the church.[16] The Sai Kung region remained relatively peaceful because there was no tradition of hostility towards Europeans, and the mission made great progress: chapels were been built in Pak Tam Chung, and new Catholic groups formed in Lung Shuen Wan, Pak Tam Chung and other places.

Following a pastoral visit in 1875, Bishop Raimondi visited Sai Kung again in early 1879. After staying in Tseung Kwan O and Tai Wan Tau for a day, he and his travelling companion Rev. Chu arrived in Sai Kung the next day, where villagers welcomed them with firecrackers and music. After two days in Sai Kung, Bishop Raimondi and Rev. Chu visited the parishioners in Yim Tin Tsai, Wong Nai Chau, Chek Keng, Tai Long, Sham Chung and Che Ha.

A Pastoral Visit with Bishop Piazzoli

In 1884, the Sino-French War led to the persecution of various Christian groups in Guangdong, Guangxi and even Guizhou, along with French missionaries. The Apostolic Vicariate of Hong Kong were also affected: foreign missionaries were associated with the French and faced great danger. Rev. Piazzoli, the priest-in-charge of the Continental District, was ordered the arrest by the Chinese government for holding a French passport with a bounty of 500 yuan. Soldiers from the mainland also arrived in

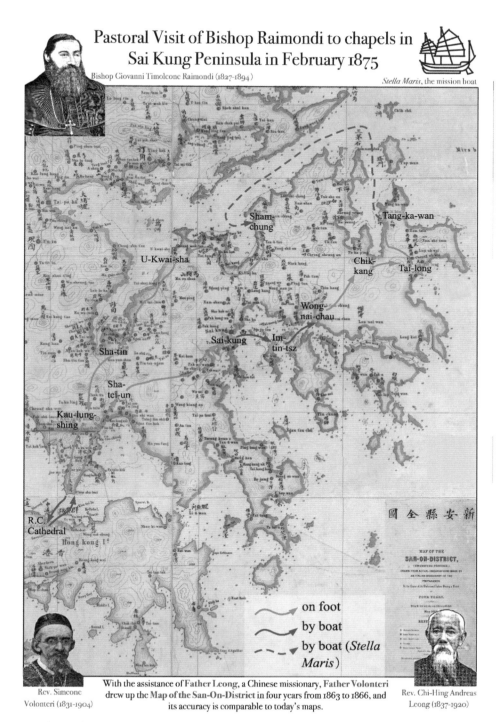

Pastoral Visit of Bishop Raimondi to chapels in Sai Kung Peninsula in February 1875

Bishop Giovanni Timoleone Raimondi (1827-1894)

Stella Maris, the mission boat

Sham-chung

Tang-ka-wan

U-Kwai-sha

Chik-kang

Tai-long

Wong-nai-chau

Sha-tin

Sai-kung

Im-tin-tsz

Sha-tei-un

Kau-lung-shing

R.C. Cathedral

Hong kong I.

~~~ on foot
~~~ by boat
- - -▶ by boat (*Stella Maris*)

Rev. Simeone Volonteri (1831-1904)

With the assistance of **Father Leong**, a Chinese missionary, **Father Volonteri** drew up the **Map of the San-On-District** in four years from 1863 to 1866, and its accuracy is comparable to today's maps.

Rev. Chi-Hing Andreas Leong (1837-1920)

Pastoral visit of Bishop Raimondi to chapels in Sai Kung Peninsula in February 1875.

Sai Kung to search for him.[17] He and another priest were forced to leave in September and returned to Hong Kong Island.[18] In the following years, missionary work stagnated and only a dozen adults were baptized each year.[19]

Nevertheless, in general the losses suffered by Catholic groups in San On County were not as severe as those in the Guangzhou Missionary District, which was governed by French missionaries. By December 1884, all missionaries were able return to live in their original places. However, between March and December 1885, Rev. Piazzoli was again forced to take leave due to illness. Rev. Giuseppe Burghignoli (MEM, 1833-1892) took over his responsibilities, but he was only able to visit the area intermittently. Much of the work was taken over by Chinese priests, and an Italian priest named Domenico Pozzoni, who had just arrived from Italy to replace Rev. Fu, who was transferred to Hoi Fung.[20] When Rev. Piazzoli was transferred to the urban areas in 1891, there were only two priests in the Continental District—Rev. Dominic Pozzoni and Rev. Leong. The former became the head of the Continental District until he was appointed as Hong Kong's Apostolic Vicar in 1905, and he then left his post.

In 1895, Rev. Piazzoli was appointed as the Apostdic Vicar of Hong Kong and ordained the bishop to succeed the Bishop Raimondi. In November of the same year, Bishop Piazzoli returned to visit old friends with whom he used to work. Since the bishop could not visit everyone, he focused on the Sai Kung Peninsula. The villagers set off firecrackers and played music to welcome the bishop and his entourage, and solemnly accompanied them into the church, where they held a welcome party. The evening was occupied with Bible teachings and the ceremony of repentance; the next morning, Mass was held and the Eucharist was received. Bishop Piazzoli had a wonderful time in Sham Chung, Pak Sha O, Chek Keng, and Tai Long. The believers then solemnly accompanied the Bishop to walk from the chapel to the seashore, from where he returned to Hong Kong Island by boat. According to the existing record, the enthusiasm of the villagers was touching, and the whole celebration was wonderful.[21]

Soon after Easter in 1896, Bishop Piazzoli visited Sai Kung again. The pastoral visit lasted only three days, he was accompanied by Rev. Giuseppe Zamponi (MEM, 1870-1925) whom had only started his serving in the Continental District for about a year. From 1897 to 1898, as Kwai Shin and Hoi Fung gradually became autonomous regions, Rev. Pozzoni, who managed the Continental District, focused on the work of San On County and reallocated the manpower under his jurisdiction to designate Sai Kung and Nantou in San On County as two mission centres.[22]

The Lease of the New Territories by the United Kingdom: Sai Kung separated from the Continental District

Following the signing of the *The Convention Between Great Britain and China Respecting an Extension of Hong Kong Territory* between the Qing Dynasty and the United Kingdom in Beijing, the United Kingdom leased the New Territories from China on 9 June 1898. In April 1899, the Union Jack was raised in Tai Po, symbolizing the official takeover of the New Territories by Britain. As San On County was politically divided into two parts, Sai Kung and Nan Tou followed different paths. From a religious point of view, the status of the former declined to only the center of the New Territories, while the latter oversaw the rest of San On County. Although the residents of the New Territories did not welcome British rule at first, it did bring a certain degree of stability and calm to the area. At that time, the members of To Yeung Catholic Church in Kwai Shin County had faced hostility from the local population for ten years. In 1879, five believers were killed and ten families and two missionaries were looted.[23] The New Territories were largely spared from the fallout of the Boxer Rebellion in China, which took place in the turn of the 20th century. The social and political turmoil and riots caused by the overthrow of the Qing Empire had little impact on missionary work in the New Territories. In addition to continuing pastoral visits to Sai Kung, subsequent bishops also visited local priests and Catholic groups in mainland mission areas, such as Hoi Fung.

On 10 November 1885, Rev. Pozzoni left Italy for Hong Kong and arrived on 19 December. Over the following two years, he traveled to Nantou, Wai Yeung and Hoi Fung in Po On to preach, mainly for the Hakka people.[24]

In the summer of 1904, Rev. Pozzoni left Sai Kung to accompany the sick Bipshop Piazzoli back to Italy, where the latter died on 26 December. In early 1905, Rev. Pozzoni returned to Hong Kong and travelled to Sai Kung, where he was in charge. In a letter written in Chek Keng in June 1905, he mentioned that he had reported to the superior about his visit to the mainland. The Holy See was considering appointing a new vicar.[25] When the names of the three bishop candidates were submitted to the Pope Pius X, the Pope asked: "Which one is working hard for the Chinese?" When he was told that was Rev. Pozzoni was doing so, he responded: "Then he is the one elected."[26] Rev. Pozzoni received the news that Pius X had appointed him as the third vicar of Hong Kong in July and was widely praised as the "holy bishop" for cultivating the spiritual life of the diocese.[27] He was ordained as a bishop in October 1905, and his duties and work in the New Territories were replaced by Rev. Angelo Ferrario (PIME, 1876-1933) who was sent to the New Territories at the end of 1900, and was assisted by Rev. Francis Chan (1869-1941). The typhoon in 1906 was one of the deadliest natural disasters in Hong Kong's history. The typhoon landed in Hong Kong on 18 September and caused more than 10,000 deaths. 38 houses in Tai Po central area collapsed, and buildings in Central were also affected. Conservative estimates indicate that the loss amounted to 20 to 30 million Hong Kong dollars. In Sai Kung and several villages, all houses, including those of missionaries, collapsed. Schools were particularly badly damaged. The missionaries had to repair them immediately to continue their services. In January of the following year, after taking over as the pastor, Rev. Pozzoni visited the Continental District presided over by Fr. Antonio Banchi (1878-1930), and he also visited the Hoi Fung area (he went there again in 1917 and 1923), he even also visited the Philippines in 1908. Rev. Pozzoni's last visit to Sai Kung took place when he was 62 years old, in December 1923.[28] During his 18-year tenure, the population of Catholics in pastoral areas increased significantly. It is estimated that there were approximately 21,000 believers, of which 15,000 were Chinese.[29]

The political turmoil before the overthrow of the Qing Dynasty in 1910 had little effect on the New Territories. The three bishops repeatedly visited Sai Kung for pastoral visits. Even though they had to climb mountains and traverse rivers—an exhausting process—they were satisfied. This reflected the important position of Sai Kung at that time. From the end of the 19th century to the beginning of the 20th century, Catholic missionary activities in Sai Kung were inseparable from the religious and social events of Hong Kong. The Catholic Church in Hong Kong was "upgraded" in 1874, and Sai Kung immediately became the centre of Continental District, and became the base of priests responsible of the inland area, as well as a training ground for foreign missionaries. Although only four priests served this large area at the time, their efforts yielded favourable results. The number of believers in Sai Kung and the Catholic community gradually increased, in tandem with the entire Apostolic Vicariate of Hong Kong. Missionary activities also suffered setbacks as a result of typhoons, hatred of foreigners, and the wider developments like the Sino-French war, but their impacts on Sai Kung was limited Sai Kung, proving the wisdom behind designating it as an administrative centre for the church.

In 1898, the British leased the New Territories, and Sai Kung's status was reduced

Group photos of Bishop Pozzoni (front centre), Rev. Andreas Leong (front right) and other Chinese priests taken in 1914/1915. (Image source: PIME)

to the missionary centre of the New Territories, but it also helped the area avoid the political turmoil and riots arisen from the collapse of the Qing Empire. During this period, even in the face of a shortage of manpower, natural and man-made disasters, missionary activities in Sai Kung still made great progress. Bishops were warmly welcomed by Sai Kung villagers during their pastoral visits, and when Rev. Pozzoni passed away, villagers languished and wept bitterly, demonstrating the depth of feeling the villagers felt towards members of the church—tangible proof of success of their missionary work. Their successors continued their efforts in dealing with adversity and spreading the gospel to the outside world.

Bishop Valtorta appointed Apostolic Vicar and Rev. Teruzzi as the Director of the District of Sai Kung

Foreign missionaries left their hometowns to introduce the gospel to those who did not yet know Christ. They devoted themselves to the improvement of Catholic communities in other countries, and often suffered and died far from home. Their experiences, devotion and sacrifice should be remembered forever.

Rev. Emilio Teruzzi (PIME, 1887-1942) from Italy was one of these greatest missionaries. He served Sai Kung for 15 years and had a great love for local customs. After this period, he returned to Italy, but revisited Sai Kung because of his love for Hong Kong—he was eventually martyred in Sai Kung. Rev. Teruzzi is still well-known in his hometown, where young Catholics deeply admire him for his great faith.[30] Rev. Teruzzi was in charge of the Sai Kung district from 1914 to 1927. During this period, he had frequent and close contacts with Catholic groups and believers throughout the district. His work was the epitome of the mission carried out in Sai Kung at the time.

Rev. Teruzzi was born on 17 August 1887 in the town of Lesmo in Milan, northern Italy. When he was young, Rev. Teruzzi asked to join the Milan Institute for Foreign Missions of Milan, and he was ordained as a priest on 29 June 1912. In December of the same year, after Rev. Teruzzi arrived in Hong Kong, he obtained the permission of his teacher and bishop to carry out pastoral work in Sai Kung District. Under the guidance of Rev. Ferrario, a senior missionary in charge of the New Territories at the time, he learned the local language and customs. While Rev. Ferrario and his assistant Rev. John Situ (1877-1947) visited communities and schools and worked as herdsmen, Rev. Teruzzi concentrated on studying Chinese, and soon he took care of the entire New Territories.

In 1915, Rev. Teruzzi managed 15 churches and chapels[31], and Rev. Angelo Grampa (PIME, 1882-1957) and Rev. Joseph Yeung Cheuk-wah (1878-1945) assisted him, in succession. In his report from 1914 to 1915,[32] he was excited about the church's missionary achievements in Sai Kung—mainly because in that year, women were baptized in Long Ke, and other villagers in Sai Wan and Pak Tam Chung asked to be baptized.[33] But this missionary was not always smooth sailing. Rev. Teruzzi also complained about insufficient funds, difficulty in finding preachers, and a lack of catechumens.[34]

Rev. Teruzzi and his Chinese assistants maintained contact with more than a dozen religious communities under his jurisdiction. In order to hold the sacrament, the priest insisted on walking the steep path to the church in the remote village, regardless of the weather. Because some villages were scattered along the seashore, they needed to be reached by boat, and priests often encountered dangers in the form of storms. Rev. Teruzzi also visited many poor villages, including Yuen Long, Pat Heung and Tai Po, where he achieved some success.

In 1917, Sai Kung welcomed another newly-ordained priest: Rev. Philip Lo Lee-

Rev. Teruzzi when he was young. (Image source: PIME)

tsung (1889-1970), who was from Shunde, Guangdong province. After being ordained, Rev. Lo was sent to Sai Kung as Rev. Teruzzi's assistant, where he also helped with teaching. The two missionaries continued to visit every village as usual, where they held Mass for loyal believers, attracted new catechumens to the church, and stayed for a longer time where needed. Rev. Teruzzi fully supported the faithful, and his reputation was so good that even heretics sought him out. The two priests also repaired buildings damaged by termites and typhoons, and built new churches, such as a chapel in Long Ke in 1918, a residence and chapel in Tan Ka Wan and a chapel in Wong Mo Ying in 1923.[35]

Rev. Teruzzi not only held Mass, preached, and established new churches, but he also put great emphasis on pastoralizing the villagers through education. Although difficulties were encountered in the process of preparing the school, he responded calmly. For example, he planned to build a large school and residential buildings in the back hills of Sai Kung Market. After he raised funds to purchase the land, he discovered that apart from financial difficulties, there were also strong objections from Sai Kung residents because they believed that the construction would destroy the hillside. It was believed that cutting down trees would also offend the local deities and bring misfortune to everyone. In the 1930s, Rev. Ottavio Liberatore (PIME, 1901-1972), who was in charge of the Sai Kung district, remembered that Rev. Teruzzi finally took a long time to convince them and even mobilized the police to quell the incident.

Rev. Enrico Valtorta was appointed as the fourth Apostolic Vicar of Hong Kong in 1926, and was ordained as Bishop on 13 June of the same year to replace Bishop Pozzoni, who died of a heart attack in 1924. There were changes not only in the leadership of the Apostolic Vicariate but also missionaries serving in the New Territories. On 1 May 1926, the New Territories was divided into the East Deanery (Sai

Group Photo of Bishop Valtorta (front centre) and a group of directors and young seminarians in 1930. (Image source: PIME)

Rev. Teruzzi (middle) and a group of Scout leaders in Anderson Valley (circa 1930s). (Photo credit: Tsang Wing-sun)

Kung), West Deanery (Tai Po) and Outlying Islands Deanery. Rev. Teruzzi was in charge of the East Deanery and focused on the Catholic affairs of Sai Kung. The number of Catholics in this district has been reduced to 1,620, and divided into 14 groups, with eight churches and chapels, all of whom are "old parishioners". This explains why Rev. Teruzzi, in his report in September 1927, began to complain about "low religious spirit", "lack of new converts" and "believers think they know more than catechists and stop listening to them."

Rev. Teruzzi was not only faced with missionary challenges, but also had to face huge financial pressures. Like all other missionaries, he could only receive a small amount of funding from the vicariate, so he must find other donors or even borrow money to cover the expenses of the whole district. Under heavy pressure, Rev. Teruzzi asked whether Bishop Valtorta could send him to other areas. In the end, he resigned due to extremely heavy financial burdens. He explained to the bishop: "Churches and chapels, missionary residences and classrooms all need to be repaired on a large scale. In addition, my personal debts and the interest are due for repayment. It will consume the small sum I saved from allowances and Mass offerings, making me unable to bear any new expenses."[36] As a result, his duties were replaced by Rev. Pietro Daelli (PIME, 1893-1965) in 1928.

After leaving the East Deanery, Rev. Teruzzi was assigned to work in the Diocesan Curia, where he held positions such as Secretary-General, Archivist and Master of Ceremonies; he was later appointed as the Chaplain to Victorian Goal prison, and also served as the parish priest in the Cathedral and St. Margaret's Church in Happy Valley shortly. He also enthusiastically supported the establishment of Catholic Action by the faithful and advocated the The Catholic Scout Guild.[37] Even though his duties were heavy, Rev. Teruzzi still kept in touch with Sai Kung, especially during special commemorative events or when financial problems in certain chapels need to be dealt with.

A New Church built in Pak Sha O Catholic Village

There were many Hakka villages on the north side of the Sai Kung Peninsula, including Pak Sha O, a Hakka walled village built during the Qing Dynasty.[38] Pak Sha O was located in a valley and was quite remote; other nearby villages at the north include Pak Sha O Ha Yeung Village, Uk Tau Village and Hoi Ha Village. These villages were built in the 19th century like Pak Sha O.[39] Pak Sha O has developed into a village for the Catholics, with a chapel built on a small hill behind a Hakka bunker. Italian priests had preached in Pak Sha O Village as early as the 1870s. After that, all villagers were baptised and became a Catholic village and no longer worshipping the ancestors or setting up an ancestral hall. Rev. Leong, Rev. Teruzzi and Rev. Francis Wong Chi-him (1894-1942) served in the village consecutively, and the chapel in the village was ordained by Bishop Pozzoni.

During the Daoguang period (1827-1850) in the Qing Dynasty, in the genealogy compiled by the Li's family of Wo Hang, Pak Sha O was also called "Pak Sha Au".[40] Probably influenced by the "Map of the San-On District, Kwangtung Province" drawn by Rev. Volonteri in 1866, the Hong Kong Government Gazette in 1899 also named the village "Pak Sha Au".[41] History of the village of Pak Sha O dated back to the early Ming Dynasty and was listed as a village under the jurisdiction of Koon Fu Si in the Jiaqing edition of "Map of the San-On District"; its villagers' surnames include Ho, Lau, Lam, Yip, Wong, Yung, and Chan, etc.[42] According to records, it was believed that the Ho Chan (Earl of Turg Kuan) family was the first to move to Pak Sha O. During the Hongwu reign (1393) of the Ming Dynasty, Lan Yu conspired a mutiny to overthrow Zhu Yuanzhang and was defeated. The Ho family was implicated and fled. It was not until the death of Zhu Yuanzhang (1399) that Ho Chan dared to settle in Sungang Village, Po On, Shenzhen with his son Ho Sung, and his family branched out to Hong Kong's New Territories, including Pak Sha O Village.[43]

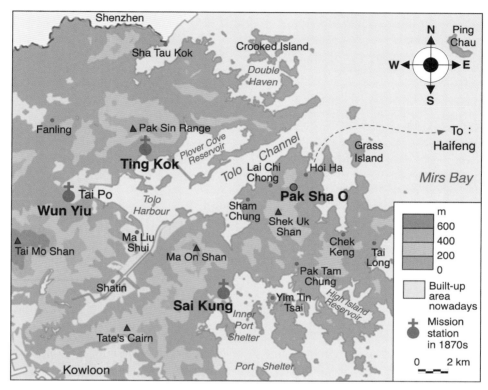

Pak Sha O and the location of the mission stations in the 1870s. (Drawn by Anthony Yeung)

The appearance of the Ho clan's Bunker-style Hakka mansion in the 1990s. (Image source: Yuen Chi Wai)

However, many of the Ho clan in Shenzhen and Hong Kong claimed to be the descendants of Ho Chan's second son, Ho Wah, or of the fifth son, Ho Sung. The bunker-style Hakka dwellings built by the descendants of the Ho clan are still in existence today and are built with green bricks, which is the signature building of the village built by the Ho family.

Lau clan moved to Pak Sha O in 1805. In addition, Lam, Yip and Wong clans also moved to this village between 1810 and 1820. Yung clan moved from Hoi Hai Village to Pak Sha O in 1855.[44] The villagers made their livings mainly by farming, wood logging and charcoal making. Some villagers also worked as fishermen and masons. According to oral history, there used to be a charcoal kiln in Pak Sha O Village, and the villagers would hire workers from the Mainland to make charcoal. The hill behind the village was called "Siu Tan Ping", which, as the name suggests, referred to a flat area on the hill for making charcoal.[45]

As mentioned in Chapter 2, as early as the beginning of 1869, missionaries from the Milan Institute for Foreign Missions had already set foot in Pak Sha O. This was because there were mission stations at Wun Yiu and Ting Kok in Tai Po at that time. Missionaries used water transportation to travel from these two places to and from Kwai Shin and Hoi Fung, both of which belonged to the Apostolic Prefecture, to preach and conduct pastoral worlc. Pak Sha O Village, near the Chek Mun Strait, became a midway stop on the waterway between Tai Po and Hoi Fung.[46] Rev. Volonteri was the first major missionary who came to Hong Kong from Europe. At that time, when he was preaching in Ting Kok Village, he often traveled to and from the Chek Mun Strait, and sometimes stayed in Pak Sha O to preach.

Pak Sha O Village was under the jurisdiction of Sheung U Tung in San On County. This area was dominated by the Liu clan in Sheung Shui, and they collected taxes on behalf of the Qing court. In the middle of the 1880s, the Liu clan in Sheung Shui had a dispute when collecting land rent from the villagers in Hoi Ha and Pak Sha O.[47] Catholic missionaries used the opportunity to assist the villagers in Pak Sha O to resolve the conflict and preach to them. Between 1869 and 1870, dozens of villagers in Pak Sha O Village were baptized, and this place became a Catholic village.[48] In 1880, a chapel with a capacity of 160 people was built in the village's valley.[49] Rev. Leong once served here from 1868 to 1882.[50]

The Apostolic Prefecture of Hong Kong sold the original Pak Sha O chapel land to the Ho clan in 1915, and then Rev. Teruzzi bought the land where the chapel is now located. He then built a new chapel to replace the dilapidated old chapel. The new church was consecrated by Bishop Pozzoni on 25 April 1916. The three priests who accompanied him were: Rev. Pietro Gabardi (PIME, 1866-1919) who presented a statute of Holy Mary and Jesus; Rev. Grampa, who was the architect and builder of the church, sometimes even acted as a stonemason, carpenter, and painter; and Rev. Joseph Yeung, who laid the foundation for the new church—the latter two had both served in the Continental District.[51] The chapel could accommodate up to 190 people, and the average number of people participating in the Mass at the initial stage of the new construction was as high as 180 people.[52] It was almost in full capacity. No wonder Bishop Pozzoni pointed out in the report that the completion of the new chapel had made the groups in Pak Sha O "regain vitality and strength".[53] The school next to the chapel was established by Rev. Teruzzi in the early 1920s, and about 30 students were

On 25 April 1916, Bishop Pozzoni consecrated the newly built Pak Sha O Chapel. (Image source: Pontifical Institute for Foreign Missions)

The entrance of the Pak Sha O Chapel in 2002. (Image source : Li Wai-kwong)

enrolled in the school in the 1930s. The curriculum of the school was determined according to the teaching scope set by the government. The subjects taught included Chinese language, letter writing, mathematics and abacus, general studies, health and other subjects. In addition to students from Pak Sha O and Nam Shan Tou, there were also children living in non-Catholic villages such as Lai Chi Chong and Hoi Ha.[54]

At that time, a priest had to serve several villages at the same time, including Tai Long, Chek Keng, and Sham Chung. Because of the considerable distance between the various places, Rev. Teruzzi and Rev. Wong could only visit Pak Sha O once a month. Whenever they arrived in Pak Sha O, believers would gather in the chapel to participate in Mass and pray. Since there was no priest permanently staying in the village, the nuns would take turns staying in the village to teach the villagers knowledge of the Bible and how to recite. Each nun would stay for no more than two months before moving to another village and being replaced by another nun. When there were no priests visiting, the nuns or the students studied in the school next to the chapel would lead the villagers to recite the Bible and pray every Sunday morning.[55]

There was a village named "Nam Shan Tung" near Pak Sha O, and it was also a Catholic village. Villagers also participated in the ceremony in the chapel of Pak Sha O. In addition, a small number of believers who lived in nearby non-believers villages also came to the chapel—some of them were originally residents of Pak Sha O, and later married to surrounding villages such as Hoi Ha.[56] The parishioners came from many villages and there were many of them. According to government statistics, the Pak Sha O Chapel, which could accommodate up to 190 people, usually had 180 people attending Mass between 1912 and 1934, which was nearly full. We can imagine the bustling situation of the sacrament at that time.[57]

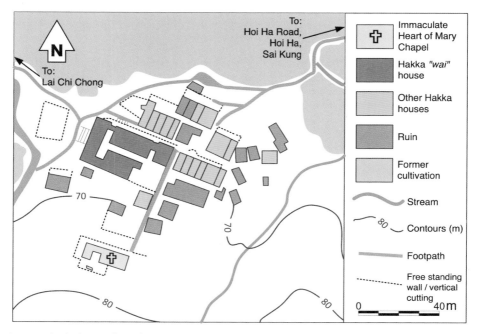

Layout of Pak Sha O Village. (Drawn by Anthony Yeung)

The appearance of the Pak Sha O Chapel after being renovated in 2018. (Image source: The Immaculate Heart of Mary Church, Tai Po)

The appearance of the Pak Sha O Chapel before its restoration in 2018. (Image source: The Immaculate Heart of Mary Church, Tai Po)

Coastal Chapels: Pak Tam Chung "Lo Ma Tong" and Lung Shun Wan "Mission Centre"

Among the chapels established by missionaries, two chapels in Sai Kung Hoi are the closest to the Sai Kung Market. One is Our Lady of the Seven Sorrows Chapel in Pak Tam Chung, and the other is Lung Shun Wan Mission Centre in Pak A. "Pak Tam Chung" itself is the name of a tributary which originates from the stream called Lung Hang flowing from Lui Ta Shek Shan. It is located presently between the end of Tai Mong Tsai Road in Sai Kung and Sai Kung East and West Country Parks. Legend has it that as there was flickering of light on the surface of the stream under the moonlight, the place name was thus originated from "Pak" (means white) Tam Chung and then turned to its present name. When there was no land connection to Pak Tam Chung in the past, the river creek was used for navigation.[58] The Pak Tam Chung was composed of six villages forming the "Luk Heung" (Alliance of Six), including Pak Tam, Tsam Chuk Wan, Wong Keng Tei (Pai Au), Sheung Yiu, Tsak Yue Wu (Ching Hang), and Wong Nai Chau (Wong Yi Chau).

Pak Tam Chung Village was strategically located in the centre of Luk Heung and was a water and land transportation hub. In the past, people from the six villages used the "Yung Pak Corridor" (the ancient road from Yung Shue O to Pak Tam Chung) to Kei Ling Ha Hoi, and travelled to Tai Po by boat, or from the small piers at Wong Keng Tei and Sheung Yiu to Sai Kung Market, Shau Kei Wan and other markets, where they would sell pigs, firewood, lime and bricks, etc., and bought grains and oil and other materials back to the village. According to the village head of Pak Tam Chung, his family used to build a grey brick house in the centre of the "Yung Pak Corridor". Apart from living, they also ran a grocery store and opened a village school in the house. More than 150 years ago, the Wong clan built a long corridor with tile roof in their homes, allowing the villagers of Sai Kung to pass through and go to the "Yung Pak Corridor". These villagers would also take shelter from the rain, rest and chat, so it is called "Ko Lo Long" (in Cantonese, passing corridor).[59] From 1900 to 1910, there would be a wooden boat transport to Sai Kung every day from Wong Keng Tei, leaving at 10 am and returning from Sai Kung at 2 pm to meet the needs of the residents. However, when the wind was not in the right direction, the boat may have to stay in Sai Kung, and often it was not possible to return to Pak Tam Chung until night, and the family would bring the lanterns to the pier to pick up the villagers.

The centre of Luk Heung is Sheung Yiu. According to the survey map when the British leased the New Territories in 1898, the village was also named "Pak Tam Chung". The history and economic activities of Sheung Yiu village are closely related to the "Alliance of Six" of Wong Nai Chau Village. More than 200 years ago, the Wong clan, Hakka people from Tam Shui of Wai Chow Guangdong province, first went to the bank of Tsam Chuk Wan to establish Wong Nai Chau Village. Many years later, as population multiplied, it was necessary for land development. Around the 1830s, the Wong clan established Sheung Yiu Village by the coast, which also belonged to Luk Heung.[60] Because the tortuous coastline of Sai Kung area forms numerous bays, and the sea was rich with corals and oyster shells, the coastal area was very suitable for the development of the lime kilns. Sheung Yiu was no exception. There were mountains nearby to supply charcoal, and Wong made good use of the geographical advantage and built an lime kiln on the beach. The kiln was about ten feet deep and still remains today. The lime could be used for construction and fertilizer. In addition, because the mountains were full with yellow clay, it was convenient for the Wong to set up a brick kiln on the opposite bank of the lime kiln to burn bricks and tiles as building materials. At the beginning of the 20th century, the villagers of the Wong clan used ships to transport bricks and lime to the neighboring villages or Shau Kei Wan from the small wharf in front of the village for sale. In its heyday, more than a hundred workers were employed here.[61] At one time, Wong clan savings of property caused frequent crimes by bandits, and even needed to reinforce the walls to prevent theft. Unfortunately, after the rise of cement in the 1940s, the demand for lime gradually decreased. At that time, the establishment of the Green Island Cement Limited dealt a heavy blow to the local kiln industry. Villagers began to leave their villages in search of a way out. Many residents returned to the mainland, and some villagers chose to move to Southeast Asia, most of them moved to the UK after the war. Although most of the residents of Sheung Yiu Village have moved to other places, the ownership of the land was still in the hands of the villagers.[62] According to the village chief's recollection, the Hakka women in the village would go up the mountains to chop firewood for fuel. They would also cultivate rice, grow vegetables, and raise pigs, etc. Therefore, there were also pig pens in the residential houses of Sheung Yiu.[63]

Not every village in Luk Heung believes in Catholicism. Instead, the missionary achievements of Wong Nai Chau and Sheung Yiu were more prominent. The former were converted earlier, and the chapel established by the latter was still existent. In 1869, missionaries opened a mission station in Tsam Chuk Wan. Bishop Raimondi made a visit in 1875 followed by the report of this trip, it was reported that the number of Catholics in Wong Nai Chau had increased significantly:

> It takes half an hour by boat from Yim Tin Tsai to Wong Nai Chau. Wong Nai Chau had only one Catholic two years ago, but there are already 25 baptized and 25 catechumens.[64]

In 1877, at the funeral of the preacher Ma Kam Sau, villagers from Wong Nai Chau went to the Sai Kung chapel to mourn this mentor who had contributed a lot to the mission of Sai Kung. In early 1879, Bishop Raimondi made another pastoral visit to the Continental District. The report mentioned that the Catholic community in Wong Nai Chau had been further expanded:

> On the 7th, the bishop went to Wong Nai Chau, one and a half hours away from Sai Kung, to visit the group of newly baptized people. This group is rapidly increasing. More than 50 people have been baptized, and nearly 20 people are ready to be baptized.[65]

According to the land survey in the New Territories completed by the government from 1898 to 1904, and subsequent records of the "Block Crown Lease", the site of the Catholic Church was "Lo ma tong" (in Cantonese, Roman Church).[66] The Church established the Our Lady of the Seven Sorrows Chapel here in 1900. Since the adjacent lands of the "Lo ma tong" were also called "Wong Yi Chau", it was almost certain that "Lo ma tong" was located in Wong Yi Chau. In addition, according to government records in 1905, Rev. Ferrario had applied to the government for exemption from the payment of Crown rents of the chapels in Sai Kung, including the chapel located in Wong Nai Chau.[67] Villagers from other villages in Luk Heung also asked for sermons and were baptized. At the end of the 19th century, the whole village of the Hakka Wong clan in Sheung Yiu Village, Pak Tam Chung was converted to Catholicism. In order to cope with the growing number of church members in Pak Tam Chung, missionaries built the Our Lady of the Seven Sorrows Chapel in Sheung Yiu in 1900, so that the

The government record on 13 October 1905, shows that Rev. Ferrario asked the government to exempt the Sai Kung Chapels from paying Crown rents but was rejected. (Image source: Government Records Office)

church members here could regularly listen to priests' sermons, confess, and attend Masses.

According to the records of The Land Registry, the "Block Crown Lease" issued by the government in 1905 indicated that the owner of the Our Lady of the Seven Sorrows Chapel was "Lo Ma Tong" as early as 1898.[68] "Lo Ma Tong" was not a villager whose surname was Lo in Sheung Yiu Village but refers to the transliteration of the Roman Catholic Church. The Wong clan of Sheung Yiu offered this place to the Hong Kong Church in that year, and the Church built a chapel.[69] Later, in 1908, the land ownership of the chapel was transferred from "Lo Ma Tong" to the name of the Vicar of the Roman Catholic Church in Hong Kong. According to government records, the manager of the chapel was Rev. Ferrario, the director of the New Territories. Generally, there were about 80 parishioners attending the Mass (it was estimated that many of them standing on the open yard outside the chapel to participate in the Mass).[70] At that time, Lutheranism, one of the Protestant sects of Christianity, first came to preach in Po On, including the Chinese Christian Tsung Tsin Mission (formerly known as the "Basel Mission"). Their dual missionaries, Rev. Theodore Hamberg and Rev. Rudolph Lechler, were the first who came to China and tried their best to preach to eliminate cultural barriers. Pastor Hamberg specialised in Hakka, and Pastor Lechler specialised in Chaozhou language, so as to facilitate access to the three counties of Tung Kuan, Kwai Shin and Po On.[71] According to historical records, since the Protestant and Catholic churches were established in Wong Yi Chau almost the same moment when the British leased the New Territories for surveying, and spread the faith or the gospel to

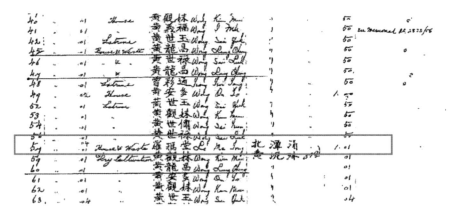

Our Lady of the Seven Sorrows Chapel of Pak Tam Chung was first registered as the "Lo Ma Tong" in the Block Crown Lease (now known as Block Government Lease) (1898-1903).

the Hakkas, it was inferred that the two churches had a certain degree of coordination during the land registration. The villagers then used Pak Tam Chung or Sheung Yiu as the village's name or address (note: the original Luk Heung did not have the village name "Pak Tam Chung"), and the villagers who believed in Protestantism still called it "Wong Yi Chau". After the opening of Our Lady of the Seven Sorrows Chapel, more people began to believe in Catholicism. In describing his missionary work in Sai Kung from 1913 to 1914, Rev. Ferrario said, "There are six families in Pak Tam Chung who have decided to join the Catholic Church. I will try my best to take care of them..."[72] Rev. Teruzzi succeeded Rev. Ferrario in 1914. The report from 1914 to 1915 wrote, "There are several Protestant families in Pak Tam Chung, and their homes still have idols (Editor's note: Buddha and deity statues of traditional Chinese religion), but some pagan families have asked me to baptize them and carried out the teaching."[73]

In addition to the increase in the number of church members, there were more exciting news in Pak Tam Chung. After years of hard work by Catholic missionaries, a person born in Pak Tam Chung received vocation and became a priest. Rev. Teruzzi wrote a letter to Rev. Giorgio Caruso (PIME, 1908-2004) on 1 March 1937, requesting him to provide about the baptism and confirmation documents of a villager who surnamed Wong and was born in Pak Tam Chung, and has studied in a seminary of Kota Kinabaru (Jesselton, the capital of Sabah). This indirectly let us know that there was once vocation in Pak Tam Chung. However, the Catholic community in the village was also facing challenges. The number of people attending Mass in the chapel fell from 80 to 60 in the 1920s, and to 40 since 1935.[74] The loss of these church members might be associated with a large number of villagers who moved to urban areas to work. It could be seen from the annual report of Rev. Ottavio Liberatore (PIME, 1901-1072), the Director of Sai Kung district, that in July 1935, there were several Catholic families in Sheung Yiu and Ha Yiu (now named "Hei Tsz Wan"), and most people in Pak Tam Chung village had been working in the urban area. When Rev. Liberatore visited Pak Tam Chung, there were only seven to eight people receive the Eucharist on average.[75] As for the capacity in the chapel, it was reduced from 120 people when it was completed to 80 people in 1939.[76]

According to documentary records, the Catholic mission in the chapel was more prosperous before World War II. At that time, most of the villagers near the chapel were already faithful and would go to the Shun Tsun School in Sai Kung Market to get food such as flour, oil, etc. — this reflects the doctrine of "Believe in me, can be saved". In addition to healing people's hearts, the way of preaching at that time was in line with the social conditions of that era, so the missionaries would satisfy the needs of food and clothing for the villagers. These material aids were very attractive to the general public, so the conversion to Catholicism upsurged. However, before converting to Catholicism, they believed in Earth God (called Pak Kung in Cantonese) and other deities. Though the villagers in Sheung Yiu believed in Catholicism, some villagers in Luk Heung still worshipped Tai Wong and even built Tai Wong Shrine on the path leading to Pak Tam Chung which was donated by villagers in Luk Heung. This reflected the church's understanding and respect for Chinese traditions. Normally before Mass, the priest would stay in the village; and on the stele of Pak Tam Chung Bridge, an amount of HK$300 donations from the Catholic Church was recorded, reflecting the priest's integration to the village life and cooperation with the villagers outside of the Catholic festival.

Our Lady of the Seven Sorrows Chapel was built on the east bank of the estuary of the stream. When the tide was high in the past, the villagers could take small boats directly ashore on the pier outside the chapel.[77] Since the neighboring Sheung Yiu Village was built on a high platform to prevent piracy, it was believed that the chapel was also built on a foundation about two meters above the ground for the same reason. It was the same typical Hakka precautionary measures as Sheung Yiu Village. For the same Hakka architectural style, both used granite masonry walls on site. The chapel had a combination of Chinese and Western architectural styles. On the one hand, it had a "hard mountain" style gable. On the upper side of the entrance of the chapel building, rectangular columns were erected, and the columns were decorated with cirrus clouds. The decoration was maroon red and the columns were white, showing the popular decorative art expression of the time. The plaque above the door was engraved with the three Chinese characters, meaning "the Catholic Church", and its style is a mixture of Chinese, Western and church elements.

Since the appearance of the chapel was the same as that of ordinary Hakka village houses, it was estimated that the chapel itself was once a residential house, which was dedicated to the church by the villagers to serve as a chapel. The chapel was of two-room style, the one on the left was used as an altar, the wall was embedded with a cross, there was a crucifixion statue on it, and the part under the statue was decorated with cirrus patterns.

There was a small area on the right side of the chapel. In the past, it was used as

Our Lady of the Seven Sorrows Chapel. (Image source: Catholic Scouts, taken in the 1980s)

The present appearance of the Our Lady of the Seven Sorrows Chapel.

a drying ground for the Hakka people to dry and pickle food, take the shade and hold banquets. On the left side of the chapel, there was a piece of farmland which owned by villagers of Wong family. After the chapel was taken over by the Catholic Scout Guild in 1982, this land became a part of the chapel and was converted into a religious gathering place. The style of the chapel was exactly the same as the Sheung Yiu Folk Museum. The latter was formerly a residential building, which was also built on a platform, and there was also a courtyard in front of it. Traditional architectural wisdom believed that the north-south orientation allows the house to keep warm in winter and cool in summer, as well as attracting sufficient sunlight. However, the two buildings in Sheung Yiu Village adopted the east-west orientation, which was in line with the local Fengshui requirements of facing the sea and backed by mountains.

In 1909, the Sai Kung District had 1,215 Catholics and 60 catechumens. Though there was turmoil in the Mainland, the law-and-order in Sai Kung did not have much impact. At that time, the Sai Kung district continued to develop missionary work. The Lung Shun Wan Chapel, located in Pak A Village, Leung Shuen Wan, was completed in 1910.[78] According to the report of Bishop Pozzoni, he ordained the chapel and recalled that he had visited the village when he was still not a bishop. All the villagers, including the elderly and the young, came to the chapel to welcome the bishop, which made him very happy. During the consecration ceremony, he met many old friends again, and they had already been baptized.[79] Shortly after the completion of the chapel, Rev. Teruzzi took over management from Rev. Ferrario. Since the village where the chapel located was populated by Hakka people with multiple surnames, the priest needed to learn the Hakka dialect to preach here. The chapel was of two-room style. The room on the right was the sanctuary, and the altar was located in the centre of the end of the chapel, facing the main entrance. The wall of the altar was designed in a typical column style, and there was a side door on the right side of the altar leading to the neighbouring sacristy. The loft of the sacristy should be the priest's dormitory. The wall of the chapel had a Chinese-style window decoration design. It could be seen that the missionaries here mostly adopted the methods of combining the traditional customs of the villagers with the Western church. There was even a Chinese-style ancestral hall built next to the chapel.

Pak A Village and Tung A Village in Leung Shuen Wan had a long-established ritual organisation at the Tin Hau Temple. Most villagers in this area believed in Tin Hau (Empress of the Heaven), so missionaries also encountered a lot of resistance in

The roof of the Lung Shun Wan chapel has now collapsed, and only part of the wall is left for people to pay tribute to. (Image source: Yuen Chi Wai)

Pak A Village where Lung Shuen Wan Chapel is located. (Image source: Paul Wong Yee-tin)

preaching in this village. The number of faithful had not been a substantial increase. However, the ancestral hall next to the chapel was the centre of ancestor worship. This showed that although the village has not formed a large Catholic group, missionaries were allowed to preach in the village. According to the indigenous villager of Pak A and parishioner Paul Wong Yee-tin, the number of church members in the village has not been so large. According to the baptismal records of the Sacred Heart Church in Sai Kung, there was still a resident surnamed Wong who was baptized on 28 December 1924, the priest responsible was Rev. Richard S. Brookes (PIME, 1892-1980); the location recorded was "Lung Shun Wan". It could be seen that the missionaries preached in the village and still achieved certain results.

After the establishment of the Apostolic Vicariate, the missionary cause in Sai Kung has developed rapidly, which is inseparable from the enthusiasm of the priests in charge of the Sai Kung district. Although there have been many obstacles, the Catholic communities in Sai Kung, especially Pak Sha O, Pak Tam Chung, etc., have become influential villages for the faithful, and demonstrated a model of rural mission in the area.

The records of the baptisms of the Sai Kung parish from 1924 to 1925 show that there should be believers baptizing from Leung Shuen Wan, Yim Tin Tsai, Long Ke, Shek Hang and Wong Mo Ying. (Image source: Sai Kung Sacred Heart Church)

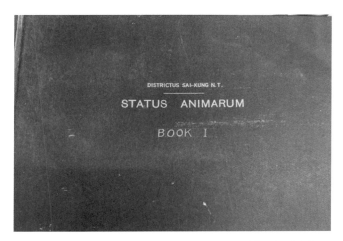

The Church records in Sai Kung District preserved by the Sai Kung Sacred Heart Church. (Image source: Sai Kung Sacred Heart Church)

When Rev. Lambertoni and his godchild Paul Wong Yee-tin visited the Lung Shuen Wan Chapel in the 1990s, the shape of the altar still existed. (Image source: Paul Wong Yee-tin)

Notes

1   Ha Keloon, *The Foundation of the Catholic Mission in Hong Kong, 1841-1894* (Hong Kong: Joint Publishing Co. Ltd., 2014), p. 229.

2   D'Elia, Pascal M., *The Catholic Missions in China* (Shanghai: The Commercial Press, 1934), pp. 55-56.

3   Ha Keloon, *The Foundation of the Catholic Mission in Hong Kong, 1841-1894* (Hong Kong: Joint Publishing Co. Ltd.,2014), pp. 158-160.

4   Sergio Ticozzi, "The Catholic Church in Nineteenth Century Hong Kong", *Journal of the Royal Asiatic Society Hong Kong Branch*, 48(2008), p. 129.

5   Brambilla, op. cit., pp. 115-118.

6   Shatin peninsula should be referring to Ma On Shan today.

7   Ryan, Thomas F., *The Story of a Hundred Years: The Pontifical Institute of Foreign Missions, (PIME), in Hong Kong, 1858-1958* (Hong Kong: Catholic Truth Society, 1959), pp. 67-71.

8   Sergio Ticozzi, "The Catholic Church in Nineteenth Century Hong Kong", *Journal of the Royal Asiatic Society Hong Kong Branch*, 48 (2008), p. 131.

9   Liu Yunxun (ed.), *The Memorabilia of the Seventy-five Years of Haifung Catholicism* (1873-1948), p. 64.

10   Murray Barracks was a former military barracks in Hong Kong, located between the current Central Garden Road and Cotton Tree Drive.

11   Vicariate Synod, 1875; The Catholic Directory 1877, Section 1V, Box 13, Folder 01, HKCAD.

12   The Daughters of Mary, the full name Daughters of Mary Help of Christians, FMA in Abbreviation, Salesian Sisters of St John Bosco/Daughters of Mary Help of Christians is the sisterhood of the Salesians of Don Bosco and one of the Catholic organizations.

13   Sergio Ticozzi, "The Catholic Church in Nineteenth Century Hong Kong", *Journal of the Royal Asiatic Society Hong Kong Branch*, 48 (2008). p. 131.

14   *The Catholic Directory 1877*, Section 1V, Box 13, Folder 01, HKCAD.

15   Sergio Ticozzi, translated by Yuen Chi Wai, "Father Emilio Teruzzi's Mission and Contributions in Hong Kong", *Hong Kong Journal of Catholic Studies: A History of the Hong Kong Catholic Church in the 20th Century*, No. 7, 2016, pp. 29-68.

16   HK-CCA, Piazzoli file; G. Tragella, Le Missioni Estere di Milano nel guadro degli avvenimenti contemporanei, Vol. III, Milano 1963, pp. 318-321.

17   G. Tragella, Le Missioni Estere di Milano nel guadro degli avvenimenti contemporanei, Vol. III, Milano 1963, p. 65.

18   Sergio Ticozzi, "The Catholic Church in Nineteenth Century Hong Kong," *Journal of the Royal Asiatic Society Hong Kong Branch*, 48 (2008),pp. 134-135.

19   1888 年 St. Martin Feast (03/21), Letter of Pozzoni in Sai Kung to Superior: Le Missioni Cattoliche, Milano, 1889. Vol. XVIII, p. 8.

20   Sergio Ticozzi, "The Catholic Church in Nineteenth Century Hong Kong", *Journal of the Royal Asiatic Society Hong Kong Branch*, 48 (2008), p. 135.

21   Report of Fr. Chu dated 18 November 1896 in Le Missioni Cattoliche, Milano, 1896, pp. 38-42.

22   Sergio Ticozzi, "The Catholic Church in Nineteenth Century Hong Kong," *Journal of the Royal Asiatic Society Hong Kong Branch*, 48 (2008), pp. 111-149.

23   Ibid.

24   HKCDA, https://archives.catholic.org.hk/In%20Memoriam/Clergy-Brother/D-Pozzoni.htm, retrieved on 27 April 2021.

25   Germani, Ferdinando, *Mons. Domenico Pozzoni, Vescovo titolare di Tavia Terzo Vicario Apostolico di Hong Kong 1861-1924 : Presentazione del Cardinale John Baptist Wu Chu Chang-Chung Vescovo di Hong Kong* (PIME), pp. 73-74.

26   HKCDA, https://archives.catholic.org.hk/In%20Memoriam/Clergy-Brother/D-Pozzoni.htm, retrieved on 27 April 2021.

27   Gianni Criveller, translated by Chen Aijie, "150 Years' Gospel of Pontifical Institute for Foreign Missions in Hong Kong"（〈宗座外方傳教會百五年在港傳福音〉）, *Ding* (《鼎》), Vol. 164, Spring 2012.

28   Bishop Pozzoni died at St. Paul's Hospital in Hong Kong on 21 February 1924. Germani, Ferdinando, *Mons. Domenico Pozzoni, Vescovo titolare di Tavia Terzo Vicario Apostolico di Hong Kong 1861-1924 : Presentazione del Cardinale John Baptist Wu Chu Chang-Chung Vescovo di Hong Kong (PIME)*, pp. 10-11.

29   HKCDA, https://archives.catholic.org.hk/In%20Memoriam/Clergy-Brother/D-Pozzoni.htm, retrieved on 27.4.2021.

30   "The 50th Anniversary of Sai Kung Fathers' Martyrdom" (〈西貢神父殉道五十周年 親友千里迢迢參禮紀念〉), *Kung Kao Po* (《公教報》), 28 August 1992.

31   *Le Missioni Cattoliche*, 1915, pp. 277-278.

32   Ibid.

33   Ibid., p. 243.

34   Sergio Ticozzi, translated by Yuen Chi Wai, "Father Teruzzi's Mission and Contribution in Hong Kong" (〈丁味略神父在香港的傳教使命與貢獻〉), *The Hong Kong Journal of Catholic Studies*, Vol. 7, 2016, p. 36.

35   Ibid., p. 39.

36   HKCDA, "Letter of Fr. Emilio Teruzzi to Bishop Valtorta", 14 March 1927.

37   Sergio Ticozzi, translated by Yuen Chi Wai, "Father Teruzzi's Mission and Contribution in Hong Kong" (〈丁味略神父在香港的傳教使命與貢獻〉), *The Hong Kong Journal of Catholic Studies*, Vol. 7, 2016, pp. 45-46.

38   Anthony Siu, *Tai Po Gazetteer* (《大埔風物志》)(Hong Kong: Tai Po District Council, 2007), pp. 62-63.

39   The villages that belong to the northern part of the Sai Kung Peninsula are located on a plateau above 300 meters and are surrounded by Shek Uk Shan and Kai Kung Shan. For example, Cheung Sheung and Wong Chuk Long Villages are connected to Ko Tong Village and Yung Shu O Village by trails, while small villages along the coast have Shum Chung, Yung Shu O, Hoi Ha, To Kwa Ping and Tai Tan, etc., see PH Hase, "Uk Tau and the Books of Cheng Yung (鄭榕)", *Journal of the Hong Kong Branch of the Royal Asiatic Society*, Vol. 47 (2007) , pp. 33-40.

40   *Genealogy of Wo Hang Lees in New Territories*(《新界禾坑李氏族譜》) in *Historical Literature (Supplement)* (〈新界文獻補編〉), *Index of Land Records of Yung Sze Chiu in Hoi Ha, Pak Sha O, New Territories* (〈新界白沙澳海下村翁仕朝地契與地契目錄〉), in East Asia Research Centre, Chinese University of Hong Kong, *Historical Literature of New Territories* (recorded in Hung On To Memorial Library, The University of Hong Kong, 1983).

41   *Hong Kong Government Gazette 1899.*

42 Antiquities and Monuments Office, Record of Historical Buildings Studies in 2002 2004: Immaculate Heart of Mary Chapel, Identification Number: AM04 2030, 2004, p.2, quoted from South China Morning Post, 31 January 1980.

43 [Ming] Sun Yi and Ho Shun Jo, *The Record of Lu Jiang Ho's Clan* (《皇明本紀：不分卷，洞庭集：四卷 / 孫宜撰，盧江何氏家記：不分卷 / 何崇祖撰》) (Taipei: National Central Library, 1985), p. 471.

44 Antiquities and Monuments Office, Record of Historical Buildings Studies in 2002 & 2004: Immaculate Heart of Mary Church, Identification Number: AM04 2030, 2004, p. 2.

45 Oral History Interview with Mr. Yip Wun of Pak Sha O, Sai Kung; Oral History Interview with Ho Yi Fat, 13 November 2003, Interviewer: Au Hin Fung. Collection of the Chinese University of Hong Kong Library.

46 Anthony Yeung, *Pak Sha O: History, Culture and Heritage of Religion* (《白沙澳：歷史：文化與信仰的傳承》)(Hong Kong: Catholic Scouts Association, 2014), p. 6.

47 [Ming] Sun Yi and Ho Shun Jo, *The Record of Lu Jiang Ho's Clan* (《皇明本紀：不分卷，洞庭集：四卷 / 孫宜撰，盧江何氏家記：不分卷 / 何崇祖撰》), p. 3, quoted from Anthony Yeung, *History, Culture and Heritage of Religion*, p. 5.

48 Sergio Ticozzi, *Historical documents of the Hong Kong Catholic Church* (Hong Kong: Hong Kong Catholic Diocesan Archives, 1997).

49 "Ecclesiastical returns: Churches and chapels of each denomination to be returned consecutively", *Hong Kong Blue Book* for the years 1908-1934 (Hong Kong, Printed by Noronha and Co., Ltd. Government Printers).

50 The chapel has been renamed several times. It was first named Holy Spirit Chapel in 1954, Sacred Heart of Our Lady Chapel in 1956, and the current name of Immaculate Heart of Mary Chapel in 1960.

51 *Le Missioni Cattoliche*, 1916, pp. 321, 336.

52 "Ecclesiastical returns: Churches and chapels of each denomination to be returned consecutively", *Hong Kong Blue Book* for the years 1908-1934.

53 *Le Missioni Cattoliche*, 1916, pp. 321, 336.

54 Interview with Ho Yee Fat, 27 April 2004.

55 Ibid.

56 Ibid. Interview with Chiu Sze, Yung Ah Lin and Chiu Yi Mui, 7 May 1981. Interviewers: Li Lai Mui, Cheng Shui Kwan, Compiler: Cheng Shui Kwan, Collection of Library of CUHK.

57 "Ecclesiastical returns: Churches and chapels of each denomination to be returned consecutively", *Hong Kong Blue Book* for the years 1908-1934.

58 Now Pak Tam Chung is a place name but not a village name. It is used to refer to the area of Sai Kung including the place from Ngau Yi Shek Shan to Sheung Yiu and Wong Yi Chau.

59 *Exploring the Villages and Cultures of Sai Kung District* (《西貢區鄉村文化探索》)(Hong Kong, Sai Kung District Council), pp. 28-31.

60 Antiquities and Monuments Section, USD, and Department of Architecture, University of Hong Kong, *Survey of Chinese historic rural architecture in Saikung district, New Territories* (Hong Kong: 1977), pp. 65-67.

61 Ibid.

62　Regarding the history of Wongs in Sheung Yiu, the Antiquities and Monuments Office had conducted a survey of the Chinese rural architecture in late 1970s. As the Sheung Yiu was abandoned at the moment, the oral history interview mainly focused on Wong Koon Sau, see Antiquities and Monuments Section, USD, and Department of Architecture, University of Hong Kong, *Survey of Chinese historic rural architecture in Saikung district, New Territories* (Hong Kong: 1977), pp. 65-66.

63　Ibid.

64　Sergio Ticozzi, "The Catholic Church in nineteenth century Hong Kong", *Journal of the Royal Asiatic Society Hong Kong Branch*, 48 (2008), p. 130.

65　See the full report in Catholic newspaper *Hong Kong Register*, vol. 2, 1879, no. 22.

66　*The Hong Kong Catholic Guide* (Hong Kong: Catholic Truth Society, 1957), p. 144.

67　Wong Yi Chau in the past did not only include the Wong Yi Chau Village we see today. Therefore, it is not surprising that no church can be found in Wong Yi Chau Village today. However, according to another land record and scholars, it is pointed out that Wong Yi Chau once had a Christian church "Gospel Church".

68　Land Registry, D. D. 257, Lot 57 Land Record (Hong Kong: Land Registrar, Sai Kung, 2016).

69　Block Crown Lease of D. D. 257.

70　"Ecclesiastical returns: Churches and chapels of each denomination to be returned consecutively", *Hong Kong Blue Book* for the years 1908-1934.

71　In 1895, Shung Tsun Church which spoke Hakka established Wong Yi Chau Church (formerly Gospel Church), then the villages joined the Protestants. Regarding the evangelization of Shung Tsun Church in New Territories, see Li Chi Kong, *History of Christian Church in Hong Kong* (Hong Kong: Hong Kong Baptist Church, 1996 (Reprinted and appended version)), pp. 8-9.

72　Sergio Ticozzi, translated by Yuen Chi Wai, "Father Teruzzi's mission and contribution in Hong Kong", *Hong Kong Journal of Catholic Studies- A History of the Hong Kong Catholic Church in the 20th Century*, No. 7, 2016 (Hong Kong: Centre for Catholic Studies, 2016), p. 35.

73　*Le Missioni Cattoliche*, 1915, p. 243.

74　*Hong Kong Blue Book 1929* (Hong Kong: Noronha & Co., Government Printer, 1930), p. 273.

75　*Report for 1924-35*, HKCDA, Sai Kung, Section IV, Box 14.

76　*Hong Kong Blue Book 1939* (Hong Kong: Noronha & Co., Government Printer, 1940), p. 344.

77　*The Catholic Guide to Hong Kong*, p. 204.

78　*Hong Kong Catholic Directory and Year Book for the Year of Our Lord 1970* (Hong Kong: Catholic Truth Society, 1970), p. 111. The chapel, demolished today, has not been rated as a historic building by the Antiquities Advisory Board of the Hong Kong Special Administrative Region.

79　Germani, Ferdinando, *Mons. Domenico Pozzoni, Vescovo titolare di Tavia Terzo Vicario Apostolico di Hong Kong 1861-1924 : Presentazione del Cardinale John Baptist Wu Chu Chang-Chung Vescovo di Hong Kong (PIME)*, pp. 105-106.

Chapter 4

**Tai Long District and the Japanese Occupation
Period: Loss of Control and Danger
(1931-1945)**

1841

1874

1931

1945

1969

1981

2000

Thanks to the unremitting efforts of the Italian missionaries and Chinese priests, including Rev. Francis Wong and Rev. Renatus Kwok King-wan (1911-1942) who had once preached in Guangdong, the number of Catholics in Sai Kung had increased gradually. According to the "Ecclesiastical Return" in the 1933 government record, there were more than 1,250 parishioners in the entire area, in particular the number of Catholics in Sai Kung, Yim Tin Tsai, Tai Long, Chek Keng and Pak Sha O had exceeded 100. The twelve chapels of Sai Kung could accommodate a total of more than

The capacity of the Sai Kung chapels and the attendance rate of Catholics in the Ecclesiastical Return of the year 1933 in the Government Records

Chapel	Capacity (people)	Attendance in 1908	Attendance in 1920	Attendance in 1933
Sai Kung	300	80	100	100
Yim Tin Tsai	400	180	180	180
Wong Mo Ying	100 (60)*	40	80	80
Pak Tam Chung	120	80	60	60
Kei Ling Ha	150 (80)	60	90	30
Sham Chung	120	90	60	60
Pak Sha O	190 (160)	130	180	180
Chek Keng	200	150	130	130
Tan Ka Wan	130	70	80	80
Tai Long	400	300	250	250
Long Ke	100	-	80	80
Lung Shuen Wan	100	20	25	25
Total	**2,310**	**1,200**	**1,315**	**1,255**

*( ) denotes the capacity of the chapels in 1908

2,300 people.[1] Comparing with the number of Catholics in 1920s (1,315), there was a reduction of 8.7%. For example, the number of Catholics in Kei Ling Ha decreased from 90 people in 1920 to 30 people in 1933. This trend reflected the impact of local folk beliefs on the development of Catholic Mission in local society. Another example is Che Ha Village which as listed in the Ecclesiastical Return of 1908, have had a chapel capacity of 100 people was no longer recorded with any Catholic population. This was probably because it had joined the worship for Tsat Sing (literally Seven Saints) Temple in Kwun Hang Village.

Among the churches or chapels in Sai Kung, Sai Kung Market, Yim Tin Tsai, Chek Keng, Tai Long and Pak Sha O had the largest number of Catholics. Therefore, villages such as Chek Keng and Tai Long formed a new "Tai Long District" which became another vibrant parish in addition to Sai Kung Market and Yim Tin Tsai. However, as the war approached, in the 1940s, the missionary activities in Sai Kung were also overshadowed. The Second World War was a dark age in Sai Kung's missionary history. Some of the priests were killed. Among them, Rev. Kwok King-wan was killed by gangsters while serving as the acting parish priest of the Sacred Heart Church in Sai Kung from 1941 to 1942. Soon Rev. Francis Wong, who was serving in Tai Long, was

Mar Cinese Meridionale

Sai Kung is the origin of Catholic Mission of the Pontifical Institute for Foreign Missions in Hong Kong. (Image source: PIME)

also murdered by the gangsters. The Italian priest Rev. Emilio Teruzzi, was abducted by unknown armed soldiers during his mission in Tai Tung in 1942. He was brought to the nearby deep bay and lost his life in a small boat. The murderers of these three incidents were still unknown. During the same period, the East River Column, which was in charge of guerrilla activities, set up its headquarters in the Holy Family Chapel in Chek Keng, while the Hong Kong and Kowloon Battalion was established in Wong Mo Ying Rosary Chapel in Sai Kung.

Tai Long District and Sai Kung Society before the Japanese Occupation

Tai Long, located in the eastern part of the Sai Kung Peninsula, was one of the earliest Catholic districts in Sai Kung, and it was also considered to be one of the Sai Kung villages with the most Catholics. As early as 1867, a chapel was built in Tai Long and Rev. Giuseppe Burghignoli baptized the first batch of believers. At the end of the 19th century, the Apostolic Vicar of Hong Kong had noticed that the flourishing catholic activities of this place. In July 1892, Rev. Dominico Pozzoni, who was not yet a bishop at the time, had just took over the management of missionary activities in the Continental District. He noticed that Tai Long had become a Catholic village and described it as one of the important Catholic groups in San On County (as the New Territories had not yet been leased, Sai Kung was still under the jurisdiction of San On County).

In 1931, Tai Long became an independent parish comprising of Chek Keng, Tai Long, Pak Sha O, Sham Chung, Tan Ka Wan and Tung Ping Chau. The Immaculate Conception Chapel in Tai Long Village was the most important amongst them as evident by her highest number of liturgy participants in Sai Kung area.[2] In official correspondences of the Apostolic Vicariate, it was also specifically mentioned that the church should take extra care of this parish, such as providing appropriate assistance and repairing the chapel.[3] Tai Long village of Tai Long District was located in Tai Long Wan, the east of Sai Kung. It is close to the sea and borders the Mirs Bay. It is surrounded by mountains on three sides and with sea on its back, and the left is Nam She Tsim (Sharp Peak).[4] According to the recollections of local indigenous residents, the villagers of Tai Long were mainly surnamed Wan, Cheung and Chan. Villagers made their living by farming and fishing, and worshiped Tin Hau (Empress of Heaven, also known as the queen of the sea). James Hayes (1930-), who was the Southern District Officer, mentioned in the record that there used to be a Tin Hau Temple in the south of the Tai Long Village, but it seemed to have been abandoned by the villagers. He estimated that as most of the villagers converted to Catholicism in the second half of the 18th century, Tin Hau Temple was then abandoned.[5]

In 1867, the chapel in Tai Long Village was completed. It was located in a fertile valley far from the sea. Rev. Burghignoli baptized the first group of believers in the village on Christmas Day, including villagers surnamed Tsam, Chan, Cheung, Lai and Lam.[6] The priest was also responsible for the Sunday Mass, weddings and baptisms. As the number of local church members increased, expansion works were carried out in 1873 due to the chapel's low capacity. After which, it was able to accommodate 200 to 300 people, making it the largest chapel in Sai Kung district at that time, and also the chapel with the highest number of church members. This proved that the number of church members in Tai Long has grown rapidly in only six years. The chapel was divided into two parts, each part had its own entrance, one side was for men and the other side was for women. Rev. Raimondi, who was not ordained as a bishop yet, considered it comparable to any church in Europe in 1873,[7] but this chapel so described was not the current one.

After being ordinated as bishop in Rome, Bishop Raimondi returned to Hong Kong and immediately went to various mission stations in the mainland to conduct pastoral visits, including Tai Long, which was destroyed by the typhoon on 22 September 1874. Three years later, he visited Tai Long again in 1877, which he had mentioned in his letter that almost all the villagers were already Catholics by that time.[8] In 1879, Bishop Raimondi visited Tai Long and other Sai Kung villages again and acclaimed Tai Long Chapel as one of the largest scale in Sai Kung, and the missionary achievements were very impressive. Bishop Raimondi visited Tai Long villagers frequently from 1875 to 1879. He not only celebrated the Lunar New Year with them, but also affirmed the missionary achievements of the village and the size of the chapel, which proved that the Apostolic Vicariate attached great importance to it. This may explain why the church sent a priest designated for Tai Long in 1893 to meet the local pastoral needs.

The New Territories was divided into East Deanery (Sai Kung), West Deanery (Tai Po) and Outlying Islands District in 1926. After five years, there was another change. On 30 March 1931, the Bishop decided to divide East Deanery into two parishes, namely "Tai Long District" and "Sai Kung District". The former was managed by Rev. Francis Wong, covering Tai Long, Chek Keng, Pak Sha O, Sham Chung, Tan Ka Wan and even Ping Chau.[9] According to a letter to the Vicariate Apostolic in 1941, Rev. Wong was very concerned about the group of nuns serving there. In July of the same year, the house where the nun lived was collapsed because of strong winds. He reported to the Vicariate Apostolic that these nuns living in Chek Keng would also go to Tan Ka Wan to teach catechumens.[10] While Rev. Richard S. Brookes (PIME, 1892-1980) oversaw the original New Territories West and outlying islands, he also had to take care of Sai Kung.

In 1932, a new chapel was built in Tai Long Village, replacing the old one, and this was the existing chapel.[11] It is located at the entrance of Tai Long Village, at the starting point of the uphill road to Tai Long Gap, adjacent to the Tai Long Wan Village Office. Villagers remembered that there used to be a stream next to the church, named "Dragon's Back." The water was gurgling and particularly sweet, but it may have been cut-off due to construction projects. Government records show that the chapel could accommodate up to 400 people, which was the largest chapel in Sai Kung. In the 1930s, it recorded a higher number of parishioners than that of the end of the 19th century. On average, there were about 250 church members participated in the liturgy, second

Rev. Francis Wong taking photo with villagers. (Image source: PIME)

to none in the Sai Kung district.[12]

As what is seen now, the Chapel of the Immaculate Conception was built in Italian or Spanish style, with wavy tiles on the top, plastered walls, and arched windows. The chapel had a front door and a side door, and the lintels of both doors had semi-circular windows. As for the internal structure, each pair of octagonal Roman columns formed a vault to support the ceiling of the chapel. The focal point of the chapel was the exquisite altar at the end. It was erected on a platform paved with Guangzhou tiles. A recessed niche in the centre of the upper wall was placed with a statue of the Virgin Mary. There was a wooden door on the right side of the altar leading to the sacristy, where the priest would prepare before the Mass. There was an attic above the sacristy, where the priest might have stayed and worked in the past.

The inner space of the church was divided into two areas by green glazed short columns. According to Sit Seng, a villager who served as an altar boy (to assist priests and related rituals during the Mass) in the 1930s, it turned out that men and women would separately enter from the side and the front entrance of the chapel and respectively sat in the front half and back half of the chapel. When receiving the Eucharist, men and women would also receive it separately, and the female church members needed to wear a headscarf when receiving the Eucharist. The entrance of the chapel was destroyed by a typhoon in the 1970s, so the current porch was added later. Other than that, the chapel has preserved its original appearance

When Sit Seng was a child, in addition to serving as an altar boy, he also followed the priest to other villages in Sai Kung (such as Chek Keng, Pak Sha O, Tan Ka Wan, Pak Tam Chung, etc.) to serve and stay overnight, he would also cook for the priest. On Sundays when there was no Mass, villagers in Tai Long would gather and chant in the chapel at 7 am, while Sit Seng was responsible for ringing the bell hanging at the entrance of the church to notify the faithful, but this bell has now been removed.

I was serving as an altar boy in Mass at the time, and I was the only altar boy at that time. It was the 1930s. The candlestick was very tall, strike a match, light a candle... all done by me. The priest came to Ta Long Village only once in two or three months. Every week, I would ring the bell... to remind the villagers to chant the scriptures. The bell hanging at the entrance of the church was very high and required a lot of force (to ring). I was a born Catholic. My parents were Catholics, for a long time. The old church was at the centre of the field. The typhoon destroyed it. Now this is the new one.[13]

There were two nuns who taught the villagers to recite, they also taught knowledge, and taught the villagers... (Did they live in the village?), two of them lived in Tai Wai. They taught the villagers to recite the scriptures because the villagers did not know how to. Serving sacraments, respectfully receiving the Eucharist...just teaching chanting: Our Father, who art in heaven, hallowed be thy name...like this.[14]

This reflected the daily life of the villagers: their work and rest time matched the sunrise and sunset, and they generally went to bed early and got up early, at 6 o'clock in the morning. The Yuk Ying School was built next to the chapel. According to Sit Seng's memory, the school had been established before the war. At that time, the priest hired a teacher, offering subjects such as Chinese, Mathematics and Chinese history, but English was not taught. The school taught students to sing hymns every week.

By comparing the data of church documents and government records, we can see that the flourishing Catholic activities in Tai Long Village in the decades before the war: after the first group of villagers were baptized in 1867, the number of church members increased steadily, and it exceeded 160 in the 1870s. In the 1930s, there were as many as 250 people participating in the Catholic rituals, and increased to 500 in the 1950s. In the 1870s, the village's chapel could accommodate 200 to 300 people, one of the largest in Sai Kung. The church newly completed in 1931 had a capacity of 400 people, much higher than other village chapels. The Chapel of the Immaculate Conception is located next to the Tai Long Village Office, the core of the village. In fact, it also played an important role in Tai Long Village in the past: every Sunday morning, the villagers gathered to participate in the Mass. If the priest had to take care of other villages and was not able to come to celebrate the Mass, the Catholic villagers would still go to the chapel to chant together. It was undoubtedly a gathering place for villagers and was socially important, in addition to its religious function. Moreover, the nearby Yuk Ying School not only provided school-age children with education, but also preached them through lessons, and nurtured more young faithful. Although there was a well-established Catholic community in Tai Long, Catholism did not take root in Sai Wan, the neighbouring village, until after the war. Therefore, Sit Seng, who was once an altar boy, did not have much impression about the impact of Catholicism on there and thought folk beliefs prevailed thereat. However, his son added that this may be because not the whole village of Sai Wan believe in Catholicism:

> It might not be the whole village, but only a certain group of people. As Tai Long village and Sai Wan had no tight connection, there had even been conflicts, fighting, robbing "encirclement", and in short, robbing everything. Even if we were very close to Sai Wan, there was rarely marriage between the two villages. Most of their villagers married those from Chek Keng and Kei Ling Ha. We didn't go to Sai Wan very often, because we had conflicts with each other, so we rarely went there (Sai Wan). I heard that there was rinderpest, and the "Sai Wan Guys" would not let us cross the road, making everyone needed to use the mountain road and had to walk a long distance.[15]

Since the 1960s, due to inconvenient transportation and far from working places, villagers have moved to the urban area gradually, and many people have chosen to immigrate to the UK to make a living. Looking through the newspaper cuttings, fresh water pipes were first installed in Tai Long in 1960,[16] and it was only in 1977 that telephone services were introduced for the first time.[17] The slow pace of development helped us understand the reasons why the villagers moved out. As the number of residents in the village decreased, Tai Long gradually declined. Some village houses began to collapse due to lack of maintenance, and the number of church members declined sharply. In 1962, Tai Long District was under the management of the Tai Po District. By 1980, Tai Long District was abolished, and the chapels in the district were placed under the jurisdiction of the Tai Po Parish. Due to the decreasing number of faithfuls participating in Mass, the Immaculate Conception Chapel was suspended and abandoned after 1988.

In the past, the missionaries exerted their best endeavours in taking care of spiritual needs and even daily life of Tai Long villagers. Although the missionaries have left, the statue of Our Lady of Immaculate Conception still stood firmly inside the church, symbolising that the missionary's efforts will not be obliterated. Even if the villagers had moved away from Tai Long and lived scattered, the Catholic faith rooted in their hearts will continue to sprout.

Sai Kung Society during the Japanese Occupation: the Murder of a Chinese Priest

The flourishing Catholic activities in Tai Long and Sai Kung in the pre-war period did not last long and have drastically declined due to Japanese invasion. Rev. Teruzzi resumed his post before leaving Hong Kong, including the Secretary-General, the Director of the Archives, the Ritual Director, the Prison Special Priest, and the priest of the Catholic Scout. In his account on 26 May 1940, he had this feeling about the Hong Kong defense war that was about to break out at that time.

> Today we celebrate the Corpus Domini in a consistently solemn way. This is also a special day for praying for war. I took up the post of Fr. Garbelli in the Bishop's Office: I still go to St. Joseph's College every morning as their priest. Nothing has happened in the seminary so far, and if Italy does not participate in the war, we will not have too many problems.[18]

But this situation has become increasingly fragile. Since the Lugou Bridge Incident on 7 July 1937, Japan has formally invaded China, and when Italy allied with Nazi Germany and Japan as the Axis power, the situation of Italian missionaries in China was even more dangerous. Beginning in April 1941, the Communist guerrillas formed by the Guangdong People's Anti-Japanese Guerillas, which later became one of the East River Columns, founded in 1939 by General Zeng Sheng (1910-1995). In order to carry out activities in Hong Kong, their headquarters was located in the Catholic Church in To Yeung on the north bank of Mirs Bay.

Although communication with Italy was difficult before the war broke out, Rev. Teruzzi was able to maintain contact with certain friends and the association's magazine *Le Missioni Cattoliche*. This magazine published news from various places provided by the clergy, including an article contributed by Rev. Teruzzi, written on 21 June 1941, from which we can learn more about his and other clergy's experiences in dangerous situation on the brink of war:

> We are cut off from the priests in the Chinese territory. No one dares to make a statement because there are officers, soldiers and bandits in control. While we are preparing for the worst in Hong Kong, we also hope that the storm will not

Hong Kong and Kowloon Independent Brigade of East River Column proceeding along the Sino-British Border of Hong Kong.

hit us. We also celebrated the fifteenth anniversary of the ordination of Bishop Valtorta... Let us thank the Lord, after all, He is still blessing us in this year's worries and fears, especially when we are confined to our residence. There are several people who need to leave the colony, including the five who are still in Macau and the three who are in the Chinese territory. Our priesthood duties in these two cities has not shrunk because of the war this year. In fact, we continue to expand our charity work and our commitment to society.[19]

In the Sai Kung area, there were still two Chinese priests serving in the area controlled by the Japanese army. They were the young Rev. Renatus Kwok King-Wan and the more experienced Rev. Francis Wong. Rev. Kwok was the first Hoklo priest. By that time he was in his thirties and had only five years of evangelization experience. After working in Wai Yeung for three years, he started working in Sai Kung in November 1941, taking care of Sung Tsun School. Rev. Wong was nearly 60 years old and had 25 years of pastoral experience. He has been preaching in Tai Long since 1930. On Christmas Eve in 1927 in Shanwei, Hoi Fung District, he was taken captive by the communist regime of the "Hoi Luk Fung Soviet" along with Rev. Lorenzo Bianchu (PIME, 1899-1983), Rev. Robba and seven Canossian sisters. As a Chinese, he was first sentenced to death, but then fortunately, Rev. Valtorta stepped in and used the British battleship "Angel" to launch a surprise attack. They were lucky enough to escape. Due to the turbulent situation, the residence and activities of the two priests in the Sai Kung district were also kept secret, and they acted cautiously. Whenever they had to leave their residence, they must first plan carefully.[20]

In September 1941, in a letter reported by Rev. Francis Wong of Chek Keng to the superior, it was mentioned that he had visited Pak Tam Chung, Long Ke and Lung Shuen Wan. The local believers asked him for help and this was the reason for continuing to serve Sai Kung. Villagers in Chek Keng and Tai Long could not get enough food and clothing, and the scattered living quarters made it difficult to take care of each other. Rev. Wong then urged the Vicariate Apostolic to consider the situation of these Catholics.[21]

On 8 December 1941, Japanese troops bombed Kai Tak Airport and formally offended the British colony. After the first five days of attack, the Japanese army invaded and occupied the entire New Territories. Since Italy had formed an alliance with Japan earlier, the British Hong Kong government at the time regarded Italian personnel in Hong Kong as war criminals and sent them to the concentration camp in Stanley. At Christmas, the British surrendered and the Japanese occupation of Hong Kong officially began. On 10 December, several detachments of the Japanese Army entered Sai Kung and looted the villagers' crops and food. After staying there for a while, they advanced towards Kowloon, during which they ransacked the villages around Ho Chung and Pik Uk. After the colonial government surrendered, the Japanese returned to Sai Kung to take over the area. At the same time, bandits had appeared in Sai Kung before Christmas. On the winter solstice they were equipped with firearms, plundered all the residents' valuables, and forced the farmers to carry the grains to Kei Ling Ha so that they could leave by boat there. It was reported that bandits were rampant throughout the area, divided into factions of eight to ten members, engaged in smuggling activities, and regularly looted materials and money everywhere.

After the courageous resistance within 18 days, the British army stationed in Hong Kong finally succumbed to the attack of the Japanese army. The then Governor Sir Mark Young surrendered to Japan at The Peninsula on 25 December 1941, the Christmas Day. Japan proclaimed officially the occupation of Hong Kong, commencing the Japanese rule of "Three Years and Eight Months". For the entire colony, the Japanese rule was a nightmare, but also a period of suffering, fear, and famine. Food was already in short supply at that time, and the Japanese authorities even urged urban residents to leave. Everyone tried to escape to other places. From January to April 1942, a total of 600,000 people left Hong Kong, and the population gradually decreased to 500,000. Many Catholics also fled to Macau, and the number of local believers decreased from 21,000 to only 4,000. Those who did not leave might starve to death, as each person could only receive 90 grams of rice per day. As a result, 50,000 people died of starvation during this period, and the work of burying them fell on the church. The Catholic Church and Rev. Teruzzi were in charge of this work. They used the funds provided by the Vatican to support the victims of the war and distributed materials to those in need. However, unfortunate incidents occurred. In August 1942, when Rev. Kwok seven or eight other people (including several teachers) were talking in a square in Sai Kung, they were suddenly taken captive by heavily armed forces. At first, people thought it was a kidnapping for ransom. However, by September it was known that they had been killed — someone had seen them tied to a boat and then taken to the mountains to be killed and buried.[22] Later, Rev. Wong was driven by Rev. Teruzzi's enthusiasm and visited even more villages. According to the Catholic Diocesan Archives, Rev. Wong still visited Chek Keng in October 1942 to serve the local Catholics;[23] and Sit Seng, the Tai Long villager who followed Rev. Wong touring the villages, described Rev. Wong's disappearance in Chek Keng in a certain evening.[24] Later, people gradually suspected that he was also murdered. After being abducted by the guerrillas, he was taken to the mountainside near Tai Long, killed and buried, around the end of November to early December.[25]

Apart from the priests that still served the villagers during the Japanese occupation, the "East River Column" formed by the Hong Kong and Kowloon Brigade of the former Guangdong Anti-Japanese Guerrilla also tried its best to gain the trust of the villagers and recruited members from the village. Through patriotic advocacy, the guerillas protected the remote villages from the attacks of the bandits by all means so as to evade the control of the Japanese; they also assisted those in need to leave Hong Kong.[26] The guerrillas used the Holy Family Chapel as a dormitory in Chek Keng and recruited local residents mainly from Hakkas. In early 1942, there were 300 guerrillas, and they used this to launch "people's activities" in each village. They set up a training base in Luk Wu, which was close to Sai Wan Village; they also guarded against bandits in remote villages in a systematic manner, and successfully controlled and took over the smuggling of owners and materials. The East River Column gradually became more confident in its own organization and started more work. In order to retaliate against the Japanese army, they launched: (1) ambush of the Japanese boats and killed the Chinese who were regarded as accomplices (between 1943 and 1944, they killed the three most important Japanese-Chinese translators), (2) collection of intelligence, (3) destruction of trains and attacked Japanese police stations.[27] In addition to Chek Keng, the guerrillas also used the favorable terrain of Wong Mo Ying Village to carry out anti-Japanese activities.

Wong Mo Ying Chapel and the Sacrifice of Anti-Japanese Villagers

Wong Mo Ying Village in Tai Mong Tsai District of Sai Kung was a typical Hakka village in the mountainous area. At the beginning of the 20th century, almost all the villagers of Wong Mo Ying converted to Catholicism, and they participated in Mass in Wong Mo Ying Chapel, which was built before 1880. According to the government archives (*Hong Kong Blue Books*, v. 1908-1939), from 1908 to 1911, the Wong Mo Ying Chapel, which could accommodate 60 church members, had 40 people participating in Mass at ordinary times; by 1912 to 1939, the chapel could further accommodate 100 people, and the number of participants has increased to 80. It is believed that the chapel was expanded around 1912. In order to cope with the growth of church members, the new chapel was built in 1923, but it has been too small after just several years. In addition to the natural increase in the population of converted families in the village, it was also due to the efforts of the missionary group established in 1923, i.e., the efforts of the Chinese Catholic youth group.

In 1930, Rev. Teruzzi of the Pontifical Institute for Foreign Missions (PIME) replaced the Apostolic Vicar of the Roman Catholic Church in Hong Kong as the trustee of Wong Mo Ying Chapel. Wong Mo Ying was one of the few villages that had their own school before the 1930s. Run by Rev. Teruzzi, the school mainly offered Bible study and Chinese classics where students attended classes inside the chapel. In addition to the students of Rev. Teruzzi, some of them came from the Tai Mong Tsai area. According to a report in the *Kung Kao Po* on 16 May 1939, "The New Territories Wong Mo Ying Church was built on the abandoned site of the old church."

Rev. Emilio Teruzzi.
(Image Source: PIME)

As the number of church members was increasing day by day, a larger church was built on the original site of the chapel in 1939, which was today's chapel (the Rosary Chapel), and it was completed under the auspices of Bishop Valtorta on 29 May 1939 to celebrate the ceremony and Mass. Although there was a typhoon and heavy rain that day, more than 300 church members did not even had breakfast, and had walked several miles to the new chapel in the morning to receive the Eucharist at Mass. Before the Japanese occupation, Rev. Teruzzi and Rev. Richard Brooks would hike to Wong Mo Ying and other Sai Kung chapels every two to three months. The priests would stay in the village, during which Masses and prayers would be held every evening until they left the village.

After the fall of Hong Kong in December 1941, Sai Kung was in a dangerous situation under the Japanese occupation as riots, looting and murder occurred from time to time. Japanese occupied Sai Kung and used Sai Kung Market as their military base, while the East River Guangdong People's Anti-Japanese Guerrilla Group entrenched the mountainous area to organise villagers to resist such as destroying Japanese military facilities, and rescuing cultural celebrities. Wong Mo Ying was closely linked with the neighbouring villages like Cheung Sheung, Chek Keng and Tai Long and became a guerrilla base. On 3 February 1942, the Hong Kong-Kowloon Independent Brigade of the East River Column was established in the chapel, and together with various guerrilla

The old look of Wong Mo Ying Chapel completed in 1923.
(Image source: *Kung Kao Po*)

公 教 報	1939 年 6 月 1 日

西貢黃毛應
新堂落成典禮
新界一帶教友
冒雨前往參加

本港消息‧新界黃毛應聖堂，於上月廿九日舉行落成典禮，恩主教於廿八日下午偕同一部份神父先往籌備一切，本港教友亦預租小輪一艘，定於是日晨前往參加典禮，後因颶風，該輪不得開行。惟該堂落成典禮仍照常舉行，參加者約三百餘人，多為新界教友，有晨起即步行數里，不進早膳，以便領聖體者。查是日彌撒聖祭係自晨六時開始，恩主教則於九時舉行彌撒，領聖體者約達二百餘人。至下午一時，且有一百教友，領堅振云。

Report on the inauguration ceremony of Sai Kung Wong Mo Ying Chapel on 1 June 1939. (Image source: *Kung Kao Po*) teams in the New Territories, they held a banquet in the open space next to the chapel. In two years, about 70 guerrillas settled and stationed in the chapel of Wong Mo Ying Village to store supplies, weapons, and ammunitions for the guerrillas. Therefore, the chapel played an important role in the anti-Japanese activities. If they travelled to southwestern China, the guerrillas were also supported with water, material and shelter in the chapel.

The indigenous register of Wong Mo Ying Village recorded the anti-Japanese history and establishment of a base by Hong Kong Kowloon Independent Brigade in the Catholic Church.

Today's Rosary Chapel of Wong Mo Ying. (Image source: Following Thy Way)

In the autumn of 1944, a tragedy took place in the chapel. A Sai Kung villager who was once a member of the guerrillas became a spy for the Japanese army and led them to a place where the guerrillas might be hiding. The Japanese army learned of the activities of the guerrillas in the village and besieged Wong Mo Ying Village. The Japanese army detained about 20 villagers in the chapel for interrogating, while the remaining about 50 villagers were guarded by other soldiers in the open space nearby. Inside the chapel, five of the villagers whose relatives or family members being guerrillas were executed by burning. The Japanese army failed to obtain any information about the guerrillas during the siege, nor did they capture the guerrillas. They ransacked the house, took away the livestocks and valuables, and then left the village.

Rev. Teruzzi's Martyrdom: an Unbearable Burden

Apart from Rev. Kwok, Rev. Wong and villagers of Wong Mo Ying, Rev. Teruzzi also lost his life during the Japanese occupation period. In April 1937, Rev. Teruzzi's family asked him to return to Italy for a rest. He then asked Bishop Valtorta for a temporary leave from Hong Kong and was approved. Later, he was appointed as the Dean of Villa Grugana Brianza by the President of the PIME. In addition, Rev. Teruzzi also went to London to explore whether the Hong Kong church could open a new priest's office in England to facilitate the new missionaries to learn English, and conducted a feasibility study for this — but found that the possibility was extremely low. Bishop Valtorta then wrote to him, "If this is the case, you'd better take the earliest ship back to Hong Kong. Your new office has been expanded and beautified, and there is a group of scouts waiting for you to come back." We could see how much the bishop and the followers of Hong Kong longed for Rev. Teruzzi's return. It was a pity that the President has entrusted Rev. Teruzzi with another duty, which stopped him from making the trip for the time being.

Rev. Teruzzi has always been concerned about the missionary work in Hong Kong, so when Bishop Valtorta wrote again to persuade him to return to Hong Kong to serve, he immediately put aside his work and returned to Hong Kong. According to the "Chronology of Events in the Hong Kong Mission District" in 1940, Rev. Teruzzi resumed his duties after returning to Hong Kong, including Secretary-General, Archivist, Ritual Director, Prison Special Priest, and Missionary Scout Priest.[28] When Rev. Teruzzi returned to Hong Kong by ship, he must have been eagerly looking forward to setting foot in this colony that he had been served for many years, and also excitedly looking forward to meeting every familiar Sai Kung villager again. But he did not expect that this trip back to Hong Kong would lead to his sacrifice.

Since being sent to Sai Kung for pastoral work, Rev. Teruzzi has forged an indissoluble bond with this area throughout his life. He was praised as "a priest who acts according to God's will... Rev. Teruzzi's true humility comes from his talent for silent work, without complacency".[29] This reflected that he often encountered different challenges in Sai Kung, but still worked sedulously and served his faith.

Rev. Teruzzi had been preaching there for many years because of his deep love for this area. Although he was worried about the changes in the situation, he, during discussion with the Bishop, said he was the most suitable candidate to replace Rev. Kwok who lost his life to serve Sai Kung. because he was very familiar with the people and things there, and was willing to become a resident priest in Sai Kung district. Bishop Valtorta took a wait-and-see attitude towards this, but Rev. Teruzzi still insisted. Bishop Valtorta could only grant him a short visit permission and asked him to complete it within a time limit.[30]

At about 6 o'clock in the evening on 5 October 1942, Rev. Teruzzi set out to Sai Kung. The next morning, he conducted the sacrements of confession and the Eucharist for the Catholics. Later, he visited the Japanese authorities to obtain permission to stay and preach in Sai Kung. He discovered that some rooms had been occupied by the "Sai Kung Autonomous Committee" organized by pro-Japanese residents—this was the tacit approval of Rev. Kwok. He also visited some Catholic families to try to find clues about the murder of Rev. Kwok and wrote about the local difficult situation and the urgent needs of the villagers, as well as the news he received about Rev. Kwok, "It seems that the main consideration here is to wipe away all the traces of the captives... this evening I went to the market and received a sincere welcome from everyone, especially the students from the school I taught..." After staying in Sai Kung for two days, he then went to Wong Mo Ying, which was controlled by the Hong Kong Kowloon Brigade. He reported that he had visited Wong Mo Ying on the previous Thursday and Friday. He was originally expected to revisit on Sunday, but he was discouraged from going back because of fear of the sudden appearance of guerrillas. When he arrived, he found that the damage to the church was not serious. On the following Saturday, he visited Kei Ling Ha and noticed the disastrous condition there. He described that there was nothing left there, not even the wooden stairs. On Sunday, he went to Wo Mei to observe.[31]

Rev. Teruzzi continued to report to the Bishop and asked him to extend his stay in Sai Kung. He also hoped to travel to Lung Shun Wan, Yim Tin Tsai, Tseng Tau, Tai Tung, Wu Kai Sha and other places to visit local church members—but if the Bishop did not allow the extension, he would follow. If approved, he would write a brief letter in Chinese and hand it to the head of the Japanese police in exchange for a license for protection or missionary work. He thought that his stay in Sai Kung was after all an encouragement to the local Catholics.

With the permission of Bishop Valtorta, Rev. Teruzzi was able to visit other villages, but he had to take great risks. He spent three days in Pak Tam Chung (14-16 October):

> Because of my loyalty and trust in me, I was helped by a few conscience people. I spend two nights in Long Ke every Saturday...no one gives me any trouble in these two places. Unfortunately, I was not able to carry out sacraments of confession and Eucharist for everyone in Long Ke: from December 1941 to October 1942, no missionaries visited the village. When I left Long Ke to Sha Tsui Kok, I met five guerrillas, one of whom was from this village. They stopped and questioned me, and considered me as "a monster without fangs and claws", and they let me pass by safely. When we parted ways, we were more like good friends-thanks to the Lord. The next day, because of God's will, I visited the island of Yim Tin Tsai, and Rev. Francis Wong still held Sunday Mass here 15 days ago. I only want to stay for two days before going to Wo Mei, because I plan to stay in Sai Kung to deal with a few things... There are many people who are sick, but there are more abuses of power that need to be resolved. There is an urgent need for missionaries to station here permanently.[32]

On 23 October, although Rev. Teruzzi was on the way to Wo Mei to prepare for the "Feast of Christ the King", Bishop Valtorta wrote to him:

> First of all, thank you for what you have done. Deo Gratias (Thanks be to God)! I still hope you can return to Hong Kong, not later than All Saints' Day. On 8 November we will have a devotional practice. I still don't want you to stay in Sai Kung. I believe that in the end another Italian priest will be permanently sent

there. I suggest you—in fact, I am ordering you to always exercise caution so as not to be exposed to the danger of captivity.[33]

When Rev. Teruzzi returned to Hong Kong, he confirmed his assessment of Sai Kung more positively. Rev. Quirino De Ascaniis (PIME, 1908-2009), who lived in the dormitory of the priest near the Cathedral,[34] wrote, "I met him once. He is completely satisfied with his missionary work and has great confidence in the conditions of the place where he lives. Between the lines in his words, he thinks that where he stayed is fine and free of danger."[35] It could be seen that Rev. Teruzzi was still very insistent on returning to Sai Kung. Although the Bishop completely ignored his request before the spiritual practice, Rev. Teruzzi was still very keen on meditation. Although he could not persuade the Bishop, the Bishop still agreed to let him return to Sai Kung as he wished and appointed him as the Director of Sai Kung on 16 November. Just before his departure, the Bishop gave him a large sum of money, which was provided by the Holy See to assist the victims of the war so that Rev. Teruzzi could distribute it to poor families. In addition, the Bishop also asked him to stay in Hong Kong for ten days per month. On the same day, Rev. Teruzzi set off to Sai Kung for the last time with unknown future.

On 18 November, Rev. Teruzzi sent a messenger back to the Cathedral to retrieve the belongings he had left in the room and brought a letter, which has record the violent scenes he witnessed in Sai Kung:

> In the week of our spiritual practice, there was change of Japanese military personnel in Sai Kung. The officers and soldiers here are the worst. They robbed, they hitted others, and have killed several people. The others were torn apart by six fierce dogs. The ferry that carried villagers from neighboring villages has been suspended. It (Japanese Army) is a terrifying dynasty. I'm thinking about what I can do to help these poor Chinese people.[36]

Although the situation was quite difficult and dangerous, Rev. Teruzzi did not think about changing his plan to continue visiting Catholics. He visited some Catholic families living in Kei Ling Ha, and then headed towards Tai Tung. In the meantime, he needed to stay overnight in the Catholic family and celebrate Mass, because there was no chapel in that district.[37] On the morning of 25 November, he had just stayed with a catechist and servant at the home of a believer in Tai Tung Village to prepare for Mass and head to the neighboring village. While he was putting on the chasuble, a group of armed guerrillas suddenly broke into the house and ordered him to follow them to leave. The priest asked them to give him some time to send the Eucharist to the Catholics but was refused. The guerrillas asked him to leave immediately. Rev. Teruzzi and the catechist had to follow them, but they did not know where to go and why. The group of guerrillas ignored the servants' hold back, only saying that they would be sent back soon. Someone witnessed the guerrillas walking from the village to the beach, boarding a boat and sailing to the north coast. Soon some soldiers returned and took away the servants who were still waiting there.[38]

From subsequent investigations, it was discovered that Rev. Teruzzi had already been killed on the boat, and his skull was fractured. It was believed that someone attacked his head with a hard object such as a rock which caused direct death. His body was tied to a large rock and sank to the bottom of the sea. As the rock loosened, the body floated to the surface and was washed up by the waves on the shallows of an inner bay to the north of Sham Chung. When the tide receded about a week later, the women (some of whom were Catholics) picking up shells discovered his body was floating on the shore tied with a rope. They immediately recognized Rev. Teruzzi because he was wearing European-style socks, black and white soles, and noticed one of his gold teeth. They immediately ran to inform the other church members and buried his body on a hillside, not far from the beach.[39]

According to another source, it was the Communist Party members who first discovered Rev. Teruzzi and asked nearby farmers to bury him. In this case, two church members were very careful to bury it in a higher position, not on the beach, as suggested by the Communist Party members. However, as for the accompanying preachers and servants, no one knows their whereabouts.

Investigation into the Murder of Priests

On 2 January 1943, the representative of the church in Tokyo of the Roman Ministry of Communication sent a telegram to Bishop Valtorta, announcing that Rev. Kwok, Rev. Wong, and Rev. Teruzzi were all "killed by Chinese bandits in Sai Kung", but neither the date, location, nor details of any murders was known. The source was a report in Latin, dated 3 December 1942, probably written by a Chinese priest.

Rev. Teruzzi was killed after being taken to the sea in Kei Ling Ha Hoi in 1942. (Image Source: PIME)

Rev. Renatus Kwok (the third left in the front) was abducted and killed in August 1942. (Image source: PIME)

Eight days ago, or even earlier, Han Ah-Kung (the steward of the Sai Kung Church) advised Rev. Teruzzi not to venture into the remote village. Because he said there were guerrillas who regarded Rev. Teruzzi as a traitor to China. Rev. Teruzzi disagreed and said he was a priest and not a traitor. He just took care of the souls of Catholics and was not worried. On the same day, the priest visited Tai Tung, Tseng Tau and Wu Kai Sha and said that he should be back in two days. But he never returned. Last night, a Catholic who lived on the island and often went to Sai Kung for business transactions told Ah-Kung that Rev. Teruzzi had been killed and his body had been found and buried. But no one knows when or how.[40]

When everyone confirmed that Rev. Teruzzi and his companions had been killed, Bishop Voltarta held a memorial Mass. The church was crowded with believers, and they all shed tears at the sacrifice of Rev. Teruzzi. It was impossible to investigate and search for the burial site during this period of Japanese occupation. Until October 1945, Bishop Valtorta and others went to Sai Kung to collect more information

When life in Sai Kung resumed normal, Rev. Joachim Chan Tang-shue (1890-1975, ordained as a priest in 1917), who was born in Yim Tin Tsai, successfully traced Rev. Teruzzi's tomb with the help of some Sham Chung Catholics. They cremated the bones, put them in a wooden box, and took them back to the Cathedral. On 15 November 1946, a group of priests, members of religious and Catholic groups, and the Catholic Scouts, together paid their last tributes to Rev. Teruzzi, and buried him in the area especially for priests in the St. Michael's Catholic Cemetery in Happy Valley. The ceremony was presided over by Fr. Antonio Riganti (PIME, 1893-1965), the Vicar General of the Diocese, and D. W. Luke, the director of the Catholic Church Scouts, without the presence of the Bishop. They were the close partners of Rev. Teruzzi when he promoted the Catholic Scouts, and they read aloud

Obituaries of Rev. Teruzzi.

a glorious tribute.[41] However, the details of the murders of Rev. Teruzzi and other priests still remain a mystery today.

In order to commemorate Rev. Teruzzi, Bro. Vittorio Polo (PIME, 1915-1984, who supervised the construction work) and Bro. Mario Colleoni (PIME, 1910-1988) established the Father Teruzzi Memorial Hall in Tung Tsz Scout Centre, Tai Po.

Chek Keng Holy Family Chapel: Escape and Rescue

Chek Keng is located in the eastern part of the Sai Kung Peninsula, southwest of Nam She Tsim, facing the sea and surrounded by mountains on three sides. There was a lot of arable land near Chek Keng Village, and the water source was sufficient, favorable for irrigation. There had been records of this village in the *San On County Chronicles* in the 24th year of Jiaqing period in the Qing Dynasty (1819). According to the *San On County Chronicles*, Chek Keng was a Hakka village with multiple surnames, with a history of more than 200 years. The villagers were named Chiu, Li, Fan, Cheng and Wong. The villagers surnamed Chiu moved from Tang Tou Xia, Shilong, Tung Kuan,

Holy Family Chapel of Chek Keng. (Image source: Following Thy Way)

Guangdong province to Chek Keng, and they were the first villagers to settle in Chek Keng. According to oral tradition, when the village was built, Chek Keng was paved with red stones on the seashore, hence the name "Chek Keng", meaning red path. Early villagers lived on farming. The Chiu clan lived in Sheung Wai (upper walled village), while the Li, Fan, Cheng, and Wong clans lived in Ha Wai (lower walled village).

In 1866, Rev. Giuseppe Burghignoli moved from Tai Po to Chek Keng to preach. After a year of hard work, the villagers in Chek Keng gradually converted, and there was the first batch of baptised people. They were all villagers surnamed Chiu and Wong. Seeing the success of the missionary work and the substantial pastoral needs, the chapel was built in 1867 and became one of the three mission centres of the Catholic Church in the New Territories. Since the priest would only stay in Chek Keng for a short time, the missionary work relied heavily on the Sisters of the Precious Blood. Since the late 1860s, two or three Sisters of the Precious Blood had been living in a village house called "Priest's House" outside the Chapel of the Holy Family. They would teach female villagers to read and write, and also encouraged villagers to participate in Mass.

On 23 September 1874, a strong typhoon hit Hong Kong and many buildings were damaged, including the Holy Family Chapel. Due to the small scale of the original chapel, it could no longer meet the needs of the believers. At that time, the Italian missionaries, who was in charge of the Holy Family Chapel, hired Chek Keng villagers to rebuild the chapel into a larger church with 200 seats.

In February 1879, Bishop Raimondi, who was then the Apostolic Vicar of Hong Kong, visited the villagers in Chek Keng and held Mass for the villagers in the newly built Holy Family Chapel. According to records, except for three people in the village, all the villagers were already catholics or catechumens preparing to be baptised. Among them, 62 Chek Keng villagers had been baptised. Most newborn babies in the village were baptised and received the sacrament of Confirmation in their teenage. Between 1909 and 1912, about 130 to 150 people participated Mass in the chapel. In 1928, the administration of the Holy Family Chapel was changed to Apostolic Vicariate.

Chek Keng before and after the War

According to the list of the "Chek Keng Village Member Prayer Society" in the 1930s, there was a prayer group in Holy Family Chapel. The members who had received Confirmation ranged from 8 to 15 years old. Their Christian names included "John",

"Antonio", "Joseph", "Paul", "Jacob", "Thomas" or "Louis". Most of the Catholics were members of the Chiu clan from nearby Chek Keng Sheung Wai and those of other main surnames in the village such as Fan and Li. The 22 members of the prayer group, in addition to young people, including adults in their twenties, were believed to be active members of the church.[42] The priest once set up a special room for the Catholics for spiritual practice and prayer.[43]

In December 1941, Hong Kong fell, and Sai Kung was in a dangerous situation under the Japanese occupation. The Japanese army used the Sai Kung Market as a military base, while the East River Column Anti-Japanese Guerrilla entrenched the mountainous area and organised villagers to resist, support, destroy Japanese military facilities, and rescue

The Holy Cross on altar in Holy Family Chapel, Chek Keng.

cultural celebrities. Apart from Chek Keng, other villages in Sai Kung, such as Cheung Sheung, Wong Mo Ying and Tai Long Village, had become the guerrilla bases of the Hong Kong and Kowloon Independent Brigade of the East River Column.

During the War, the guerrillas stationed in the Holy Family Chapel, and the priest dormitory became the office and bedroom of the captain and political commissar. The guerrillas would meet in the open space next to the chapel to formulate combat strategies. In addition, as the Luk Wu Field Hospital was behind Chek Keng, the injured were sent to the chapel for treatment from time to time. At the same time, many Chek Keng villagers joined the East River column and fought bravely against the enemy. Among them, the names of villagers Chiu Wah, Fan Fat and Li Yu Cheung were recorded in the list of martyrs.

Rev. Francis Wong, Parish Priest of Tai Long was Killed

In the early days of the War, priests would still go to the Holy Family Chapel to celebrate Mass. However, riots, looting and killings occurred from time to time in Sai Kung under Japanese occupation. Rev. Francis Wong who served Tai Long chose to stay in Sai Kung to preach. The security in Tai Long Village was very bad not only due to the scattered Japanese troops, but also bandits active in the whole Sai Kung area. Bandits armed with guns usually consisted of eight to ten people, and they went to Tai Long Village to rob money and food every few days.

Sit Seng, the then altar boy of Rev. Wong, recalled that on 15 November 1942, the guerrillas assumed Rev. Wong was a traitor, and therefore captured him. Later, Rev. Wong disappeared and was not heard until after the war that he had been killed. Sit Seng speculated that Rev. Wong was killed because he was accused of serving the Japanese army. In addition, he himself was also captured by the guerrillas because he had followed the priest to provide rituals and services in different villages. Fortunately, he was released under the guarantee from the villagers of Chek Keng, but then he was asked to join the guerrillas. Sit Seng served as a "political warrior" in the guerrillas, responsible for depicting the Japanese invasion of China and encouraging the villagers to resist. In addition, he also participated in the Anti-Japanese War in Tam Shui, Lung Kong, Shek Lung and other places in Guangdong. After the war, Sit Seng did not retreat with the troops to the North, and chose to return to Tai Long.[44]

According to Sit Seng, many young people in Tai Long were forced to join

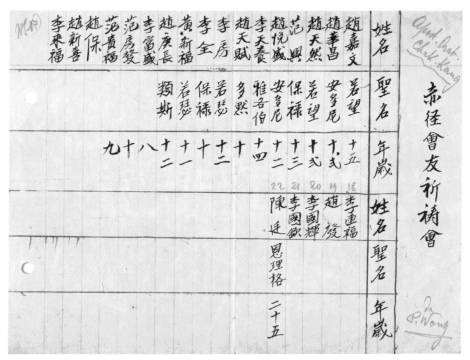

Membership record of the Chek Keng prayer group in the 1930s.
(Image Source: Hong Kong Catholic Diocesan Archives)

Village Houses in Chek Keng.

the guerrillas at that time, and many of them were killed in the war. Some villagers participated in logistical work to help the guerrillas transport explosives to areas such as Chek Keng and Ko Tong. Sit Seng returned to Hong Kong after the Japanese surrender. Before leaving the team, he was reminded by his superiors that he must not disclose to anyone about his participation in the East River Column, otherwise he would be pursued by the Kuomintang. Therefore, he remained tight-lipped and only revealed it to his son 60 years later.[45] Sit Seng's personal experience proved the important role played by Tai Long Village during the War and also explained the great fear that war brought to the people.

In addition, the village chief Tsam Kwai Shing, who was still young during the war, also joined the "Little Devils" to deliver news for the guerrillas. Once when he sent a letter to Chek Keng, he saw a Japanese tugboat on the sea, and heard noises from a nearby bay, so he hurriedly swallowed the letter and almost choked to death. Later, he discovered that the sound came from troops of his side.

Mr. Lam Kap Sou, another Tai Long villager, was also a Catholic. He once served as a clerk in the guerrillas and was responsible for writing letters to inform his teammates about the whereabouts of the Japanese. He mentioned that guerrilla members were banned from believing in any religion, otherwise they would be punished. In the last three months before Liberation of Hong Kong, the Japanese army stationed in the chapel of the Immaculate Conception and hired villagers to dig air-raid shelters in the mountains adjacent to the village. Fortunately, neither the altar nor the chapel was severely damaged. When the Japanese army left, the anti-Japanese guerrillas lived in the chapel for several days.

The period from the establishment of Tai Long District in 1931 to Japanese occupation during 1941 to 1945 saw the missionaries leading the villagers to convert to Catholicism in a precarious situation. Tai Long District was once an important Catholic community of the Hong Kong Vicars Apostolic to which the local Church attached great importance. However, Catholic activities drastically declined during the Japanese occupation period. Rev. Teruzzi strived persistently to overcome all the hardships which set an exemplary model to others. Additionally, Rev. Teruzzi was devoted to serving the community and therefore was recognized as a beloved priest by the Chinese people and became a genuine member of their society. Unfortunately, he and other Chinese priests were martyred. These regrettable events made the names of these missionaries inscribed in the pioneers' footpaths in Sai Kung so as to remind us the association between history and faith.

The altar in Immaculate Conception Chapel of Tai Long .
(Image source: Immaculate Heart of Mary Church, Tai Po)

Notes

1   "Ecclesiastical Return", *Hong Kong Blue Book for 1933*.

2   *Hong Kong Blue Book 1935*, p. 310; *Hong Kong Blue Book 1939*, p. 345.

3   Letter dated 2 April 1931 concerning some directions regarding Tai Long District: 1/ Taking care of the District, 2/ Some material items: subsidies, church repairs, etc., HKCDA, Section IV, Box 13, Folder 02.

4   From 1997 to 1998, a survey conducted by the Antiquities and Monuments Office found that more than 90% of the village houses in Tai Long Village have a history of more than one hundred years, and the entire village has retained its traditional architectural pattern in Hong Kong, constituting a rarity of the territory. See *Affection for Tai Long Wan* (《情牽大浪灣》) (Hong Kong: Hong Kong Observes of wildlife & Londsrape, 2001), p. 152.

5   John Strickland (ed.), *Southern District Officer Reports – Islands and Villages in Rural Hong Kong, 1910-60* (Hong Kong: Hong Kong University Press, 2010), p. 280.

6   HKCDA, Sai Kung and Tai Long files.

7   HKCDA, Section I, Box 08, Folder 02.

8   *Le Missioni Cattoliche*, 1877, pp. 324-325.

9   *Hong Kong Catholic Directory and Year Book 1958*, p. 26; *Hong Kong Catholic Directory and Year Book 1959*, p. 30.

10 Francis Wong's letter from Catholic Mission, Chik Kang, 4 July 1941. HKCDA: Section IV, Box 13, Folder 02.

11 The chapel was renamed as Immaculate Conception Chapel in 1954. It was uncertain as to the original name of the chapel.

12 *Hong Kong Blue Book 1935*, p. 310; *Hong Kong Blue Book 1939*, p. 345.

13 Interview with Sit Seng of Tai Long Village. Interviewers: Yuen Chi Wai, Lam Suet Pik and Cheung Chun Kin, 9 June 2018.

14 Ibid.

15 Ibid.

16 "Fresh water pipes installed in Sai Kung" (〈西貢大浪村居民裝水管輸送山水〉), *The Kung Sheung Daily News*, 8 June 1960.

17 "Telephone service started yesterday, villages and tourists found convenient" (〈大浪村昨日有電話服務鄉民遊客便〉), *Overseas Chinese Daily*, 22 March 1977.

18 Letter of Fr. Teruzzi, 26 May 1940, published in Hong Kong, Missionee Martirio (Tiemme, Milano 1992), p. 30.

19 *Le Missioni Cattoliche*, p. 42.

20 Sergio Ticozzi, "A Brief History of the Martyrs of the Three Fathers in Sai Kung" (《西貢三神父殉道簡史〉), *Kung Kao Po*, 28 August 1992, p. 1.

21 Francis Wong letter dated Sep 10, 1941 from Catholic Mission Chik Kang, HKCDA: Section IV, Box 13, folder 02.

22 Sergio Ticozzi, "A Brief History of the Martyrs of the Three Fathers in Sai Kung" (《西貢三神父殉道簡史〉), *Kung Kao Po*, 28 August 1992, p. 1.

23 Vicarius Apostolicus, Datum Hong Kong, die 2 Octobris 1942. HKCDA: Section IV, Box 13, Folder 02.

24 *Interview with Sit Seng of Tai Long Village*, Yuen Chi Wai, Lam Suet Pik and Cheung Chun Kin, 9 June 2018.

25   Sergio Ticozzi, "A Brief History of the Martyrs of the Three Fathers in Sai Kung" (《西貢三神父殉道簡史》), *Kung Kao Po*, 28 August 1992, p. 1.

26   The Hong Kong Independence Brigade, belonging to the East River Column of the Communist Party of China, was established on 3 February 1942 at Wong Mo Ying Chapel in Sai Kung.

27   Centre for East Asian Studies, Chinese University of Hong Kong, *Saikung, 1940-1950: The Oral History Project* (1982), p. 49, 52, See HKCDA, Sai Kung, Section IV, Box 14, Folder 02.

28   Sergio Ticozzi, translated by Yuen Chi Wai, "Father Teruzzi's Mission and Contribution in Hong Kong", *Hong Kong Journal of Catholic Studies – A History of the Hong Kong Catholic Church in the 20 th Century,* No. 7, 2016 (Hong Kong: Centre for Catholic Studies, The Chinese University of Hong Kong, 2016), p. 49.

29   A. Lozza, *Sangue Fecondo* (EMI: Bologna, 1981), pp. 146-147.

30   Sergio Ticozzi, "A brief history of the martyrdom of the three priests in Sai Kung", *Kung Kao Po*, 28 August 1992, p. 1

31   HKCDA, Section IV, Box 14.

32   Ibid.

33   Ibid.

34   Rev. Quirino De Ascaniis came to Hong Kong in 1933 as a fellow of PIME. He served as the priest of the Sai Kung District from 1953 to 1961. After his retirement, he lived in the St. Joseph's Home for the Elderly in Ngau Chi Wan, Kowloon. See Hong Kong: Current Status of the Association, *Kung Kao Po*, 28 August 1992, p. 1, http://kkp.catholic.org.hk/coko2956.htm, retrieved on 18 December 2016.

35   "Quirino De Ascaniis", PIME Archive, Hong Kong.

36   HKCDA, Section IV, Box 14.

37   This is based on the knowledge of Rev. Quirino De Ascaniis. After a Catholic traitor knew about Rev. Teruzzi's journey plan, he informed the guerrillas in Shum Chung. The guerrillas then hired a non-Catholic man and his boat from this village to carry Rev. Teruzzi to an unknown destination.

38   Sergio Ticozzi, "A brief history of the martyrdom of the three priests in Sai Kung", *Kung Kao Po*, 28 August 1992, p. 1.

39   Ibid.

40   HKCDA, Sai Kung, Section IV, Box 14, Folder 01.

41   On August 23, 1992, the Sai Kung Sacred Heart Church held the Requiem Mass to commemorate the 50th anniversary of the martyrdom of Rev. Kwok, Rev. Wong and Rev, Teruzzi in Sai Kung. The then Vice-Bishop Lam Cheuk-Wai Gabriel and several members of the PIME attended the ceremony. Fr. V. Bruni made a special trip to Hong Kong from Milan, Italy. In addition, more than a dozen members from Rev. Kwok's family and Rev. Teruzzi's Italian hometown also came to Hong Kong to attend. See Kung Kao Po, 28 August 1992, p. 1.

42   HKCDA, Section IV, Box 13, Folder 2.

43   Letter of the Vicar Apostolic of Hong Kong dated 28 November 1934 concerning a Centre for prayer apostolate to be erected at Chek-kang, HKCDA, Section IV, Box 13, Folder 2.

44   Interview with Sit Seng. Interviewers: Yuen Chi Wai, Lam Suet Pik and Cheung Chun Kin, 9 June 2018.

45   Ibid.

1841

1874

1931

1945

1969

1981

2000

Chapter 5

Establishment of the Diocese and Post-war Social Services (1945-1969)

On 15 August 1945, Japan surrendered unconditionally. The British navy army landed on Hong Kong for reoccupation and proclaimed the end of the Japanese rule.

After the war, many of the priests returned to their original Catholic villages to continue their services. However, as the number of Catholic villages was declining due to parishioners' emigration or moving to the urban area, the original parishes such as Tai Long District were gradually abandoned and the chapels fell into disrepair. Some of the chapels were included in the plan of charitable organizations for providing social services, which changed their development use and became new religious sites.

As time flies, although these chapels had been in operation for a period of time after the war, they had gradually been abandoned due to changes in the social environment, migration of villagers, and reduction of believers. In 1949, Bishop Enrico Valtorta (PIME, 1883-1951) went to Sai Wan to serve sacraments of initiation for more than 30 villagers. Afterwards, construction of the Sai Wan Star of Sea Chapel was officially completed. It was the only newly built chapel after the war in Sai Kung. In addition, the Epiphany of Our Lord Chapel in Sham Chung, a Hakka village, was rebuilt after the war. The missionaries also set up a village school in the chapel named "Kung Man School" or "Catholic Citizen School" so access to education was available to children in the village. Missionaries went to Hakka villages to preach on a daily basis, and often brought daily necessities such as blankets, milk and bread to succour the villagers. They even took photos to record the Hakka people's participation in rituals and life at that time, which showed that they were very concerned about the needs of the villagers and built a close relationship with them.

There were many fishing boats docking near Sai Kung Market. In the 1960s and 1970s, priests from Sai Kung visited the boat people. They acted like the district officers who understood boat people's needs, and sought a place for them to build houses from the government, which they could be settled ashore to improve lives. For example, the

Peter's Village, located on the Tui Min Hoi of Sai Kung Market, was a fishermen's village built by missionaries and Caritas-Hong Kong (Caritas). After completion, the church helped with the allocation of flats to boat people. The children of fishermen could therefore continue their learning on weekdays, and the place is still a village of faithful fishermen nowadays.

The Development of Catholic Mission in Post-war Hong Kong

By the end of the war, the situation in the mainland became uncertain in the late 1940s. Many people had concerns about the new regime and escaped to Hong Kong. According to the records of the Hong Kong government, the population of Hong Kong was less than 600,000 in September 1945. By 1949, it had soared to 1.85 million, and in March 1950 it was increased by 500,000 to 2.31 million.[1] The rapid demographic change affected the scale and direction of Catholic missionary activities at that time.

Faced with the huge number of refugees, the British Hong Kong government lost its bearings. When the Governor David Trench (1915-1988) recalled the welfare policy of the time, he pointed out:

In 1953, Hong Kong had a small population and could not even be called a society, because for many people it was only a temporary residence. They were highly mobile, and they came back to their hometown after staying in Hong Kong for a period of time. In this case, social services were only provided for those who have stayed in Hong Kong for a long time.[2]

His claim that Hong Kong had a small population is obviously inconsistent with the social situation of more than 2 million people in 1953. It could be seen that the government only regarded these people as temporary residents. The reason behind it might be because the colonial government was worried that providing generous benefits will attract more refugees to Hong Kong and increased the burden on society.[3] In fact, after the influx of these refugees into Hong Kong, they did not just stay for a while and then returned to the mainland as mentioned above but wanted to settle down. According to a survey, only 0.6% of people who arrived in Hong Kong from the Mainland wanted to go back, that is, most of the refugees became the population of Hong Kong.[4] The post-war population boom created a huge demand for social services, which has already caused various problems. Worse still, the government's neglect of it put pressure on the society, but prompted the Catholic Church to intervene in providing social services through which missionary work could be carried out.

The Catholic Diocese of Hong Kong at that time was led by Bishop Lorenzo Bianchi (1899-1983), who was called "the bishop of the world's largest refugee concentration camp". The missionary work that was forced to be suspended during the war gradually resumed, and the sudden change in social situation and demography injected impetus for the revitalising the ecclesiastical affairs. As Bishop Bianchi mentioned: "Every day, hundreds of refugees arrive in this British colony. This is an astonishing wave of fleeing, and there is no sign that it is about to end. These desperate people are displaced and starved, looking forward to finding shelter and daily food. We can't waste time any longer."[5] Missionaries set up humanitarian aid centres near the churches to provide material and spiritual assistance, such as distributing food and medicine, and assisting refugees in finding jobs.[6]

In the 1950s, the Catholic Church opened about 20 social service centres, built more than 4,000 shelters, 55 food and clothing distribution centres, and 17 clinics.[7] Due to the fact that many civilians starved to death during the occupation and there were shortage of rice caused by the increase in Hong Kong's population, the government controlled imported rice to prevent hoarding and price increases, and established a grain distribution agency to directly purchase rice and grains for rationing. However the rice rationing system was abolished in 1954, and all the rice imports were handed over to the retailers in the following year with 30 to 40 batch importers. Sai Kung Sacred Heart Church had once assisted the government wholesale office in issuing villagers' shopping permits in Sai Kung. At that time, the villagers could only purchase a certain quota of rice at designated shops in Sai Kung Market with the valid ration cards sealed by the "Sai Kung Catholic Church". One of the retail stores was "Tai Yik" at No. 13 Sai Kung Centre Street.

In addition, the religious congregations who originally served in the mainland were expelled because of the founding of the People's Republic of China. They went to Hong Kong and asked for residency. However, the Holy See instructed the Hong Kong Catholic Diocese to only help these missionaries to transit through Hong Kong to other places. Bishop Bianchi finally decided to continue the policy of his predecessor Bishop Valtorta and accepted these religious congregations to commence their pastoral work in Hong Kong. These new congregations became the new blood of Catholic groups who

Sai Kung Market in the 1950s. (Image source: Sai Kung Sacred Heart Church)

Bishop Bianchi (second right). (Image source: PIME)

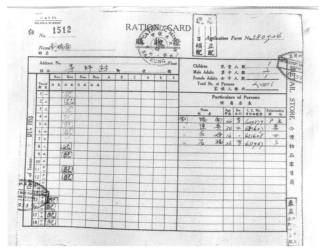

The ration card issued by the Government Wholesale Office to a family of four in Mao Ping Village in December 1953 can be seen with the stamp of the Sai Kung Catholic Church. (Image source: Heung Yee Kuk, New Territories)

catered for the social needs.[8] In 1955 and 1959, Ma On Shan and Hang Hau became separate districts and no longer belonged to the Sai Kung District.

Against this backdrop, the Catholic service in Hong Kong has expanded its scale and emphasized pastoral work to respond to social needs. The Catholic Diocese of Hong Kong grew rapidly, and missionary activities on the Sai Kung Peninsula gradually recovered. Missionaries went to the Sai Wan Village, which had been abandoned after the war, to preach and baptise the villagers. The Star of the Sea Chapel in the village was officially put into service in 1953 and was the only new Sai Kung Chapel built after the war.

The Establishment of Sai Wan Star of the Sea Chapel

Star of the Sea Chapel located in the eastern part of Sai Wan lower village, not far from the beach. Sai Wan, also known as Tai Long Sai Wan, is located at the southeast Sai Kung Peninsula. As it is located in the west of Tai Long Wan, it is called "Sai Wan" (west bay). There are three small islands in the off-shore of Sai Wan which are named, from left to right, "Lantau Pai', "Tai Chau" and "Tsim Chau". Three seamounts form a three-part screen blocking the tide. Sai Wan is adjacent to Tai Long Village and Long Ke Village, with Law Tei Tun on its back and facing the sea. Sai Wan is divided into two villages, the upper and lower villages. The villages were founded in the Ming Dynasty and their ancestors came from Jiangxi. The villagers are mainly Lais, and most of them were fishermen. In the heyday, there were about 100 villagers.[9] Before the Second World War, villagers also engaged in the charcoal industry. Some villagers built a charcoal kiln on the top of the mountain. Villagers burned wood into charcoal every day and transported it out of for sale. However, due to the popularisation of other fuels such as kerosene and petroleum gas, the charcoal industry gradually declined and thus charcoal kilns were also suspended.[10]

During the war, villagers would hide in the charcoal kiln in order to avoid the Japanese army. Afterwards, the whole village decided to seek refuge in the mainland, as relatives of the Lai's were in Guangdong Province. Their temporary departure caused the whole village of Sai Wan to be deserted. Paul Tsui Ka Cheung, the first Chinese to be appointed as a Cadet Officer who served as the Southern District Officer with Sai Wan as a part of the district under his purview, recorded after a tour, "I was surprised by the barrenness of Sai Wan. Almost all the houses were reduced to ruined roofs. I later learned that it was because the Japanese army knew that the guerrillas had set up operations bases here, so they ransacked and burnt the village".[11]

In the early 20th century, missionaries had already set foot in Sai Wan, with a small number of villagers willing to be baptised. In his report from 1914 to 1915, Rev. Teruzzi described the villagers in Sai Wan Village as "a rather mischievous character, but on several occasions they wanted to become Christians."[12] It was after the war that Catholicism became the prevailing belief in the village when Rev. Giorgio Caruso (PIME, 1908-2004) resumed pastoral work in Sai Kung. He worked tirelessly to spread the gospel and interacted with both faithfuls and non-believers in a humble manner which moved the villagers of Sai Wan and made nearly all converted to Catholicism. At that time, the village chief Lai Wan Loi discussed with the villagers and asked Rev. Caruso to help them to abolish the old faith.[13] Rev. Caruso believed that the villagers were looking for God not because of the plague or other disasters, but awakening from idolatry and no longer superstitious.[14] In addition, the villagers of Sai Wan also deeply understood the importance of education and negotiated with Rev. Caruso to set up a school in the village to teach language and other subjects. At the same time, there were also nuns who taught catechesis in the school.

In December 1949, Bishop Valtorta went to Sai Wan to baptise the first group of catechumens after the war. Teachers and students from Tai Long Village Yuk Ying School also came to welcome the Bishop. The Bishop administered the baptism and the sacrament of confirmation for the villagers, and celebrated the Mass. On that day, there were 36 people baptised, 30 people who received the First Communion, 32 people received the confirmation, and about 60 people attended the ceremony.[15]

At the beginning of the mission, there was no church in Sai Wan, and the priest had to say Masses in a house lent by a zealous believer. Later, the number of church members in Sai Wan gradually increased, and the diocesan found a place to build a church in the lower village of Sai Wan in 1953. The Chapel was a small single-storied building divided into two parts: the sanctuary and the school. The Star of the Sea Church is on the left of the main entrance of the building, and the Star of the Sea School is on the right. Both the church and the school were named "Hoi Sing" (Star of the Sea) to express the villagers' reliance on Our Lady of Star of Sea and hoped that she would lead the villagers and bring them true light. The whole building was made of granite. The forehead of the door was engraved with the words "Hoi Sing Xing Tong" (Star of the Sea Chapel) and "Tin Chu Tong" (Catholic Church).

The roof of the Chapel is a Hakka-style tile roof, which is very distinctive. In the old days, villagers sat on the benches to attend Masses at the front portion of the Chapel. The back portion was an altar with a portrait of the Virgin of Star of Sea hanging above the altar. The wall below the windows in the church was originally blue. Behind the Star of Sea School's main entrance classroom was the teacher's room, with a wooden ladder leading to the wooden attic, which was the teacher's dormitory. On one hand, the school instilled knowledge, on the other hand, it cultivated their students' faith. When students returned to school, had lunch, and were dismissed, they would recite the *Angelus* (Latin, meaning Angel) under the guidance of their teacher.

Religious Life in Sai Wan Village in the 1960s

In the 1960s, the priest visited Sai Wan Village once every one to two weeks. Sai Wan was remote and inconvenient for transportation. According to the records of Austin Coates, who served as the Southern District Officer in the 1950s, Sai Wan, Long Ke and Tai Long were the most remote villages in the New Territories at that time. Due to the undercurrents on the coast of Sai Wan, it was difficult to reach it directly by maritime transport. People usually walked from Sha Tsui which takes two hours if one brought with luggage.[16] The priest had to take a small sailing boat from Sha Tsui to the Sai Wan Sui King Pier, and then walked through the rugged mountain roads to reach the Sai Wan mission. The priest usually started walking to Sha Tsui in the morning to say the anticipated Sunday Mass and then went to Long Ke, and arrived at Sai Wan about dusk. Whenever the priest came to the nearby Lo Wu Tun, he would exclaim to Sai Wan Village. Whenever the villagers heard it, they would row a small boat to welcome the priest across the stream. The priest usually stayed overnight in a village house next to the chapel, and then held Sunday Mass on the following day. According to the current village head Lai Yan, the village house belonged to a devout believer named Wan Ngau Mui who was very enthusiastic. Whenever the priest came, she immediately informed the Catholics everywhere, reminding them to attend Mass and confess.

Villagers near Sai Wan Village (such as Ham Tin Wan, Long Ke Village, Sha Tsui Village, etc.) sometimes also participated in the ceremonies of Sai Wan Village, including baptism, the Assumption of the Blessed Virgin Mary, and the Procession of the Eucharist. According to the village chief's recollection, six priests once said the Mass of the Assumption of the Blessed Virgin Mary, and it was as lively as a wedding banquet. In addition, the villagers of Sai Wan would also cook traditional village dishes to entertain the neighboring villagers who came to participate the ceremony, making the whole day full of joy.

Due to the geographic remoteness of Sai Wan, if villagers need medical treatment, they often enjoyed the "flying doctor" service provided by the government. This service began in March 1961. The Flying Doctor Team was directly under the jurisdiction of the New Territories Medical and Health Department, providing medical services to villagers in remote areas of the New Territories. There was an open space next to the Star of Sea Chapel for helicopters of the flying doctor team to land on. At first, the flying doctor team would come once a week to provide consultations and medicines for the villagers without any fees. Villagers needed to prepare their own containers to collect medicines, which cold medicines and stomach medicines would be given a particularly large amount. Later, the population of the villagers became smaller and smaller, and the service of the flying doctor team changed from once a week to once every two weeks. However, dentists began to take a helicopter to provide dental services to the villagers in Sai Wan.

In 1962, Typhoon Wanda struck Hong Kong which seriously devastated. The villagers in Sai Wan suffered huge losses, and the Star of Sea Chapel was also destroyed. Overcoming considerable hardships, the chapel was rebuilt in 1963 and therefore "1963" was engraved under the Holy Cross above the main entrance of the chapel to commemorate it. After the expansion, a small room was added next to the chapel for priests to stay overnight. Even in the peaceful and prosperous times, the income from hard work was only enough to make ends meet. In the 1960s, the Hong Kong government built the High Island Reservoir, which greatly changed the water systems in Sai Kung and affected the livelihoods of local villagers. At the time when the British government amended the nationality law, many people from the New Territories immigrated to the UK, and the male villagers in Sai Wan also went abroad to earn a living. Only a few female villagers remained behind, and the number of church members also reduced. On 1 July 1979, the Sai Kung District was upgraded to a parish, and Rev. Ruggiero, Nicola (PIME, 1925-2012) served as the supervisor of Sai Wan Primary School, proving that the Star of Sea School was still serving the villagers at that time. By the end of the 1980s, the number of villagers was no more than ten, and there were only two students. Eventually, the village was gradually abandoned and the Star of Sea Chapel ceased service. Even so, Sai Wan Village and the Star of Sea Chapel had jointly witnessed the re-start and rapid development of the Hong Kong Catholic Diocese after the war.

Education: Sham Chung Kung Man School and Local Society

In the 1950s, when Austin Coates, the then Southern District Officer of the New Territories, visited the Sai Kung Peninsula he mentioned in his memorandum:

The Catholic Church is powerful in the whole (Sai Kung Peninsula) region, chiefly in the remote part. Through their middle school at Sai Kung they are the principal education institution, and in view of the care given to pupils subsequent to their studies (in finding employment) they rival the Government in the services they offer.[17]

In fact, in the face of the influx of refugees that flooded Hong Kong after World War II, the Hong Kong government finally had to face up to the various problems of the swelling population and provide relief to social poverty, including the promotion of education. The government invited all institutions that were interested in running schools to open new schools and sponsored them through various means, including granting land at low fees or even for free, and providing financial assistance to build various buildings. James Hayes, who served as the District Officer of the Southern District from 1957 to 1960, also stated that the government hoped to provide sufficient primary schools for the entire New Territories after the war.[18] Bishop Bianchi responded to the government's call and vigorously promoted Catholic education. He firmly believed that every parish needed a school and said: "Now that the people need schools, and we must provide them with schools."

Bishop Bianchi entrusted Rev. Ottavio Liberatore (PIME, 1901-1972) to be responsible for the construction of the school. Br. Mario Colleoni (1910-1988) who assisted Rev. Ottavio Liberatore at the time, recalled that the entire Catholic Church in Hong Kong had become a "construction site". The two often visited schools and churches under construction, and they also jointly planned how to finance these projects. Although there were worries about the rumor that the Communist Party might rule Hong Kong, Bishop Bianchi did not stop the project. Instead, he believed that people needed education and insisted on carrying out the projects. When other religious groups withdrew their funds away from Hong Kong, Bishop Bianchi still appealed for donations from all over the world.[19] As a result, the number of local Catholic schools increased significantly: from 70 in 1950 to 251 in 1969; at the same time, the number of relevant students increased from 20,570 to 211,548.[20] In less than 20 years, the number of schools and students has tripled and tenfold respectively. This showed that the Catholic Church's emphasis on education and its determination to invest resources in the post-war era, which also reflected the courage and optimism of Bishop Bianchi.

The above-mentioned government policy and the direction of church pastoralists had injected impetus to the Catholic education in Sai Kung area. Among them, the Sham Chung Kung Man School was particularly worthy for discussion. Traditional discourse believes that Catholic schools were popular with the public and promoted the rapid spread of religious beliefs, but Sham Chung was an atypical example, revealing the relationship and interaction between missionaries and villagers due to village school issues with intervention by government education and the home affairs departments.

History of Sham Chung

Sham Chung was originally a Hakka village under the San On County during the Qing Dynasty. It had the clans Lees and Wongs with the former as the majority. The history of the village can be traced back to the Qianlong period (1736-1795) of the Qing Dynasty. Sham Chung is located on the west coast of the Sai Kung Peninsula, where the Tolo Strait enters the Tolo Harbour, and its western part faces Three Fathoms Cove. The village was located in a remote location. In the early days, it mainly relied on waterways to connect with neighboring areas as it takes more than an hour walking distance to reach nearby villages Sham Chung was still almost isolated after World War II. Even though the ferry service connecting Sham Chung, Tai Po and Ma On Shan was established for the first time since 1952, the waterway transportation to and from Sham Chung was still extremely inconvenient because the village had no pier at that time and the ferry could only stay in the middle of the sea.[21] Passengers and agricultural products transportation needed to be connected by small boats to reach the ferry for boarding.[22]

Sham Chung Kung Man School is now vacant.

In the event of wind and rain, there would be multiples danger. The situation did not improve substantially until the Sham Chung Public Pier was completed in 1962.[23]

Despite her geographical remoteness, as early as the late nineteenth century, missionaries had set foot in Sham Chung: Bishop Luigi Piazzoli (1845-1904), who became the second Apostolic Vicar of Hong Kong in 1895, and was ordained as a bishop in the same year, travelled from the mission station in Ting Kok, Tai Po to Sham Chung in 1870 to start his missionary work. By 1872, there were 30 parishioners in Sham Chung. In November 1872, Rev. Raimondi, the future Bishop, visited areas including Sham Chung. At the time, there were two nuns in Sham Chung working at the Women's Centre. They were the first two nuns sent to work in the area.[24] The Diocese also built the Epiphany of Our Lord Chapel during 1875 to 1879. In 1879, Bishop Raimondi visited Sham Chung again, and the number of church members had been increased to 34.[25] In July 1892, Bishop Pozzoni stated in his report on San On that Sham Chung was one of the four main Christian groups in San On at the time. "All the residents were Catholics and only a few were not baptised", reflecting that the missionaries' efforts bore fruits.[26]

However, there was a tragedy during the constructions of the chapel in Sham Chung: the project was undertaken by Fr. Antonius Tam (1850-1875), who belonged to the Apostolic Vicariate of Hong Kong at the time. After being ordained for only six months, he took a fisherman's sampan from Ting Kok on 30 November 1875, with him he brought a carpenter to transport the masonry to Sham Chung. However, they encountered strong winds in Ting Kok Bay, the boat inclined, and the three fell into the sea. They could only hold a piece of wood and float in the sea, but the wind was too strong for them. Before the carpenter foresaw that he would be buried in the raging sea, he asked the priest to baptise him, and the two eventually drowned. Fortunately the fishermen survived, allowing the story to be passed on.[27]

The villagers had also built a long embankment with the assistance of the priest. It was 210 meters long, over 6 meters high, and 9 to 12 meters wide. It was a large-scale project that mobilised nearly 50 families and used nearly 25,000 tons of stones.[28] The construction was built in the swells, could only be done with the strength and cooperation of the villagers and the courage of the missionaries. A gate was set on the embankment to prevent the farmland from flooding during the upsurge, and the gate could also open when the sea level dropped to discharge the accumulated water of the farmland into the sea.[29] Bishop Raimondi went to Sham Chung for a pastoral visit in

1875, and expressed his appreciation for the project:

"The village (Sham Chung) is located in a large shallow bay. At high tide, large areas of land are covered by water thus untillable. Motivated by Rev. Piazzoli, villagers built a large dike to separate the sea so that the land within the dike can be reclaimed. The crops grown on this land are enough to feed half of the population. The recent typhoon damaged a large section of the dike. But the priest summoned all the Catholics to rebuild the embankment, and it was stronger than before."[30]

In addition, there was oral tradtion that due to the influence of the church, the pirates and thieves who had always swarmed there no longer gathered so that the villagers could live a stable life.[31] Rev. Giuseppe Burghignoli also preached in Sham Chung and he thought it was an excellent group of church members.[32]

Church-managed Kung Man School

There was a school built in Sham Chung as early as the 1930s.[33] According to land records, the land where the school was located was registered under by the Apostolic Vacariate of Hong Kong since 1908. Due to the retirement of Rev. Angelo Ferrario (PIME, 1876-1933), the land trustee was converted to Rev. Emilio Teruzzi (PIME, 1887-1942) in 1930. In the post-war era the Catholic Church in Hong Kong was committed to the development of education. Against this backdrop, a number of Catholic schools were established in Sai Kung including this new Kung Man School was completed in 1956.[34] The new Epiphany of Our Lord Chapel with Kung Man School was opened to replace the old chapel with many years of history.[35] Bishop Bianchi presided over the opening ceremony of the consecration and performed the sacrament of Confirmation. The parish priest of the church was Rev. Paul Tsang Chi-Kwong (1908-1984), who also served as the supervisor of the Kung Man School.

Kung Man School was a subsidised primary school. The name of the school was inscribed by Chan Pun Tsiu, the principal of the Tai Po Vernacular Normal School (TVNS). Although the school is now closed down, the name of the school and the inscription on its facade are still clearly identifiable. The building included a school and a chapel at the same time. Its spatial distribution was: the middle of the room was a church, and there were two classrooms on both sides. There was no court in the school.[36] On weekdays, there was only an open yard in front of the chapel for students' extra-curricular activities. As recalled by the former principal Joseph Kwong Kai-to of the school, students could only play football in the field during the autumn harvest. If there were physical education classes on other days, the teacher would lead the students to a nearby embankment for running and sports.[37]

According to newspaper reports, the population of Sham Chung villagers in 1956 was about 250, most of them were working class, among them there were more than 100 parishioners.[38] As shown in the Hong Kong Diocesan Archive, there were already 120 parishioners in the village in 1959.[39] The mix of parishioners and non-believers

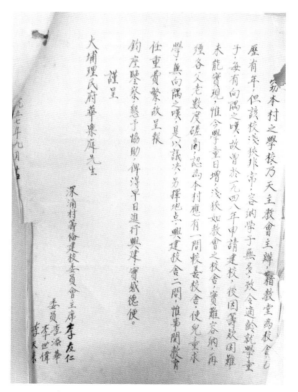

In 1957, Lee Yau Yan, Chairman of the Preparatory Committee for the establishment of Sham Chung Village School, stated to John Charles Creasey Walden, District Officer (Tai Po), that because the church school premises was small, it was recommended to build another school to accommodate the children in the village. (Image Source: Government Records Office)

in the village also reflected the composition of students: in 1958, less than half of the school's students believed in Catholicism,[40] but this may be one of the reasons why the villagers had different views on the running of the church.

Villagers-initiated Sham Chung School

Only one year after the completion of the Kung Man School, Sham Chung Village Representative Lee Yau Yan and several villagers wrote to the Department of Education, stating that the newly built Kung Man School had a limited space and could not accommodate all school-age children in the village the opportunity to receive education. In addition, the Kung Man school had never run the upper primary class, thus students had no chance of completing primary education. They then applied to the authorities to build an additional Sham Chung Public School that was subsidised by the government. Officials from the Department of Education believed that the original Kung Man School's space was sufficient for children in the village to enroll, and new classes could be opened if necessary, so they rejected Lee Yau Yan and others' applications. After that, the villagers converted part of their houses into temporary school premises, and raised funds to build private school.[41]

Tai Po District Office once suggested to the villagers that the Catholic Church should be responsible for the establishment of a new school to save the villagers' efforts to raise the cost of building new school, but the villagers were not interested in this. Government officials believe that dissatisfaction with the church's management of Kung Man school was one of the reasons why villagers wanted to build new schools. Newspaper reports also revealed that villagers were dissatisfied with the church's preaching in school.[42] Therefore, the authorities met with the school supervisor, Rev. Tsang, and expected him to listen to the villagers' opinions and cooperate with them.[43]

After that, the Sham Chung Public School, which was set up in a temporary school premises, started running in September 1958. It was named "Sham Chung Public School", and Lee Yau Yan served as the school supervisor. The village representative and the Catholic representative in the village entered into a contract for the opening of the school, which stipulated that both parties agreed that Sham Chung Village "do not allow a second school to exist in addition to the Public School", as if the original Kung Man School should be abolished (note: even after the contract had been signed and the Sham Chung Public School commenced classes, the Sham Chung Kung

Man School still continued to operate).[44]

It is worth mentioning that Sham Chung Public School did not seem to oppose to Catholicism, as it offered a weekly Bible lesson, where students could participate freely, and had a school board with three out of five members being Catholic. In the first year of its opening, the Sham Chung Public School had enrolled 29 students, more than twice of that of the Kung Man School with only 12 or 13 students. Unfortunately, the former suffered financial difficulties after less than a year of operation, even if it was donated by overseas Chinese and subsidized by ancestral trust.[45] It was difficult to sustain in the long term. The school submitted an application for subsidies to the Department of Education, which was supported by the Sai Kung North Rural Committee.[46]

Proposed Solution

The authorities finally proposed to build another subsidised new school to replace both Kung Man School and the Public School. Its school management committee was composed of one supervisor and four school managers. The head of committee concurrently the supervisor was appointed by the Education Department, while the four managers were the combination of two church nominees and two villager representatives,[47] and the Kung Mun school and Public School would cease running. The plan was accepted by the Diocese and the villagers. The new school was subsidised by the government, and its construction and operating costs were also paid by the government. It was registered in September 1959 and the school was named "Sham Chung School".[48] The school floor plan in the archives of the Tai Po District Office shows that the school building contained two classrooms, a staff room, and a playground. There was also a toilet not far from the school. Its supporting facilities were better than those of Kung Man School which lacked a court, and the Public School which was temporarily accommodated in village houses.

In just three years from 1956 to 1959, there had been three schools in Sham Chung, which showed the interaction and tension between the government, the Diocese and the villagers. Despite Catholicism had been introduced as early as 1870, Sham Chung never became a Catholic village. Although non-Catholic villagers had coexisted with the Catholic faith for decades, they showed resistance after the Diocese taking over Kung Man School in the village, and even asked the authorities to approve another subsidised school in the village. Even without the approval of the government, the villagers still insisted on funding by themselves for the establishment of private schools in order to replace the Kung Man Schools. Obviously, they had concerns on the running of Catholic schools. The government seized the opportunity of financial difficulties faced by the private school, and built a new subsidised school, the Sham Chung School, which was jointly managed by the Education Department, the Diocese, and the villagers, and the conflicts were alleviated.[49]

After the war, the Diocese echoed the government's policies and devoted itself to the development of education in response to the needs of the society at that time, and to use this opportunity to preach to the public. However, the process inevitably encountered challenges, just like running a school in Sham Chung but aroused the resentment of the villagers. The missionaries then accepted the government's Sham Chung School proposal. Although the autonomy in running Kung Man School was lost, the Church was, still able to participate in the management of the new school under the model accepted by the villagers. They continued to exert their influence through education and nurture the villagers of Sham Chung. Even though the Kung Man School has long been closed, its school building has always stood in the village, witnessing the missionaries' hard work in preaching and running schools over the years.

Tan Ka Wan: A Unique Catholic Clubhouse

Tan Ka Wan is located on the south bank of the Chek Mun Strait in Tai Po, adjacent to Ko Lau Wan (or Kao Lau Wan). It is a small bay where several small villages gather, including Tse Uk, Lau Uk, Lam Uk and Mo Uk from east to west, which were all named after the surnames of the villagers. Among them, Mo Uk had the largest number of villagers. The ancestors of the Mos were originally from Sha U Chung, Po On County. About a hundred years ago, they crossed the Mirs Bay to the Tan Ka Wan Village with their family. In the early days, they made their living by fishing in Tai Po Sea, and transported the catches to Sha Tau Kok Market and Yim Tin Market for sale.

As early as the middle of the nineteenth century, Catholicism had taken root here. In 1865, when Rev. Volonteri and Rev. Origo first went to the villages of Sai Kung to preach, they passed through Tan Ka Wan. The *Map of the San-On District, Kwangtung Province* drawn by Rev. Volonteri in 1866 marked the location and name of Tan Ka Wan, which could be regarded as evidence of their visit there. In 1872, when Bishop

Raimondi visited the villages of Sai Kung, he also arrived at Tan Ka Wan and started a new mission station here. At that time, there were 12 parishioners of the village. The Tan Ka Wan Chapel (later named "St. Peter's Chapel") was completed the following year.[50] In 1874, Hong Kong was struck by a typhoon. The entire Sai Kung peninsula, including Tan Ka Wan, was severely damaged. The following year, Bishop Raimondi visited Tan Ka Wan and pointed out that the roof of the new chapel was blown away by the typhoon and needed to be rebuilt. By 1880, another chapel in Tan Ka Wan was built. During his visit to Sai Kung in 1895, Bishop Lurgi Piazolli also visited Tan Ka Wan. He conducted sacrament of confession and preached to the villagers. Mass was held the next morning, and after he was sent by the Tai Long villagers to the beach and boarded the boat back to Hong Kong.

After its reconstruction in the early twentieth century, the chapel also housed a primary school named "Shung Ming School". On 23 October 1908, the Catholic Diocese signed a land exchange agreement with the government, giving up the land in No. 6 of Lot 271, that is, abandoning the chapel originally built on this lot, in exchange for the land in Lot 366 for building the new chapel, St. Peter's Chapel, on a hill as it now locates, with a dormitory. In 1918, the Diocese repaired the chapel and dormitory in order to consolidate the foundation structure of the building. Bishop Valtorta visited the chapel in the 1930s and took a photo with the student band. However, during the Japanese occupation, as the priest had already left, the school was once managed by Education Officer Tse Tai, who was appointed by the authorities, until his lodging of resignation to the government education inspector after the war. Then the school was returned to the management of the Diocese.[51] Shortly after Bishop Valtorta's visit, Tai Long District was established in 1931. From 1931 to 1941, the St. Peter's Chapel in Tan Ka Wan was subsumed under the District and was managed by Rev. Francis Wong who would go to Tan Ka Wan Chapel to celebrate the Mass.

During the war, the law and order in Sai Kung was extremely poor and the priest's mission was at great risk. From the end of November to the beginning of December 1942, according to Sit Seng who lived in Tai Long at the time, Rev. Francis Wong was taken away by the guerrillas. According to the church records: One evening, he disappeared while in Chek Keng, and soon his dead body was found on a hill in Tai Long. It was investigated that he was taken to the hill and killed and buried secretly. Later, Rev. Quirino De Ascariis (PIME), after a cross-examination and interrogation, and based on the testimony of eyewitnesses, concluded that Rev. Francis Wong, Rev.

Bishop Valtorta took a group photo with the Shung Ming School Band during his visit to Tan Ka Wan in the 1930s.

Shung Ming School (Catholic Clubhouse). (photographed in 2020)

Kwok King Wan, and Rev. Teruzzi were all killed by the guerrillas, probably because of hatred to the Catholic believers.

After the war, the chapel was not seriously damaged. In 1946, there were nearly 100 parishioners in Tan Ka Wan. Between 1946 and 1947, priests visited there for 11 times and 13 babies were baptised, the number of homilies delivered was 30 times, and there were two pairs of Catholic marriage partners.[52] But there was no priest taking care of the chapel on a regular basis. At that time, the villagers asked Francis Feating, a British sergeant who visited the village of Sai Kung, to make petition to the Catholic missionaries to return to the village. Later, the Catholic Church sponsored the renovation of the Tan Ka Wan Chapel. On the other hand, Shung Ming School was returned to the management by the Diocese upon resignation by the education officer. At that time, Shung Ming School was called "Tai Ka Wan School." In 1954, the St. Peter's Chapel in Tan Ka Wan was under the management of the priests of the Holy Family Chapel in Chek Keng. By the end of the 1950s, Catholism was still prevailing in Tan Ka Wan. In 1959, there were 118 believers in Tan Ka Wan. In the 1950s, Shung Ming Primary School was a co-education school, managed by two nuns from the

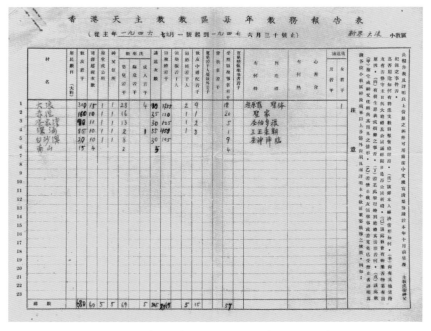

The Annual Report on Parish Affairs of Tai Long District of Hong Kong from 1946 to 1947. (Image Source: Catholic Diocesan Archives)

155

The exterior and interior of St. Peter's Chapel in Tan Ka Wan in the 2000s (rebuilt).

Sisters of the Precious Blood. The following year, the chapel was managed by the priest of the Sai Kung district. From 1962 to 1970, the Tan Ka Wan Chapel was transferred to the Church in Tai Po Market. After the 1960s, the villagers gradually emigrated to foreign countries. Rev. Narcissus Santinon (PIME, 1916-1995), the parish priest of the Immaculate Heart of Mary Church in Tai Po, visited the chapels in the Tai Long district, including the Tan Ka Wan Chapel. Later, due to the decrease in the number of villagers, the chapel was gradually abandoned and Shung Ming School was also closed in 1967.

In the 1970s, villagers left and moved to other places or urban areas. In 1977, Rev. Paul Wan Yee Tseng, who served at the Immaculate Heart of Mary Church of Tai Po, was appointed by the then Bishop John Wu Cheng-chung to manage the abandoned chapels in the Tai Long district, including several remote chapels on the south bank of Tolo Harbor at Tan Ka Wan, Sham Chung, Chek Keng, Tai Long, etc. He went to these places by boat every week, and converted them to Catholic camps so that Catholic youths could use them for camping activities. Among them, Tan Ka Wan Shung Ming School was also used as a clubhouse for Catholic students and believers. Today Shung Ming School still hangs the nameplate with "Catholic Clubhouse" written on it. Until 1997, because the villagers had already left, the Finnish Mission of the Christian Lutheran Church had repaired the village houses and used them for gatherings in the Ling Oi Gospel Drug Rehabilitation Centre. Since the main building of the chapel has been destroyed, the Finnish Mission also rented village houses in Tan Ka Wan for several male drug addicts to live in, converted the collapsed chapel into a place of worship, and developed into a drug rehabilitation village. On 1 July 2019, the "Following Thy Way" working group took back St. Peter's Chapel. So far, Shung Ming School is still the only Catholic building in Hong Kong named "clubhouse."

Social Services in Sai Kung: Rev. Adelio Lambertoni and the Faith Community of Fishermen

The Second Ecumenical Council of the Vatican (Vatican II) was convened from 1962 to 1965. The reformation it strived to advocate reaffirmed the bottom-up ecclesiastical perspective of the church, emphasized localisation and social justice, and stressed the charities promoted by the local church should suit the contemporary societal need.[53] The torrent of "Vatican II Spirit" swept across Hong Kong along with

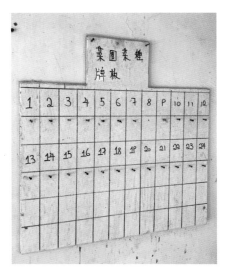

The resident at Ling Oi Drug Rehabilitation Centre recorded the use of vegetable seeds in the vegetable field.

the global wave of appeals for justice and service to the poor. Inspired by this, young missionaries wanted a breakthrough of the conventional mode of service delivery and to actively participate in social issues, help the oppressed, and strive to reclaim injustice. These "new methods" included caring for the disabled, the elderly, the marginalised and fighting for their rights by working in factories, living with the floating population in boats, living with blue-collar workers and the exploited, and fighting for their rights.[54] Among them, Rev. Adelio Lambertoni, who once served in Sai Kung, was the most conspicuous with great influence in social commitment. During his service, he also adopted eight children and brought them up.

These clergies have assumed new roles in social affairs, bringing new impacts to the way the church served the public in Hong Kong, and also laying down a new direction for the church in the development of Hong Kong's society. The idea was tally with that of Caritas, which was established in 1961.[55] According to the *Hong Kong Catholic Directory* of the year, the goals of Caritas included:

1. It is one of the branches of the Catholic International Charity Society.
2. It is a Hong Kong Catholic social welfare institution.
3. Engage in planning and handling the social welfare institutions of the Diocese, and in accordance with the instructions of the Pope and the bishop of the

Rev. Lambertoni when he was young.
(Image Source: Paul Wong Yee-tin)

Rev. Lambertoni (second right) temporarily resided in a hut in Tai Po when he just came to Hong Kong. (Image source: Paul Wong Yee-tin)

diocese, to promote the development of charitable units in each parish.

4. Promote the coordination of Catholic social welfare through the committee appointed by the bishop and the Hong Kong Catholic Social Welfare Association.

5. Make every effort to raise funds in Hong Kong and abroad in order to develop local public education and social welfare undertakings.[56]

This shows that Caritas shouldered the responsibility of coordinating, promoting and expanding social services. The establishment of St. Peter's Fishermen's Village in Sai Kung explains exactly how the priest and Caritas worked together to fight for the rights of the poor, and lived their faith through social service.

Priest's Assistance in Establishing Fishermen's Village: St. Peter's Village

Rev. Giuseppe Famiglietti (PIME, 1916-2004) served as the parish priest of the Sai Kung district from 1954 to 1956 and 1962 to 1964 respectively.[57] In addition to serving at the district centre, he also visited the nearby villages, eagerly addressing villagers' living and accommodation needs and distributing materials such as flour, bread and condensed milk. Poor households can dilute condensed milk to replace expensive milk powder to feed their babies. In addition, Rev. Famiglietti also cared for Sai Kung fishermen who had been discriminated against. In the 1940's and 1950's, these fishermen were considered to be uncivilized as they lived in boats for a long time and were ridiculed as "Tanka people" and "Tanka barbarians". The fishermen ashore would be bullied by the people, forbidden to wear shoes, scolded and beaten, and even been driven back to the boat.[58] This shows that fishermen were marginalised and needed assistance. In addition, the education of the children of fishermen was also worth worrying. As fishermen did not have a fixed residence on land, whenever they went fishing, their children have to ask for leave from school and set sail with their parents. The low attendance greatly affected their academic performance. Rev. Famiglietti has

Fishing boats in Sai Kung Market Bay in the 1960s.
(Image source: Sai Kung Sacred Heart Church)

noticed the needs of floating population and considered their "going ashore" would allow the older generation to take care of the children who could continue their education. Moreover, the livelihoods of fishermen were greatly affected if typhoon hit Hong Kong. Rev. Famiglietti therefore helped them lease land from the government, and cooperated with Caritas to build the St. Peter's Village.

St. Peter's Village, located on the Tui Min Ho, Sai Kung, was built by Caritas in 1964 and was completed in May 1966. The village was initially managed by Caritas which provided life skills training to the villagers. Active young villagers were recruited to form a youth association and encouraged to organise activities to serve other villagers. Caritas did not fade out of management until 1997, and transferred the management ownership to the "Life Improvement Cooperative Limited Liability Cooperative" formed by villagers. It was one of the cooperative houses in Hong Kong that could only live in but cannot be bought and sold.[59] There were 69 units in the village, each with only 100 to 300 square feet. Villagers needed to share public toilets and bathrooms outside the house. The village house was designed like a Tic-Tac-shaped public housing, and the residents on the opposite side could be seen so that they took care of each other. As households were connected will cement walls, the units were adjacent to each other, creating a close and responsive neighborhood.[60] Fishermen and their descendants liked to walk to the end of the corridor and look at the sea and reminisce the memories of the past. The village was a repository of its common history and memories. Everyone cherished this simple and rich life content.[61]

As the fishermen were able to "go ashore" with the help of missionaries, many of them believed in Catholicism, and the village of St. Peter became a community of faith. After the village was built, the missionaries still kept in touch with the villagers. Rev. Paolo Morlacchi (PIME, 1936-2016) has served as the parish priest of the Sai Kung parish since 1979, and he would visit St. Peter's Village on Wednesdays. In the late 1980s, the village held regular prayer meetings on weekdays.

Sai Kung "Father Fei Tsai"[62]

Rev. Adelio Lambertoni (PIME, 1939-2006), who took over the Sai Kung district after Rev. Famiglietti has left, also cared about social issues and was very influential in social commitment. Some of the current defenders of the human rights, civil rights and labor rights in society all were inspired by him.[63] Rev. Lambertoni was born in Velate in the Diocese of Milan, Italy in 1939 and was ordained on 30 March 1963. After two years, he came to Hong Kong and temporarily resided in Tai Po Church to learn Cantonese. Since 1967, he has been appointed as the assistant priest of the Sai Kung district.[64] In the meantime, he loved to drive around the villages on a motorcycle and explored Sai Kung, so he was called "Father Fei Tsai" (in Cantonese).[65] He cared about the livelihood needs of villagers and fishermen, as if he were a "District Officer" in the colonial era.

According to Mr. Paul Wong Yee-tin, a parishioner of Tai Po Parish, also one of Rev. Lambertoni's adopted children, Rev. Lambertoni would go to the mountains and the countryside in Sai Kung, where he ate and lived with the villagers in that area. He has visited countless villages, including Chek Keng, Shap Si Heung, Wong Mo Ying, Leung Shuen Wan, Tai Mong Tsai, etc.[66] Whenever he saw orphans in the village whose parents had died, or children whose parents were completely unable to take care of them, he immediately applied for them into children's homes and visited them frequently. On these busy days, Rev. Lambertoni often set off early in the morning, climbing mountains and ridges to different villages, and returning home before sunset.[67] Rev. Lambertoni also introduced the Legion of Mary into the Sai Kung district, hoping that the parishioners could practice their faith through service to the community, which was consistent with his beliefs in caring for the society. Sai Kung villagers Chan Shui-ying and Chan Yun-lin were the first members to join. They followed Rev. Lambertoni across the sea to visit the houses of the villagers, and they would also go to different chapels in Sai Kung to assist in cleaning and other tasks.

Like Rev. Famiglietti, Rev. Lambertoni paid special attention to the rights of fishermen. In order to improve the living environment of fishermen in Sai Kung, he directly liaised with the District Office on the establishment of a fishermen's village from the District Office. Although he could speak Cantonese, but he was not good at writing Chinese. His friend Mak Hon-Kai, who had taught at the Sung Tsun Catholic School in Sai Kung, usually wrote on his behalf to the government.[68] In the end, Rev. Lambertoni and Caritas cooperated to build Taiping Village and Ming Shun Village (details of the two villages are set out in Chapter 6).

In addition, Rev. Lambertoni concerned the growth and development of children and young people, and more keenly noticed that the summer vacation was a good opportunity to nurture these children. Every summer, school children had long vacations, but there were generally seven or eight children in a family that year,

Fishermen rowed sampans in Sai Kung Hoi in the 1970s. (Image source: Sai Kung Sacred Heart Church)

Taiping Village under construction. (Image source: Sai Kung Sacred Heart Church)

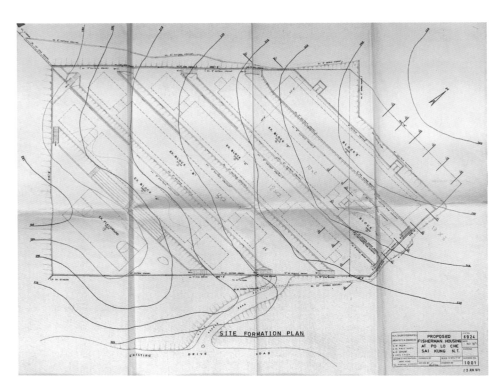

The plan for the construction of Po Lo Che Taiping Village in 1971. (Image source: Paul Wong Yee-tin)

and most of the parents did not have time to arrange activities for their children, so either they were asked to help their families, or they were allowed to run through the mountains and down the sea, but accidents often occured. In view of this, Rev. Lambertoni organised summer training courses for the secondary school students living in Sai Kung Centre, and travelled with them to Yim Tin Tsai, Tai Long Sai Wan and other places.[69] He also organised various summer activities for primary school students in the district, including tuition, campfires, children's centres, and holiday camps. These activities were not only carried out in the Sung Tsun Catholic School, but would also reach the villages of Kau Sai Chau, Sai Wan, and Leung Shuen Wan. According to villagers Chan Shui-ying and Chan Yun-lin, Rev. Lambertoni even invited young people outside Sai Kung district to help organise summer activities. He encouraged young people to organise and arrange activities for themselves, hoping to cultivate their leadership training skills and spirit of social responsibility.[70] In his mourning for Rev.

Lambertoni, Rev. Gianni Criveller mentioned that there was no better way to embody his charisma to "make community" than his adoption and nurturing of eight children with family problems or without parents, allowing them to receive education and integrate into society.[71]

Due to the tragedy of the murder of Rev. Valeriano Fraccaro, the parish priest of Sai Kung at the end of 1974, Rev. Lambertoni left Hong Kong to serve in Thailand and Italy (refer to Chapter 6 for Rev. Valeriano Fraccaro's service in Sai Kung). He returned to Hong Kong in 1978 and served successively in the parishes of Wong Tai Sin, Kwai Fong, and Shek Lei. During this period, he led the Social Concern Group of the PIME to protest against the social and economic policies of the colonial government. He has also fought for squatters, hawkers and boat people, and concerned various social issues in Hong Kong, such as the Ma Chai Hang incident, the Yau Ma Tei Boat People incident, the Kowloon Bay Temporary Housing incident, the Vietnamese Refugees problem, etc.,[72] and often stood at the front line of the protest team to fight for their rights.[73] At the same time, he also served the Society for Community Organization, a social organization dedicated to improving local marginal groups and poverty issues.

The descendants of the fishermen living in St. Peter's Village today may not know Rev. Famiglietti, and the name of Rev. Lambertoni might not be remembered. But they were dedicated to serving the most needy people in society and were considered to be the model of faith.

The church resumed its missionary work after the war, and its policy was closely linked to the social situation, which affected the relationship between the church and the Sai Kung villages. Refugees from the mainland China flooded into Hong Kong in the late 1940s, and Hong Kong's population soared. However, the government initially ignored this and failed to provide corresponding social services. In response to social needs, one of the priorities of the Catholic Church in Hong Kong at that time was to take care of a large number of refugees. In addition, the missionary expelled from the Mainland injected impetus into the missionary work. Driven by this post-war environment, the work of the church was restarted. Missionaries went to Tai Long Sai Wan Village, Sai Kung to preach, and established a church and school in the village.

The arrival of refugees in Hong Kong after the war caused a great demand for education in the community. The Catholic Diocese was willing to invest a lot of resources in running schools, but the plan was not always implemented smoothly. For example, the Kung Man School ran by missionaries in Sham Chung Village was not welcomed by the local villagers, and as a result, the government had to intervene. Although the church was constrained by the government's education policy and could not maintain its original full-autonomy in operating schools, it could continue to participate in the management of the village school in a form acceptable to the villagers.

Missionaries not only contributed to education, they were also more active on other social issues. The Vatican II held in the early 1960s reaffirmed social justice and drove some missionaries, including Rev. Famiglietti and Rev. Lambertoni, to care for the disadvantaged. They cared about the living needs of Sai Kung residents, worked with Caritas to fight for the "go ashore" of Sai Kung fishermen, established a fishermen's religious community, and followed up social injustices. When compared with the pre-war era, the scope of work in the Diocese of Hong Kong became wider and deeper. Missionaries combined Catholicism with social services and brought them into Sai Kung villages so that the religion could continue to spread.

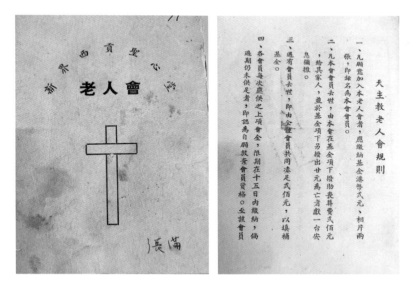

Membership card of Sai Kung Senior Citizens' Association. (Image source: Sai Kung Sacred Heart Church)

Notes

1　*Hong Kong Government Gazette*, 1950, pp. 452-453.

2　Hong Kong Government, *Official Record of Proceedings of the Legislative Council in 1970-1971* (Hong Kong: Hong Kong Government Printer, 1971), pp. 8-9.

3　He Xin-Ping, *Catholic Foreign Mission Society of America and Hong Kong* (《美國天主教全教會與香港》) (Hong Kong: Centre for Catholic Studies, The Chinese University of Hong Kong, June 2011), p. 136.

4　Edward Hambro, *The Problem of Chinese Refugees in Hong Kong* (Leyden: A.W. Sijthoff, 1955), p. 154.

5　Piero Gheddo, *Lawrence Bianchi of Hong Kong* (Hong Kong: Catholic Truth Society, 1988), p. 117.

6　*Sunday Examiner*, 26 June 1959.

7　Gianni Criveller, *From Milan to Hong Kong: 150 years of mission: Pontifical Institute for Foreign Missions, 1858-2008* (Hong Kong: VOX AMICA PRESS, 2008), p. 134.

8　Piero Gheddo, *Lawrence Bianchi of Hong Kong* (Hong Kong: Catholic Truth Society, 1988), p. 118.

9　Cai Zijie, *Gazetteer of Scenery in Sai Kung* (《西貢風物志》) (Hong Kong: Worldwide Publishing, 2008), p. 105.

10　Cai Zijie (ed.), *Scenery in Sai Kung* (《西貢風貌》) (Hong Kong: Sai Kung District Council, 2003), p. 84.

11　John Strickland (ed.), *Southern District Officer Reports – Islands and Villages in Rural Hong Kong, 1910-60* (Hong Kong: Hong Kong University Press, 2010), p. 212.

12　*Le Missioni Cattoliche*, 1915, p. 243.

13　"Sai Wan Village, Sai Kung District, New Territories, Hong Kong, Celebration of Baptism and Confirmation by new Catholics" (〈香港新界西貢區西灣村 新教友領洗領堅振誌慶〉), *Kung Kao Po*, 18 December 1949.

14　Oral History Interview with Rev. Giorgio Caruso on 20 May 1981. Interviewer: David Faure, Collection of CUHK Library.

15　"Sai Wan Village, Sai Kung District, New Territories, Hong Kong, Celebration of Baptism and Confirmation by new Catholics" (〈香港新界西貢區西灣村 新教友領洗領堅振誌慶〉), *Kung Kao Po*, 18 December 1949.

16　John Strickland (ed.), *Southern District Officer Reports – Islands and Villages in Rural Hong Kong, 1910-60* (Hong Kong: Hong Kong University Press, 2010), pp. 277-278.

17　Ibid., p. 216.

18　Ibid., p. 26.

19　Piero Gheddo, *Lawrence Bianchi of Hong Kong* (Hong Kong: Catholic Truth Society, 1988), p. 138.

20　Ibid., p. 136.

21　"Tai Po-Shum Chung Route, Lok Lo Ha Wo Sha Route, Ferry Coming" (〈大埔深涌線 落路下和沙線 將有渡客小輪〉), *Overseas Chinese Daily*, 5 April 1952.

22　"Sai Kung North Lai Chi Chong, Shum Chung builds Public Pier" (〈西貢北約荔枝莊 深涌建公共碼頭〉), *Overseas Chinese Daily*, 23 November 1960.

23　One in Shum Chung, One in Lai Chi Chong, Tolo Harbour Two New Piers, Opened both Yesterday Morning (〈一深涌一在荔枝莊 吐露海峽兩新碼頭 同於昨日上午啟用〉), *The Kung Sheung Daily News*, 27 April 1962.

24   G. Brambilla, *Il Pontificio Istituto delle Missioni Estere e le sue Missioni* (Milano: Milan Institute for the Foreign Missions, 1943), Vol. V, pp. 115-118.

25   HKCDA, Records of Bishop Piazzoli, Luigi Maria; also see the entire report in *Catholic Newspaper* (《香港天主教紀錄報》), Vol. II, 1879, p. 22.

26   *Le Missioni Cattoliche*, 1892, p. 460.

27   *Catholic Guide to Hong Kong*, p. 197.

28   *China Mission Station 1970*, p. 35.

29   *Catholic Guide to Hong Kong*, p. 197.

30   G. Brambilla, *Il Pontificio Istituto delle Missioni Estere e le sue Missioni* (Milano: Milan Institute for the Foreign Missions, 1943), Vol. 5, pp. 115-118.

31   Letter of Bishop Raimondi, 26 March 1875. *See Les Missioni Cattoliche* (Milano, 1875), Vol. IV, pp. 247-250.

32   Letter of Rev. Burghlignoli, 19 November 1877. *See Les Missions Catholiques* (Lyon, 1878), Vol. X, p. 125; Letter of Rev. Burghlignoli, 19 November 1877. *See Les Missions Catholiche* (Milano, 1878), Vol. VII, p. 28.

33   Hong Kong Public Records Office Archive. HKRS1075-3-82. Sham Chung School, Sham Chung.

34   "Bishop Bianchi visiting Shum Chung, Blessing the New Chapel", *Kung Kao Po*, 1 June 1956.

35   *Catholic Guide to Hong Kong*, p. 197.

36   Hong Kong Public Records Office Archive. HKRS1075-3-82. Sham Chung School, Sham Chung.

37   Luo Huiyan, *Under Blue Sky and Tree: Village School in New Territories* (《藍天樹下：新界鄉村學校》) (Hong Kong: Joint Publishing (HK) Co. Ltd, 2015), p. 128.

38   "Shum Chung Village Chapel and School Completed, Unicorn Celebrates, Bishop Bianchi Inaugurates" (〈深涌村堂校落成 舞麒麟誌慶 白主教主持開幕典禮〉), *Overseas Chinese Daily*, 2 June 1956.

39   HKCDA, Section I, Box 05, Folder 01; Section I, Box 08, Folder 02.

40   According to the records of the *Diocese Handbook* (1958) (p. 26), among the 26 students in the Kung Man School, 12 were Catholics and 14 were non-Catholics.

41   Hong Kong Public Records Office Archive. HKRS1075-3-82. Sham Chung School, Sham Chung.

42   "Church evangelise in School, Shum Chung villagers dissatisfied" (〈教會在學校佈道 深涌村民表不滿〉), *Kung Kao Po*, 8 September 1958.

43   Hong Kong Public Records Office Archive. HKRS1075-3-82. Sham Chung School, Sham Chung.

44   Ibid.

45   "Villages collect money to organize, Private School opens, Students double compared with Subsidised School" (〈村民集資籌辦 私立學校開課 學生倍逾津貼學校〉), *Overseas Chinese Daily*, 8 September 1958.

46   "Financial Problem with Shum Chung School Building, Villages Petition for Subsidy by Authority" (〈深涌學校經費困難 村民籲請當局津貼〉), *The Kung Sheung Daily News*, 21 July 1959.

47   Since taking office in 1962, Rev. Narciso Santinon, the priest of Tai Po and Tai Long District, has served as one of the school directors.

48   Hong Kong Public Records Office Archive. HKRS1075-3-82. Sham Chung School, Sham Chung.

49   Ibid.

50   According to the Catholic Directory published in the 1960's, missionaries first established a chapel in the area in 1873.

51   Letter of Tse Tai, Education Affairs Officer of Tai Ka Wan School to Inspector Wan (〈泰家灣學校教務主任謝帶致尹視學官〉), HKCDA, Section IV, Box 13, Folder 2. It is believed that Tse Tai was indigenous villager of Tse Uk in Tan Ka Wan.

52   See the Annual Parish Affairs Report, HKCD (From Year 1964.9.1 to 1947.6.30), Tai Long Small District, HKCDA, Section IV, Box 13, Folder 2.

53   Louis Ha Keloon, Li Peihua, "The First Chinese Bishop: Catholic Main Church and Hsu Chen-Ping Francis Xavier", Victor W. T. Zheng and Chou Man Kong (eds.), *Mid-Level Elevator: Soaring to Qingyun Road* (Hong Kong: Chung Hwa Publishing (Hong Kong) Co., Ltd., 2019), pp. 70-71.

54   Gianni Criveller, Angelo Paratico, *500 Years of Italians in Hong Kong & Macau* (Hong Kong: Dante Alighieri Society of Hong Kong, 2013), p. 70.

55   Caritas-Hong Kong was founded by Bishop Bianchi in July 1953 by the Catholic Diocese of Hong Kong to express the need of the Diocese to coordinate the enormous refugee work. It was formerly known as Catholic Social Welfare Bureau which named Caritas – Hong Kong associated with Caritas International. See Chang Sau Han, Joyce, "The Development of Social Services in Hong Kong Catholic Church (1901-2000)" in Yuen Chi Wai (ed.), *Hong Kong Journal of Catholic Studies – A History of the Hong Kong Catholic Church in the 20th Century* (Hong Kong: Centre for Catholic Studies, CUHK), No. 7, 2016, pp. 93-132.

56   Sergio Ticozzi, *Anecdote of Catholicism* (《天主教掌故》) (Hong Kong: Holy Spirit Study Centre and Holy Spirit Seminary Extramural Studies Office, 1983), p. 258.

57   HKCDA, Rev. Giuseppe Famiglietti, https://archives.catholic.org.hk/In%20Memoriam/Clergy-Brother/PIME/FAMIGLIETTI%20Giuseppe.pdf.

58   Ma Muk Chi et al., *History and Heritage of Sai Kung* (《西貢歷史與風物》) (Hong Kong: Sai Kung District Council, Sep 2003), p. 133.

59   "Sai Kung St. Peter's Village Ming Sun Village Fishermen's Responsible Cooperative for Improving Lives" in Hong Kong Council of Social Welfare, Scenario, July 2016.

60   Ibid.

61   Hong Kong Jockey Club Heritage x Arts x Design Walk (H.A.D. Walk), "Sai Kung Fishermen Sailing Through the Big Waves of the Modern Times", http://had18.huluhk.org/article-detail.php?id=211&lang=tc.

62   "Fei Tsai" in Cantonese means rogue.

63   Gianni Criveller & Angelo Paratico, *500 Years of Italians in Hong Kong & Macau* (Hong Kong: Dante Alighieri Society of Hong Kong, 2013), p. 70.

64   "Caring for the Poor during His Life, Italian Father Lambertoni Rests in Peace" (〈在世期間關懷貧苦者意國神父林柏棟安息〉), *Kung Kao Po*, 16 July 2006.

65   "In memory of Father Lambertoni" (〈念林柏棟神父〉), *Kung Kao Po*, 8 July 2012.

66   "Following Thy Way – Initiative on Historical Research Lecture – Commemorate Fr. Lamberton", *Kung Kao Po*, 30 June 2019.

67   "Writing before the 30th Anniversary of Ordination of Fr. Lambertoni", *Kung Kao Po*, 26 March 1993.

68   In an interview with Alumni Publications (September 2019) of United College, Chinese University of Hong Kong, Mak Hon-Kai mentioned that under the encouragement and leadership of Rev. Lambertoni, he led students to participate in volunteer services. A good example was to assist in the establishment of the "Hong

Kong Auxiliary Medical Service" in Sai Kung District. Mak tried his best to bring students to understand the society, which all contributing to society today, which showed that Rev. Lambertoni influences life with his life.

69   "In Memory of Fr. Lambertoni", *Kung Kao Po*, 8 July 2012.

70   Leung Kam-Chung (ed.), *Sung Tsun Middle School, Sai Kung, 70-72* (Hong Kong: Sai Kung Sung Tsun School, 1972), p. 85.

71   "Father Lambertoni, a life lived in love", *Sunday Examiner*, 16 July 2006.

72   "Writing Before the 30th Anniversary of Ordination of Fr. Lambertoni", *Kung Kao Po*, 26 March 1993.

73   Gianni Criveller, *From Milan to Hong Kong : 150 years of mission : Pontifical Institute for Foreign Missions*, 1858-2008 (Hong Kong : Vox Amica Press, 2008), p. 157.

1841

1874

1931

1945

1969

Chapter 6

**Localisation and Rejuvenation Period
(1969-1981)**

1981

2000

In 1969, the Catholic Diocese of Hong Kong entered a new era: Rev. Francis Hsu Cheng-Ping became the Bishop of the Diocese, and was the first Chinese bishop of Hong Kong. This was a historical moment of special significance, marking a turning point in the Hong Kong church's transition from being dominated by foreign priests to localisation. The local Chinese priests gradually began to take on the task of leading the Diocese, while the Pontifical Institute for Foreign Missions (PIME) who led the Diocese all the way through were changed to work as pastoralists to serve the Diocese.

At the same time, due to the innovations brought about by the Second Ecumenical Council of the Vatican, the priests have also begun to explore more possibilities and strive to find "new methods" of evangelization; Rev. Lambertoni, who has been committed to improving the living environment of fishermen, was an obvious example. Just like "God's District Office", Rev. Lambertoni became a bridge between the fishermen's community and the government. In addition, the political situation during this period was turbulent. The amiable image displayed by Rev. Fraccaro at the time, even many non-Catholics people in Sai Kung felt most cordial. His influence was as deeply imprinted on people as the bread he made. The tragic death of Rev. Fraccaro in 1974 shocked the whole of Hong Kong and silenced the mission of Sai Kung. It was not until the early 1980s that the missions in Sai Kung district recovered from depression.

From Land to Water: Sai Kung District's Service to Fishermen

Rev. Lambertoni succeeded the management of Sacred Heart Church, Sai Kung in 1968, and extended his missionary work to Pak Sha Wan in 1969. He was deeply aware of the serious housing problems of the boat people and the general public. With the support of the government and local squire, the two villages named "Tai Ping" and

"Ming Shun" were planned and established.

In 1969, Sunday Masses were mainly held in Sai Kung, Wo Mei and Pak Sha Wan, and held every two weeks in Yim Tin Tsai. Many people immigrated to other countries in that period of time, causing a significant change in the population distribution of Sai Kung District. In order to solve the problem of the shortage of fresh water supply caused by the population growth in Hong Kong, the government began the construction of a seawall between Plover Cove and Pak Sha Tau on the north shore of Tolo Harbour in the 1960s, to pump sea water in order to store fresh water, and established the Plover Cove Reservoir. The authorities then started the construction of High Island Reservoir in 1971 to increase Hong Kong's fresh water supply. Due to the reservoir project, the two villages of Lan Nai Wan and Sha Tsui were submerged. The government moved the villagers from these two areas to a new reclaimed land in Sai Kung Market for resettlement. At the same time, various community facilities were built in the surrounding area to meet their needs.[1]

Population growth and community construction have promoted the overall development of Sai Kung, making it gradually a convenient place for living. Under this trend, other villagers who originally lived in the countryside have gradually moved to live in the urban area. In view of this, the church began to change the focus of pastoral

Sacred Heart Church was completed in 1959 at the current site of Yau Ma Po Street, Lot 1762, DD 221, ordained and opened. (Image source: Sai Kung Sacred Heart Church)

work from the old village to the densely populated Sai Kung Market. The frequency and time of pastoral visits by priests to the village gradually decreased and shortened. However, during important patron feasts, people who worked in the urban areas would return to the village to celebrate and reunit with their families. The priests were also invited to celebrate Mass in these rural chapels. For example, in Wo Mei Village, in addition to the Masses on Sundays, the Immaculate Conception Chapel of the village would still hold a special Mass on the first day of the Lunar New Year and the beginning of December every year. In order to cope with the increase in the population of the market, the church built a new campus for the primary section of Sung Tsun School in Yau Ma Po in 1969. The school which originally included primary and secondary sections, was officially divided into two separate departments, for handling the two different sections. In the same year, the secondary section started the English course. In 1971, the school hall and the new wing of the secondary section were completed. In 1973, the English department of the secondary section began to have a complete five-grade secondary school system; while the AM and PM sections in the primary school were divided into separate administrations. In 1974, Sung Tsun School added an English evening school to provide more learning opportunities for Sai Kung residents. Since the establishment of the English section of the secondary school, parents would

The school building of the old Sung Tsun School (now renovated). (Image source: Sai Kung Sacred Heart Church)

Cardinal John Wu Cheng Chung took a photo with the Catholics in front of the Sacred Heart Church. (Image source: Sai Kung Sacred Heart Church)

prefer sending their children to the English section, while fewer and fewer students were applying for the Chinese section. Therefore, the Chinese section was gradually cancelled from Secondary One in 1976, and Sung Tsun Secondary School changed to English teaching. In 1978, the school applied to the government for expansion into a standard secondary school of 24 classes, which was approved by the authorities, and the expansion project was launched the following year, while the evening school was taken over by the adult evening colleges run by the government.

Construction of Tai Ping Village and Ming Shun Village

At the same time, Rev. Lambertoni also began to cooperate with the Catholic Social Welfare Bureau (the predecessor of "Caritas Hong Kong") to improve the living environment of fishermen in Sai Kung. Following the completion of St. Peter's Village in 1965, Tai Ping and Ming Shun Village under the charge of Rev. Lambertoni were also completed in 1971 and 1977 respectively.

The fishermen of Sai Kung in the past were crowded to live on boats. Whenever fishermen needed to go fishing, it was difficult for their children to stay on land to go to school, and it was also difficult for the elderly to get proper treatment and recuperation when they were sick. Therefore, Rev. Lambertoni decided to help them build houses on the shore, hoping to provide them with a better living environment.[2]

However, it was impossible for the government to allocate land for private individuals to build temporary housing. Therefore, the priest negotiated with the relevant authorities, and he set up a housing committee and served as the person in charge. In the first two weeks of the project, the priest had received three hundred and twenty families' registrations. The priest first conducted a detailed investigation of the status of these applicant families, and then invited their representatives to Sung Tsun Secondary School for a meeting to discuss the details of the housing plan. After the meeting, the committee was divided into nine groups, and each group elected a leader to further study the types of houses to be built and where to build them. The committee was finally merged into two major groups, one group belonged to Po Lo Che, the other group belonged to Tui Min Hoi. The housing project fund raising began. According to the priest's original plan, each family would save $20 a month. After ten years, everyone's savings would be combined to build enough houses so that each family had its own house.[3]

In an occation, Rev. Lambertoni talked to David L. Osborn (1921-1994), the Consul General of the United States of America in Hong Kong and Macau about this housing project. The consul was very interested in the plan and went to Sai Kung to

The article mentions Tai Ping Village was built in Po Lo Che, Sai Kung. (Image source: *Overseas Chinese Daily News*, 6 October 1971)

study the details. Rev. Lambertoni asked for a loan, hoping to build the houses for the fishermen to move in as soon as possible, and the consul simply donated HK$600,000 to him to show his support. At the same time, the government allocated space for Rev. Lambertoni, and the housing project started smoothly. The construction project was finally completed in 1969, but due to inflation, the budget that was originally enough to build 100 houses, could only build 63 houses as a result. Fortunately, the German Catholic Church also donated HK$250,000 to Rev. Lambertoni and lent another HK$250,000 to him, and thus the housing project was able to continue.[4]

After the hard work, the first batch of houses was finally completed in 1971, with a total of 62 units. Each unit had an area of 400 square feet, and each was equipped with kitchen and bathroom, which was quite private. The house was backed by the mountains and face the sea, villagers could enjoy the scenery of Sai Kung's coast at home. There was a recreation area provided by the government for free, and was used as the place for children in the village to play. On the whole, Tai Ping Village was indeed a very ideal living environment at the time.[5] At the same time, the expansion project was also continuing, adding 124 units to Tai Ping Village. In addition, facilities such as a community hall and office buildings would also be built to make the housing estate more complete.[6] In addition to providing an ideal living environment for fishermen, Caritas also organized various recreational activities in the village from time to time to make their lives colorful and help them learn new skills.[7] By 1977, Ming Shun Village (the second part of Rev. Lambertoni's housing project) was also completed at Tui Min Hoi, providing 30 housing units for fishermen.

Tai Ping Village implemented a cooperative system, with one share per family, costing $3,000 per share. According to the agreement between the two parties, villagers could live in Tai Ping Village permanently, but they could not transfer or rent their houses to others. If the villagers needed to move out, they had to return their houses to the cooperative, and the cooperative would return their responsible funds to them, and the conceded houses would grant to other residents under the same conditions. In addition, each household needed to pay a monthly maintenance fee of $20, half of which was used for housing maintenance, such as cleaning and public electricity, and the remaining half was used for the next progress of housing construction funds.[8] Under the guidance of Caritas, the cooperative not only managed Tai Ping Village, but also played a role in connecting the villagers. It was a platform that allowed villagers to cooperate with each other, help each other, and work together for everyone's welfare.

The lively situation at the opening of Tai Ping Tsuen. (Image source: Sai Kung Sacred Heart Church)

In 1978, the Tai Ping Village Mutual Aid Committee was established. On one hand, it continued the work of the cooperative in the past, and at the same time assumed more important responsibilities: took over the management of Tai Ping Village from Caritas, and fully managed the future village affairs and the development of the village.[9] In addition, the management and property rights of Ming Shun Village and St. Peter's Village were also transferred to the cooperative formed by the villagers of the two villages in the same way.[10] The fishermen changed from living on fishing boats to living on land, and then learned to cooperate with each other to improve their living environment, and finally be able to manage all the affairs of the village on their own. This depended on the efforts of Caritas and the villagers over the years. When talking about Tai Ping Village, Rev. Lambertoni pointed out that it was qualitatively different from St. Peter's Village. "In St. Peter's Village, we first had money and only invited people to live in after the houses were built; but in Tai Ping Village, we first observed the actual needs of the fishermen before formulating a corresponding housing plan." For Rev. Lambertoni, the latter was the ideal way to carry out social assistance.[11]

Although some people would think that the priest built Tai Ping Village was to attract people to profess Catholicism, it was actually and entirely up to the villagers to decide whether they would be baptised, and it was the fact that in Tai Ping Village, there were only 16 families that professed Catholicism, where ten families professed in Protestantism, and the rest were infidels. The priest named this place "Tai Ping Village" (meaning peaceful village) because he hoped that residents of different backgrounds could cooperate with each other and live in harmony.[12]

Turbulent Situation: the Murder of Rev. Valeriano Fraccaro

Rev. Valeriano Fraccaro (1913-1974), with the nicknames "Pope John" and "Father Bread", has served others unselfishly for many years. He was born in Castel Veneto, Treviso, Italy on 15 March 1913, became a friar on 20 September 1934, and was ordained as a priest in Milan on 4 April 1937.[13] Rev. Fraccaro, at the age of 24, was sent to Shaanxi, China for missionary work shortly after he was ordained, and arrived in Hanzhong in the same year. It was the period when Japan launched aggression against China, and Rev. Fraccaro's luggage was also detained due to the war and could not be retrieved until 1945.[14] For Rev. Fraccaro, who had just started his missionary career, it was not an easy start.

When preaching in the Mainland, Rev. Fraccaro mainly relied on his heavy and worn bicycle to travel to various places. The road he travelled was uneven and often covered with gravel, making the journey dangerous. Not only that, if it rains, the road in the mountain would become muddy, and at this time the priest could only carry his bicycle with his shoulders and walked across the dirt road on foot. Although the bicycle was worn out and often needed parts replacement and repairs, Rev. Fraccaro still relied on it to travel throughout the diocese of southern Shaanxi and visit different villages. Even though the days of preaching in mainland China were difficult, Rev. Fraccaro's heart was still filled with joy and amazing courage. In one of his letters in 1939, he said this to his brothers:

> I feel happy all the time and I am healthy. My feet are still strong enough to cope with the long journey. My room is quiet, allowing me to sleep every night without dreaming. There is too much work here, enough to make people breathless.[15]

The missionary work in China during the war was extremely dangerous. Although the bell tower of the church was painted in the colors of the Italian flag, it still could not escape the fate of being bombed by the Japanese Air Force. The seminary, the monastery and the houses where the missionaries lived were destroyed by bombs. When the Japanese soldiers arrived, Rev. Fraccaro was sent to a concentration camp, and he was freed two years later.[16]

However, Japan's surrender did not mean that all difficulties would end here. In 1949, the Chinese regime changed and the Communist Party, which advocates materialism, came to power. Different religious groups were severely persecuted. All actions of the church were closely monitored by the police; believers were prohibited from going to the church, and missionaries were also prohibited from carrying out missionary activities. At this time, Rev. Fraccaro was arrested again. He was originally sentenced to imprisonment, but was later changed to house arrest at home. According to Rev. Fraccaro's record, the CCP government squeezed the church by charging huge taxes, trying to make the church surrender to the government and became a governance tool to serve the government. Rev. Fraccaro once opened a clinic with two domestic nuns to treat eye diseases, but after more than a month, he was unable to make ends meet due to huge taxes and was forced to close the clinic.[17]

After a long period of persecution, Rev. Fraccaro, who was labeled as the enemy of the people, was finally deported permanently by the Chinese Communist authorities in 1951. After leaving the mainland, Rev. Fraccaro decided to settle down in Hong Kong temporarily, and had been hoping to wait for the day when he could return to Mainland China, but that day had never come. Hong Kong, the small city, had become a place where Rev. Fraccaro dedicated the rest of his life to the gospel.

When Rev. Fraccaro first came to Hong Kong, it was a period of rapid population expansion. Many people fled from the mainland to Hong Kong, and the local fertility rate continued to be high, which brought great challenges to the church in Hong Kong. Rev. Fraccaro first served as the assistant parish priest of St. Peter's Church in Aberdeen in 1954, and then served as the parish priest of the Sacred Heart of Jesus Church in Sha Tin and St. John the Baptist Church in Castle Peak from 1955 to 1960 and from 1961 to 1966. In 1966, Rev. Fraccaro was appointed as the Rector of Sai Kung District and Supervisor of Sung Tsun School.[18]

"Pope John" of the Villagers

Not long after Rev. Fraccaro arrived in Sai Kung, he intensively gained the love of the local villagers. A villager living in Sha Tsui once said:

> I will always remember the day he (Rev. Fraccaro) first came to this village (Sha Tsui). My house is located in front of a small pier. There are ships from Sai Kung every two days, so I can see all the people coming to Sha Tsui. That day, I saw a short and fat man coming ashore. As soon as he got off the boat, he opened the umbrella to block the sun, and then took a firm step, running towards the village. It didn't take long before he saw me standing in front of the house. "Mama! I'm the new priest!" He yelled at me. I really like him calling me Maa Maa (he has been calling me Maa Maa since that day), and his smile gives me confidence. I gave him some tea and two fresh eggs, and he immediately ate it unceremoniously.[19]

Rev. Fraccaro's short and chubby appearance and amiable smile made the villagers to come up with his nickname "Pope John".[20] In addition, the priest's gentle personality also made him loved by Sai Kung villagers. A preacher who has worked with Rev. Fraccaro for several years said this:

> There is a smile on his face all the time. His rustic glasses that often slip off the bridge of his nose make him look funny. The first thing that caught my attention was his brilliant smile. At first, he looked like an innocent child who don't aware of human suffering; however, after living with him for a period of time, I began to discover that he had a deep insight into the real world, and he could touch the problem in every discussion essentially. He is loved by everyone, old people, children and young people love him, this is an indisputable fact. He is good at adapting to various environments and getting along well with different people. He has special care for the elderly, because he knows that they are the most neglected, the loneliest and the most in need of help. He often visited the old villagers and talked with them in detail. How much effort did he spend to make them feel happy to talk![21]

Rev. Fraccaro and Rev. Lambertoni and the Catholics of Sha Shui Catholic Church pose for a photo. (Image source: Paul Wong Yee-tin)

Rev. Fraccaro visited the fishermen's community. (Image source: PIME)

Rev. Fraccaro (front row middle) and other priests in Sai Kung district. (Image source: Sai Kung Sacred Heart Church)

Considering that many people would go to the urban areas to celebrate during the Lunar New Year, but the elderly villagers were left at home. Rev. Fraccaro specially established the "Respect for the Aged Day" during the Lunar New Year, hoping to make these elderly villagers to be more respected and bring joy to them. He also set up a banquet to entertain these old villagers, share with them some interesting stories, sang songs to them, and even offered fine wines to enjoy. In the eyes of the villagers, the wine given by the priest was a very precious gift.[22]

Rev. Fraccaro used to walk through the entire village every morning, visiting the villagers house by house, and preaching them the gospel. This habit was formed early before he arrived in Sai Kung. He attached great importance to the relationship with the villagers, and spent a lot of time with them every day. He also visited the fishermen who live and work on the fishing boats, and even held Mass on the boats. As the space on the ship was very small, the top of the ship was very low, and the table was only a few feet high, the priest needed to kneel every time when he held a mass on the ship. Even so, the priest was happy to enjoy each visit on the boat. For priests, this was an important way to cultivate faith communities.[23]

The fishermen liked this priest who often visited them on the boat. Although they were all illiterate and often used the wrong vocabulary when chatting, the priest always got along with them patiently and never been impatient. In order to make the fishermen feel comfortable, priests sometimes imitated their words and ways of speaking. The priest's cordial and caring method of preaching made him welcomed by local residents wherever he went.[24]

"Father Bread"

Speaking of Rev. Fraccaro, Sai Kung villagers would inevitably at first think of the bread he baked. The priest was used to baking all kinds of bread by himself and gave them to villagers during the visit. Since Rev. Fraccaro's family operated a bread business in Italy, he also mastered the skills of baking bread. His family sent him an old oven from Italy so that he could make bread. After receiving the oven, Rev. Fraccaro arranged a small house near the Sacred Heart Church in Sai Kung and used it as a place to bake bread.[25] The priest would make bread at night, so that he could give fresh bread to the villagers in the next morning, and regardless of whether the person was a believer or not, the priest would be very happy to deliver the bread he made. On one hand, Rev.

Fraccaro nourished the souls of the villagers by preaching God's doctrine. On the other hand, he satisfied their physical needs by giving bread. At that time, villagers in Sai Kung generally lived in poverty, and many children suffered from malnutrition due to lack of adequate food. Therefore, for the Sai Kung villagers at that time, the bread presented by Rev. Fraccaro not only symbolized the care for them, but also one of the food they depended on for their livelihood.

In addition to making bread by hand for gifts to the villagers, Rev. Fraccaro also took care of their food needs in other ways. The priest sometimes sent some redemption cards to the villagers. With these vouchers, the villagers could go to the "Chan Fuk Shing Bakery" in Sai Kung Market at that time to exchange for bread. This bakery had closed nowadays. Rev. Fraccaro had a funny image because of his short and chubby body, and the sense of humor. In a letter to his niece Paula, the priest wrote:

> Today I needed to explain the parable of the Good Samaritan, but I skipped it and told the villagers that this passage was too difficult. In fact, this is because in this parable, the priests give people a bad impression, so I asked myself, why should I say bad things about the priests? ...What do you think your uncle is like? But Paula, you know, even though I use ants instead of raisins and use expired

Rev. Fraccaro attended the parish activities. (Image source: Sai Kung Sacred Heart Church)

flour to make cakes, your uncle is also a kind-hearted person![26]

People liked to talk to him because of his humor, they were surprised by his optimistic and positive personality, too. In the eyes of the priest, the world was indeed very beautiful; immediate difficulties was just opportunities to make people become stronger. The preaching process was full of hardships, but every time he thought of the faithfulness of the laity in Sai Kung, he would be happy about it. Although there were many things that Rev. Fraccaro needed to deal with every day, he was used to pray in the church at night. Once Rev. Lambertoni met Rev. Fraccaro who happened to be praying, and said to him, "Please help me to pray too!" Rev. Fraccaro said to him, "Everyone should pray by themselves to the Lord." For Rev. Fraccaro, prayer was very important. It was the source of his inner peace and strength, and it supported his missionary work all the time.

Villagers' Memories

According to Lai Yan, the village representative of Sai Wan Village, once Rev. Fraccaro had to walk up a very steep slope when leaving Sai Wan. Rev. Fraccaro was obese and the roads were rough and difficult to navigate. It was absolutely difficult for the priest to walk on the slope by himself. Because of this, the students tried every means to help the priest. At that time, two students would be at the top of the slope, holding a rope together, and the priest held the other end of the rope, and they pulled Rev. Fraccaro up. In addition, two students behind him also joined forces to push the priest up the slope. In the end, after everyone's efforts, the priest finally walked up to slope smoothly and left Sai Wan. The village representative described the scene at that time as very funny, and he is still impressed until now.

For the village representative Lai Yan, Rev. Fraccaro was not only a very "funny" person, but also a person he was very grateful for. When he was a child, Lai Yan hoped to be able to enter Sung Tsun School, but he was inferior to others in terms of ability and academic qualifications, he knew that he had slim chance. Rev. Fraccaro and Rev. Lambertoni, who were in charge of the affairs of Sung Tsun School at the time, knew of Lai Yan's desire and decided to let him be exempted from interviews and could directly enter the school. Thankful to their kindly support, Lai Yan got the chance to receive formal education. Rev. Fraccaro kindly invited Lai Yan to his bakery, saying that he would teach him how to make bread and cakes. These little things are unforgettable to Lai Yan.

On one occasion, Rev. Fraccaro learned from the students in Sai Wan that there was a charcoal kiln in Sai Wan for making charcoal. He was very surprised and asked the students to take him there to have a look. Although the process of going up the mountain was very difficult for the priest, and the students also spent a lot of effort to help the priest climb to the top of the mountain, but the priest was very excited along the way and did not complain at all. After finding the charcoal kiln, the priest felt very happy, and walked into the charcoal kiln to observe and admire it carefully. He was surprised that there was such a beautiful charcoal kiln in Sai Wan. Now that the charcoal kiln has collapsed, and Rev. Fraccaro was the only priest who has been to the Sai Wan charcoal kiln. Perhaps the reason why Rev. Fraccaro was so excited about the charcoal kiln is he who liked making bread has a yearning for such a huge kiln!

The Killing that Shocked the Whole Hong Kong

On 28 October 1974, Rev. Fraccaro, who was beloved by the villagers, was brutally murdered. In that day, Rev. Fraccaro, Rev. Lambertoni and Rev. Frontini had dinner together and arranged an early mass together. Later, Rev. Lambertoni and Rev. Frontini went out to visit the villagers, leaving Rev. Fraccaro alone in the priest's dormitory. At 11:45 that night, Rev. Frontini returned from Pak Hok Village and saw Rev. Fraccaro's door was left opened, so he stepped forward to check. After he pushed the door and entered, he saw Rev. Fraccaro naked and falling in a pool of blood. Rev. Frontini immediately stepped forward and found that Rev. Fraccaro had already lost his consciousness. Rev. Fraccaro's arms and feet were tied back with a bath towel, his hands were swollen, and his mouth was stuffed with a face towel; his head and back were stabbed for more than 30 times, he was seriously injured and died when he was found. While discovering Rev. Fraccaro's body, Rev. Frontini saw that the bathtub in the bathroom was filled with water, Rev. Fraccaro might be preparing to take a bath when the murderer broke into the dormitory and killed the priest.[27]

The place where Rev. Fraccaro, Rev. Lambertoni and Rev. Frontini lived together, was a two-storey building on the ramp of the Sai Kung Bus Terminal. Below the dormitory was the Catholic Church. The second floor of the dormitory was divided into three small rooms. The three priests all lived on the second floor, while Rev. Fraccaro lived in the bedroom on the right side of the stairs on the second floor. In addition, there was a bakery near the dormitory, where a security guard surnamed Li and two children lived in it. However, on the night of the incident, the two children went out on holiday, and the security guards was already asleep. In addition, the bakery was far away from the priest's dormitory. Therefore, no one was awared when the murder happened, and the assailant and the process of the attack were unknown.[28]

The police detective stated that the assailant should have sneaked in from the bathroom window, and there were traces of struggle left at the scene.[29] It was believed that the priest had resisted the assailant before he was killed; a kitchen knife taken from the dormitory kitchen was left on the scene, which was the murder weapon. However, in order to allow people who needed food to get bread at any time, the door of the dormitory kitchen was always open for them, so the murderer might also enter the dormitory through the kitchen.[30] In addition, the telephone line downstairs of the dormitory was cut off and the lights were destroyed. It was believed that the murderer did it.[31] The purpose might be to block the priest's method of seeking help from outside, and at the same time made it difficult for him to escape. However, it was impossible to confirm whether they were destroyed before or after the priest was killed.

Sister Kwok, who taught at Sung Tsun School, claimed that there was a man's voice in the dormitory at 10 o'clock that night, but she was not sure what language it was, but it didn't sound like Cantonese. She returned to her residence at 11 o'clock and saw the light in Rev. Fraccaro's room was still on.[32] In addition, according to the testimony of nearby residents of Sai Kung, three private cars were parked in the open space near the dormitory at 10 o'clock on that night, but only two of them were left in the same place after the incident. One white private car was already missing. The two private cars were owned by the priest,[33] and Rev. Fraccaro had said that he would not learn to drive,[34] so the disappeared private car was probably owned by the murderer and used it to quickly escape the scene after the attack.

Rev. Fraccaro had always worked tirelessly to serve Sai Kung villagers, and generously took care of their material needs, so he had always been loved by Sai Kung villagers, and had never complained with others. After hearing the news of Rev. Fraccaro's murder, all the villagers felt very sad, even more indissoluble. Why was such a kind priest killed? What was the reason for the murder? There were different speculations about the cause of Rev. Fraccaro's murder, but after all, there was no definite conclusion. As the priest was killed very close to the wage period of Sung Tsun

School, some people speculated that this case was a robbery: the assailant sneaked into the priest's dormitory, intending to use torture to force the priest to give out the wages, but the priest did not think of surrender, therefore the murderer decided to kill him in the end.[35]

However, according to another speculation, Rev. Fraccaro was killed because Rev. Lambertoni had actively sought to build fishermen's villages on land for Sai Kung fishermen, which undermined the plans of some developers to build luxury houses in the local area and provoked retaliation. However, it was Rev. Lambertoni, not Rev. Fraccaro, who was mainly in charge of the fishermen's village plan. Therefore, according to this speculation, Rev. Fraccaro was killed because the murderer admitted the wrong target. It also meant that Rev. Lambertoni had a chance to face danger to his life.[36] Until now, the perpetrators who killed Rev. Fraccaro were still at large, and the reason why the priest was killed remained an unsolved mystery.

Rev. Fraccaro's memorial mass was held at the St. Margaret's Church in Happy Valley at 3 pm on 1 October. There were a large number of priests, nuns and church members who participated in the Mass, and the Hong Kong Anglican Church Bishop Baker also came to pray for the dead. The memorial mass was presided over by Rev. Gabriel Lam and more than 20 other priests, while the sermon was presided over by Rev. Fraccaro's classmate, Rev. Speziali, Cirillo PIME. At 4 pm that day, the funeral ceremony at the Happy Valley Catholic Cemetery was held, and according to the wishes

The villagers' memories of Rev. Fraccaro after his death were included in the Italian book *Sai Kung*. (Image source: PIME)

of Rev. Fraccaro's family, his body was transported back to his hometown of Italy for burial.[37]

The death of Rev. Fraccaro made the villagers of Sai Kung grief, and it also caused a great psychological impact on Rev. Lambertoni and Rev. Frontini who were practicing Cantonese in Sai Kung at that time. Considering the dangers that may be encountered in continuing to stay in Sai Kung, the two priests were forced to leave the area temporarily. As a temporary measure, Rev. De Ascaniis, Quirino (PIME), was again appointed as the supervisor of the Sai Kung District, assisted by Rev. Morlacchi, Paolo (PIME), to manage the church affairs in the district, but was not responsible for the management of Sung Tsun School. In 1975, Rev. Ruggiero, Nicola (PIME) became the Rector of Sai Kung District and concurrently as Supervisor of Sung Tsun School.[38]

High Island Reservoir: Village Resettlement and Church Development

The rapid population expansion of Hong Kong in the 1960s and 1970s, coupled with the booming industrial development, led to a huge increase in the demand for fresh water. Although there were already many reservoirs in Hong Kong at that time, the water storage capacity was still insufficient to meet such a huge demand; the government implemented fresh water control from time to time to ensure water supply. In order to ensure that Hong Kong has sufficient fresh water resources, the government began planning for the construction of a new reservoir in the late 1960's, and in 1971 the construction of the High Island Reservoir began. The reservoir was finally completed in 1978, with a water storage capacity of 60 billion gallons. The entire project cost a total of 1.35 billion dollars.[39] Because of the High Island Reservoir project, the villagers of Lan Nai Wan and Sha Tsui Village bid farewell to their original homes, where the Immaculate Heart of Mary Chapel in Sha Tsui Village had been submerged under the water forever.

The Immaculate Heart of Mary Chapel was completed in 1953 and mainly served the believers along Kun Mun Waterway. In 1956, the Sacred Heart Primary School was installed in the chapel as a place for nearby villagers to receive education. When the priest toured Sai Kung and visited various villages, he would also stay overnight in the chapel. The construction of the High Island Reservoir has affected villagers in various places in Sai Kung, especially Lan Nai Wan and Sha Tsui Villages: after the completion of the reservoir, these two villages would also be submerged under the water forever. Therefore, while planning to build the High Island Reservoir, the government had to provide compensation plans for the villagers in these two affected villages.[40]

At first, the government divided the affected villagers into two groups and made corresponding compensations according to their degree of impact. The first group consists of three villages located in the Lan Nai Wan area near the dam site in the west. These villages had been built locally for several generations. Once the villages were flooded, it meant that the villagers would lost their homes and could no longer live in the village, so they were classified as the most affected group. The second group were villagers in Sha Tsui Village near the east dam site. They had not moved to this area for a long time, so they could move back to their original place of residence in Long Ke Wan and continue their rural life. The transportation in Long Ke Wan would also be more convenient due to the reservoir plan. For the sake of fairness, they received less compensation than the former. According to the original arrangement, each affected villager could get a new housing unit in Sai Kung Market and several allowances, while the villagers in Man Yee Wan could get a shop under the house as additional compensation for losing their ancestral land.

At 10 o'clock in the morning on 8 December 1972, a group of Sha Tsui villagers protested in the village, claiming that they had not received reasonable compensation and prevented workers from implementing projects within the village. For the unmarried women of Lan Nai Wan villagers, half of the housing unit could be obtained, while the unmarried women of Sha Tsui Village did not. The villagers of Sha Tsui Village believed that this arrangement was unfair to them, and had repeatedly expressed dissatisfaction with the relevant authorities and demanded a compensation plan that they believe was fair, but they had never reached a consensus, so they forcefully prevented the project from proceeding. As the villagers struggled to stop the construction, the workers were unable to construct, so they had to send someone to report the incident to Sai Kung District Office. After that, more than a dozen police officers and District Office staff arrived at the scene to mediate and persuade the villagers to leave. After a round of confrontation, the villagers gradually left. Finally, the village representative Tang Seng led several villager representatives to the District Office and the police station to discuss and negotiate with relevant people.[41]

It was not an easy task to reach an agreement with many affected villagers on the conditions of relocation. After long negotiations between the two sides, the villagers

The Immaculate Heart of Mary Chapel in Sha Tsui Village in the past.

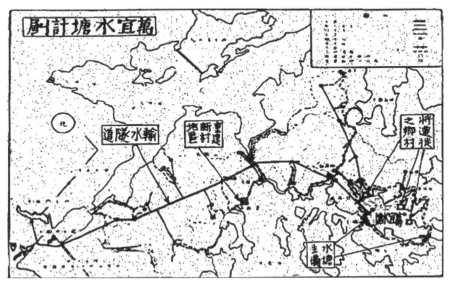

High Island Reservoir Plan.[42]

and the government finally reached a consensus: the villagers in Lan Nai Wan and Sha Tsui villages could all get the same compensation. Every family (monogamous) could get a shop unit on the ground floor. If they didn't accept the property, they could cash out $190,000; each male could get a unit upstairs, and if they didn't need a house, they could cash out $80,000. Female could get a half-storey upstairs residence, if she didn't want a residence or could not make it into one floor, she could cash out $40,000. In addition, every household could get various allowances such as occupation and decoration expenses, relocation expenses, and water expenses.[43]

In addition to taking care of the housing needs of the villagers, the government had also made proper arrangements for the rehousing of their ancestors. Because of the reservoir project, the seven ancestral halls in Lan Nai Wan needed to be relocated.[44] The new ancestral halls were all allocated and constructed by the government, and all construction costs were paid by the government. In order to respect the traditions of the villagers, the government hired geomancer to measure the feng shui of the new site, and the construction of the new ancestral halls was started with the villagers' consent was obtained. The seven newly-built ancestral halls were located in Muk Min Shan, with a toilet and a road connecting Sai Kung Highway. The total construction cost was about $1.3 million.[45]

However, the residents of Lan Nai Wan and Sha Tsui were not the only ones affected by the reservoir project. The construction of the High Island Reservoir prevented ships from passing through the Kun Mun Strait to and from Mirs Bay, which harmed the livelihoods of local fishermen. In order to compensate for the losses suffered by these fishermen, the government had invited all fishermen to conduct consultations since 1971 and carefully studied their requirements and the extent of the impact of the reservoir project. After investigation by the Agriculture and Fisheries Department, the affected fishermen were classified into A, B and C grade according to the degree of impact.[46]

For the fishermen of Grade A who were the most affected, the government had built a batch of two-storey buildings at Tui Min Hoi as a settlement for them. These buildings were completed in 1975, with a total of 30 units, which could accommodate a total of 260 fishermen. Every five fishermen could get a 500-square-foot unit as their property free of charge, and they would also receive corresponding allowances. In addition, the government had also built a number of four-storey buildings at Tui Min Hoi for the fishermen who were relatively less affected. Regardless of their population,

Overseas Chinese Daily News, 18 December 1974.

each household could only be allocated a floor of about 46 square meters, and they also needed to pay $6,000 before they could move in. As for the fishermen of Class C who were the least affected, they did not receive housing compensation.[47]

The completion of the High Island Reservoir alleviated the shortage of water in Hong Kong and brought benefits to the general public. At the same time, Lan Nai Wan and Sha Tsui villages were flooded. This might remind us that what we have now was not easy to come by, and we need to cherish it with gratitude.

Symbol of Ecumenism: Long Ke Nativity of Our Lady Chapel and Gospel Drug Rehabilitation Village

The Nativity of Our Lady Chapel in Long Ke was established by the PIME Missionary Rev. Teruzzi in 1917, applying for land allocation to the District Office, North and the construction was completed the following year. After the completion of the chapel, the Catholic Church entrusted it to the management of Wong Cho Hei, a villager of Long Ke. At that time, in addition to the Wong's family, the villagers of Long Ke also included Lau's, Tang's, and Lee's, while the Wong's family was the main clan of the village at that time. It was believed that Wong Cho Hei had already become a Catholic at that time, so he was commissioned by the church to manage this newly built chapel. In 1954, the chapel was managed by priests of the Sacred Heart Church in Sai Kung and belonged to the Tai Long District. In 1955, the management of the chapel was changed to Sai Kung Sacred Heart Church, but it returned to the management of Tai Long District a year later. Finally, since 1957, the chapel belonged to the Sacred Heart Church until 1966. However, since the 1960s, due to the impact of the villagers' abandonment of farming and the construction plan of the High Island Reservoir, the villagers and believers of Long Ke moved out one after another. Village and the chapel were gradually abandoned.

On the other hand, the Nativity of Our Lady Chapel in Long Ke, which had been abandoned since the 1960s, had also been used by two Protestant groups as a place for the development of gospel drug rehabilitation. In 1968, Pastor John Paul Chan (1922-2010) established a gospel drug rehabilitation village in Long Ke Bay, with Long Ke Chapel as its meeting place, trying to use the power of the gospel alone to help drug addicts get rid of drug addiction. Pastor Chan's attempt was successful, and the emerging method of drug rehabilitation using the gospel had also gained public recognition in Hong Kong. In 1976, Pastor Chan moved the drug rehabilitation village to a new site arranged by the government, and the Long Ke Chapel was suspended. In 1980, Pastor Harold Schock (1921-1997), who founded the Christian Wu Oi Centre, founded the "Wu Oi Gospel Drug Rehabilitation Village" in Long Ke, and the Long Ke Chapel once again became the site of the Gospel Drug Rehabilitation Centre until today.

The Father of Gospel Drug Rehabilitation in Hong Kong —— Pastor John Paul Chan[48]

Pastor John Paul Chan was originally an aircraft engineer. In his thirties, he devoted himself to becoming a Protestant preacher and served as a pastor at the Beautiful Gate Baptist Church. For Pastor Chan, the gospel of Christ was a gospel that responds to people's holistic needs. In addition to leading people to know Jesus, pastors must also respond to their physical needs. Having always focused on serving the disadvantaged, he once opened mobile clinics to provide low-cost consultation services for the poor; he also opened a primary school in a seven-storey building to provide education to poor children and at the same time instilled the principles of Christianity in them. Among them, some graduates participated in the service work in the early days of the Gospel Drug Rehabilitation Village, which was later established by Pastor Chan.[49]

In the early 1960s, the drug problem in Hong Kong became more and more serious. The Beautiful Gate Baptist Church, where Pastor Chan served at the beginning, was located near the Kowloon Walled City where the drug problem was the most serious. When Pastor Chan passed by the dilapidated stone house next to Tai Chang Street, he would see many scrawny drug addicts sitting in the house; the house was full of smoke and stench, just liked "hell on earth." Once, Pastor Chan saw a few sacks containing the corpses of drug addicts being dragged out of the public toilets in the walled city, while others shouted, "Who can give a helping hand? Get some money for sweet soup!" Then someone came and took these sacks, throw them on the garbage truck. Pastor Chan was deeply saddened to see the body of a drug addict being treated as garbage. At this time, he prayed to the Lord, hoping to help these drug users, and launched his plan to promote the gospel drug rehabilitation.[50]

Pastor Chan didn't has a complete plan at the beginning. At first he just printed some gospel pamphlets and distributed to drug addicts in the walled city to preach the gospel to them. Most drug addicts were indifferent to the gospel, and they often made fun of Pastor Chan. One day, Pastor Chan met a drug addict named Chiang Wai Man. He was deeply addicted to drugs but was very interested in the gospel. Once he asked, "Pastor Chan, you don't have a drug rehabilitation centre, how can you help me with drug rehabilitation?"[51] Pastor Chan then had the idea of setting up a drug rehabilitation centre. According to his autobiography, Pastor Chan prayed to the Lord, hoping that the Lord could prepare a suitable place for him. A few days later, he came across a Christian friend in Sai Kung who ran a local grocery store. As soon as he knew that Pastor Chan was looking for a place to set up a drug rehabilitation centre, he informed Pastor Chan that there was a deserted village in Long Ke Bay, with beautiful environment and isolated from the outside world, which was very suitable as a place for drug rehabilitation. After hearing this, Pastor Chan was excited to take a boat to Long Ke to see this beautiful place.[52]

The turbulent journey did not diminish Pastor Chan's determination. After several attempts, Pastor Chan boarded Long Ke Bay. Seeing such beautiful scenery, Pastor Chan was very happy and thought this place was very suitable as the site of a drug rehabilitation village. He negotiated with Wong Kuei, the representative of Long

Ke Village,[53] and rented two village houses for an annual rent of $100.[54]

The name "Operation Dawn" came from Romans 13:12 of the Bible, which meant that daybreak was about to come, admonishing drug addicts to get rid of the dark behavior of the past, and this section of the Bible was also the motto of Operation Dawn.[55] Pastor Chan did not use medical drugs to help addicts to get rid of drugs, but relied solely on the power of the gospel to free them from the dominance of drugs.[56] Pastor Chan preached gospels to drug addicts, clearly stating that addiction to drugs was a sin, and persuaded them to confess their sins to the Lord and stayed away from drugs. Whenever the symptoms of drug addicts appeared, Pastor Chan would help them with prayer and liturgy. In addition, the geographical location of Long Ke Bay also made it difficult for drug addicts to obtain drugs, increasing their chances of getting rid of addiction.[57]

In the early stage of the gospel drug rehabilitation work, Pastor Chan encountered many difficulties and obstacles. According to the *Overseas Chinese Daily News* in 1969, there was a dispute over the right to use the village house between Pastor Chan and the villagers of Long Ke. Some villagers who had moved out of Long Ke found that their village house was occupied by Pastor Chan without consent, by the time when they returned to the village for tomb sweeping. They were very dissatisfied and asked Pastor Chan to move out of their village house, but two months later it was found that the situation continued, so they lodged a complaint with the Sai Kung Rural Committee. The committee then held a meeting for this and asked Pastor Chan to move out of the occupied village house within two weeks.[58] Since Pastor Chan's autobiography did not mention the dispute between him and the villagers, this was difficult to prove whether Pastor Chan had moved out of the village house finally.

At the same time, because of its beautiful scenery, Long Ke Bay had always attracted people from the Royal Auxiliary Air Force to go there in groups for vacation and recreation. This situation continued even when Pastor Chan established the drug rehabilitation village. The soldiers would clamor and play on the beach, causing serious disturb to drug addicts, which annoyed Pastor Chan very much. Later, the Air Force applied to Bishop Francis Hsu, the Bishop of the Catholic Diocese at that time, hoping to borrow the Nativity of Our Lady Chapel in Long Ke Village as their club address. With regard to the application of the Air Force, Pastor Chan expressed strong opposition to the Diocese, and his opposition also aroused the anger of the Air Force. On the morning of 2 December 1969, a British military helicopter landed on the beach of Long Ke Bay, alarming Pastor Chan and the addicts, causing them to rush to the beach to check. They saw soldiers from the Royal Auxiliary Air Force walking out of the helicopter and went to the church, moving out all the Bibles, books and furniture from the church, and then locked the door of the church with an iron chain, and put a seal of District Office on the door. Pastor Chan and drug addicts were prohibited from continuing to use the church. Facing the rude provocation of the Air Force, Pastor Chan and the addicts felt both frightened and angry. However, they chose to remain calm and did not make any resistance.[59]

The incident became the headline news of *The China Mail* the next day, with the headline "British Air Force Strikes on Drug Rehabilitation Centre", which shocked Hong Kong society at that time. Relevant government departments and different churches and Christian organisations all expressed their concern and condolences to Pastor Chan, and the Hong Kong Anglican Church Bishop Baker also called Pastor Chan to express his support and encouragement for his gospel drug rehabilitation work. In addition, Television Broadcasts Limited (TVB) had reported more news about the drug rehabilitation village, and made many interviews with Pastor Chan.[60] Because of the persecution by the Air Force, the previously unknown Pastor Chan and his little-known gospel drug rehabilitation work became known to the people of Hong Kong, and the drug rehabilitation village began to receive some practical assistance. In October 1970, the Kadoorie Agricultural Aid Association donated HK$1,200 to the Gospel Drug Rehabilitation Village to purchase three cattle for reclaiming wasteland, thereby increasing the production of the fields;[61] in 1971, the association also donated to the drug rehabilitation village three milk cows to improve the living environment of drug

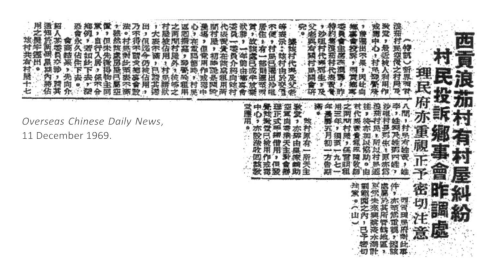

Overseas Chinese Daily News,
11 December 1969.

addicts.[62] In May of the same year, the Y's Men's Club of Kowloon donated HK$2,500 to the drug rehabilitation village to help them purchase a motorized engine as a means of transportation for travelling and from Long Ke Wan. For the drug rehabilitation village that did not has public transportation, this was indeed a very generous help.[63]

However, the conflict between Pastor Chan and the Royal Auxiliary Air Force did not end there. With the support of Bishop Baker and Commissioner for Narcotics Peter E. I. Lee, the government was willing to prepare a new place for the Gospel Drug Rehabilitation Village. In 1976, Pastor Chan, accompanied by Bishop Baker and government officials, sailed off by "Sir Cecil Clementi" to find a new location for the drug rehabilitation village. Pastor Chan finally chose Town Island in Sai Kung and officially relocated the drug rehabilitation village to this small island on 11 October of the same year. From then on, this island was named "Dawn Island". Pastor Chan's drug rehabilitation project had a brand new start, and it could continue to use the power of the gospel to help drug addicts get rid of drug addiction until now; at the same time, the small chapel of Long Ke returned to the status of abandonment.

In October 1980, the Christian Wu Oi Centre, founded by Pastor Harold Schock, was approved by the Catholic Diocese for the borrow of Long Ke chapel and changed it as the gospel drug rehabilitation centre. Since 1981, the chapel of Long Ke had been borrowed for free for five consecutive years as the place to establish a gospel drug rehabilitation village. In addition, the government had also set an annual fee of $1 as rent for Long Ke Bay to Wu Oi Centre for gospel drug rehabilitation ministry. On 20 April 1981, the Wu Oi Gospel Drug Rehabilitation Village was officially opened. The opening ceremony was co-chaired by Commissioner for Narcotics Peter Lee, Rev. Khong Kin Cheung Edward, the Deputy General Secretary of the Catholic Diocese of Hong Kong, Dr James Chien Ming-nin, Director of Social Welfare, the Society for the Aid and Rehabilitation of Drug Abusers, and Lee Hung Chak, Chairman of the Board of Directors of the Wu Oi Centre.[64] Since then, the Wu Oi Centre had continued the spirit of Pastor Chan at Long Ke Wan, relying on the power of the gospel to help drug addicts get rid of addiction until nowadays.

The chapel building had pitched roof, which was divided equally by a partition from east to west into two parts, connected by an archway. One half to the north was for prayer, meditation and rituals. The other half to the south is used for meeting and gathering while its penthouse should originally be the dormitory of the priests. It was supplemented by a loft. It was believed that the attic was a dormitory for priests when

Today's Wu Oi gospel drug rehabilitation village. (Now it has been renamed "Male Adult Training Centre")

it was still a Catholic church. The current church was called the "old church" and it was a place where Christian groups to hold worship or meet. There was a cross on the wall. The south wing was originally a dormitory for drug addicts, but now it is used as a meeting room and office, and the attic is a storage room. Another new church was built on the hillside.

In addition to witnessing the rebirth of drug addicts, the chapel of Long Ke also witnessed the cooperation between the Catholic Church and the Protestant Church in social service and evangelism. The Catholic Diocese of Hong Kong lent the small chapel to Protestant groups to run a drug rehabilitation centres, so that people bound by drugs could get help, and at the same time let the public know that the Catholic Church and other separate church groups served the people in the same spirit of Christ.[65]

In the 1970s, many fishing boats gathered in the Sai Kung Market harbour. The priests of the Sai Kung district visited the people on the water, acted like the District Officer, to understand their needs, and fight for them a place to build houses from the approval of government so that they could move into residential buildings to improve their lives. They also coordinated with the government to build fishermen's village and help allocate housing units to move in. The priests often took a boat to St. Peter's Village to celebrate masses, and the nuns taught the fishermen's children on weekdays. The village is now still a Catholic fishermen's village. Rev. Fraccaro's love for the faithful was deeply embedded in the villagers' mind. His death was a great loss for the people, and it also cast a shadow over Sai Kung's mission. Rev. Lambertoni adopted children and helped them with their early life needs, just like their biological fathers. After Rev. Lambertoni passed away, these "siblings" missed the priest's grace of nurturing and his selfless dedication to the Catholics and non-Catholics of Sai Kung. They even went to the hometown of the Italian priest to participate in commemorative activities. From the deeds of these two priests, we fully understand that faith is not purely a ritual. Therefore, after the Second Ecumenical Council of the Vatican, Western missionaries used different methods to promote their faith in Sai Kung, building trust with the villagers, and also enabling non-Catholic community to feel their selflessness. Their missionary journey is also a historical portrayal of Hong Kong's complicated political environment from the 1960s to the 1970s.

Actor Roy Chiao once went to Long Ke to share his testimony.

The Nativity of Our Lady Chapel in the 1970s.

Notes ───────────────────────────────────

1   Lung Kwok Chuen et al. (eds.), *Sung Tsun Primary Middle School Silver Jubilee, Sai Kung, (1924-1984)*(《西貢崇真中小學鑽禧紀念 (1924-1984)》)(Hong Kong: Sai Kung Sung Tsun School, 1984), pp. 99-100.

2   John Tong Hon, *In Memory of Fr. Lambertoni* (《懷念林柏棟神父》)(Hong Kong: Catholic Diocese of Hong Kong, 2006), https://www.youtube.com/watch?v=oJiCZrppCvw&feature=youtu.be, retrieved on 29 June 2020.

3   Leung Kam-Chung (ed.), *Sung Tsun Middle School, Sai Kung, 70-72* (Hong Kong: Sai Kung Sung Tsun School, 1972), p. 86.

4   Ibid.

5   "Sai Kung Po Lo Che establishes Tai Ping Village, American Consulate hosts the Inauguration Ceremony"(〈西貢菠蘿峯建成太平村 美總領事今主持開幕〉), *Overseas Chinese Daily News*, 6 October 1971, https://mmis.hkpl.gov.hk/home, retrieved on 4 June 2020.

6   Leung Kam-Chung (ed.), *Sung Tsun Middle School, Sai Kung, 70-72*, p. 86.

7   "Inauguration of Sai Kung Tai Ping Cooperative Association, Improving living environment together" (〈西貢太平村互助會就職 合力改善居住環境〉), *Overseas Chinese Daily News*, 22 September 1978, https://mmis.hkpl.gov.hk/home, retrieved on 4 June 2020.

8   Leung Kam-Chung (ed.), *Sung Tsun Middle School, Sai Kung, 70-72*, pp. 86-87.

9   "Inauguration of Sai Kung Tai Ping Cooperative Association, Improving living environment together" (〈西貢太平村互助會就職 合力改善居住環境〉), *Overseas Chinese Daily News*, 22 September 1978, https://mmis.hkpl.gov.hk/home, retrieved on 4 June 2020.

10 The Hong Kong Council of Social Service, *Scenario*, June 2016, Issue 52, http://101.78.134.197/uploadFileMgnt/0_2016722175551.pdf.

11 Leung Kam-Chung (ed.), *Sung Tsun Middle School, Sai Kung, 70-72*, p. 86.

12 *Ibid*, p. 87.

13 "Rev. Valeriano Fraccaro", https://archives.catholic.org.hk/In%20Memoriam/Clergy-Brother/V-Fraccaro.htm, retrieved on 4 June 2020.

14 Mariagrazia Zambon, *Crimson Seeds: Eighteen PIME Martyrs* (Detroit, Mich.: PIME World Press, 1997), p. 113.

15 Ibid.

16 Ibid., pp. 113-114.

17 Ibid., pp. 114-115.

18 "Rev. Fraccaro", https://archives.catholic.org.hk/In%20Memoriam/Clergy-Brother/V-Fraccaro.htm, retrieved on 4 June 2020.

19 Mariagrazia Zambon, *Crimson Seeds*, p. 115.

20 Ibid., p. 117.

21 Ibid., p.116.

22 Ibid.

23 Ibid., p. 117.

24 Ibid., pp. 117-118.

25　Ibid., p. 117.

26　Ibid., pp. 116-117.

27　"Naked priests' arms and legs tied and killed by knife" (〈赤裸神父手腳反綁遭亂刀殺死 口腔塞毛巾 背部有刀傷 死者屍橫宿舍 浴缸水滿疑入浴前後遇害〉), *Oriental Daily News*, 30 September 1974, from "Rev. Fraccaro", https://archives.catholic.org.hk/In%20Memoriam/Clergy-Brother/V-Fraccaro.htm, retrieved on 4 June 2020.

28　Ibid.

29　"Priest found murdered in his quarters," *South China Morning Post*, 30 September 1974, as cited in "Rev. FRACCARO, Valeriano PIME", https://archives.catholic.org.hk/In%20Memoriam/Clergy-Brother/V-Fraccaro.htm, retrieved on 4 June 2020.

30　Mariagrazia Zambon, *Crimson Seeds*, p. 119.

31　"Naked priests' arms and legs tied and killed by knife" (〈赤裸神父手腳反綁遭亂刀殺死 口腔塞毛巾 背部有刀傷 死者屍橫宿舍 浴缸水滿疑入浴前後遇害〉), *Oriental Daily News*, 30 September 1974, from "Rev. Fraccaro", https://archives.catholic.org.hk/In%20Memoriam/Clergy-Brother/V-Fraccaro.htm, retrieved on 4 June 2020.

32　"Priest found murdered in his quarters". *South China Morning Post*, 30 September 1974, as cited in "Rev. FRACCARO, Valeriano PIME", https://archives.catholic.org.hk/In%20Memoriam/Clergy-Brother/V-Fraccaro.htm, retrieved on 4 June 2020.

33　"Naked priests' arms and legs tied and killed by knife" (〈赤裸神父手腳反綁遭亂刀殺死 口腔塞毛巾 背部有刀傷 死者屍橫宿舍 浴缸水滿疑入浴前後遇害〉), *Oriental Daily News*, 30 September 1974, from "Rev. Fraccaro", https://archives.catholic.org.hk/In%20Memoriam/Clergy-Brother/V-Fraccaro.htm, retrieved on 4 June 2020.

34　Mariagrazia Zambon, *Crimson Seeds*, p. 113.

35　"Naked priests' arms and legs tied and killed by knife" (〈赤裸神父手腳反綁遭亂刀殺死 口腔塞毛巾 背部有刀傷 死者屍橫宿舍 浴缸水滿疑入浴前後遇害〉), *Oriental Daily News*, 30 September 1974, from "Rev. Fraccaro", https://archives.catholic.org.hk/In%20Memoriam/Clergy-Brother/V-Fraccaro.htm, retrieved on 4 June 2020.

36　Mariagrazia Zambon, *Crimson Seeds*, p. 119.

37　"Requiem Mass for Rev. Fraccaro" (〈范賞亮神父追思彌撒 濟利祿神父講道 范鐸為信仰受殉道榮冠〉), *Kung Kao Po*, 11 October 1974, from "Rev. Fraccaro", https://archives.catholic.org.hk/In%20Memoriam/Clergy-Brother/V-Fraccaro.htm, retrieved on 4 June 2020.

38　Lung Kok Chuen et al. (eds.), *Sai Kung Sung Tsun Middle Primary School Silver Jubilee, 1924-1984* (Hong Kong: Sai Kung Sung Tsun School, 1984), p. 100.

39　"High Island Reservoir Opens, Governor inaugurates" (〈萬宜水庫啓用 港督主持揭幕〉), *Overseas Chinese Daily News*, 28 November 1978.

40　"High Island Reservoir influence village relocation solved, villagers start to move"(〈萬宜水庫影響各村安置解決 開始遷村民〉), *Overseas Chinese Daily News*, 4 October 1972.

41　"Sai Kung Sha Tsui villagers resist against High Island Reservoir construction, claiming unreasonable compensation"(〈西貢沙咀村居民阻止興建萬宜水庫工程 疑因未獲得合理補償〉), *The Kung Sheung Daily News*, 9 December 1972.

42　"Now water supply is satisfied, High Island Reservoir construction proceeding fully"(〈現目供水充足 萬宜水庫正從各方面着手進行〉), *Overseas Chinese Daily News*, 6 November 1972.

43   "High Island Reservoir contruction faces great difficulty, relocated villagers already reach consent"(〈萬宜水庫建設艱鉅 遷徙村民已獲協議〉), *Overseas Chinese Daily News*, 23 October 1974.

44   There were forty families in Li Uk's family, with one ancestral hall and one family shrine. There were 23 houses in Chou Uk, with one ancestral hall and one ancestral hall. There were two families with the surname Chan, and one ancestral hall. The number of families with the surname Man is unknown, and there was an ancestral hall and an family shrine each.

45   "Seven ancestral halls relocation affected by High Island Reservoir cost over one million, inauguration host by the authorities and local squires"(〈因建萬宜水庫遷建七間祠堂共費百餘費 全由當局負責官紳剪綵開光〉), *Overseas Chinese Daily News*, 18 December 1974.

46   Ibid.

47   Ibid.

48   In fact, Pastor Chan is not the first person to use the gospel to treat drugs in Hong Kong. As early as 1956, Pastor A. Espegren of the Norwegian Lutheran Mission Society had established Hong Kong's first evangelical drug rehabilitation centre in Tiu Keng Ling, relying on the teaching of the Bible and poetry to help drug addicts rehabilitate, and at the same time provide traditional Chinese medicine to help for drug addiction treatment. She has also used fetters to prevent drug addicts from escaping. Information from Chen Ruizhang, Zhang David, Lin Xisheng, Shao Riping: "Gospel Drug Rehabilitation in Hong Kong", Caritas Philharmonic Association, https://web.archive.org/web/20190906051046/https://www.caritaslokheepclub.org.hk/7 -2-1. html, retrieved on 5 June 2020.

49   "History of Operation Dawn", Operation Dawn, https://opdawn.org.hk/zh_hk/our_history/, retrieved on 5 June 2020.

50   Ibid.

51   Ibid.

52   Ibid.

53   According to the record of Pastor Chan, Wong Kuei is the only villager in the Long Ke village that time.

54   "History of Operation Dawn", Operation Dawn, https://opdawn.org.hk/zh_hk/our_history/, retrieved on 5 June 2020.

55   Paul Chan, *Death, Die, where is your sting?* (《死啊！你的毒鉤在那裏？》) (Hong Kong: Operation Dawn, Hong Kong, 2008), p. 18.

56   Ibid., p. 2.

57   Ibid., pp. 15-16.

58   The meeting was chaired by the Chairman of the Rural Committee Li Yeun Sau, and the participants included Wong Kuei, a representative of Long Ke Village, Tang Seng a representative of Sha Tsui Village, and the villagers involved in the incident. According to the village representative Wong Kuei, Pastor Chan did rent two village houses from him through formal channels, but when he rented them, he claimed that they were used for building a farm, and he did not say that they were used to establish a gospel drug rehabilitation village. However, according to the lease, the two village houses were leased to Pastor Chan for a period of three years, from 1968 to 1971. Therefore, the villagers could not ask Pastor Chan to leave Long Ke Village, but could only ask him to stop occupying their village houses. The information is from "The Villagers' Complaints against the Rural Affairs Committee in a Village House Dispute in Sai Kung Long Ke Village", *Overseas Chinese Daily News*, 11 December 1969.

59   "History of Operation Dawn", Operation Dawn, https://opdawn.org.hk/zh_hk/our_history/, retrieved on 5 June 2020.

60   Ibid.

61   "Long Ke Healthy Village Drug Rehabilitation Association Received Grant from Kadoorie Agricultural Association yesterday", *Overseas Chinese Daily News*, 20 October 1970.

62   "Long Ke Drug Rehabilitation Centre Receives Three Dairy Cows from the Kadoorie Society", *Overseas Chinese Daily News*, 25 April 1971.

63   "Long Ke Gospel Drug Rehabilitation Centre Receives Grant from Y's Men's Club of Kowloon, *Overseas Chinese Daily News*, 13 May 1971.

64   "Long Ke Bay Drug Rehabilitation Village was opened on Monday, Peter Li Chien Ming-nin host the ceremony", *Overseas Chinese Daily News*, 17 April 1981.

65   The Edict of the Ecumenical Document of the Second Vatican Council: "The cooperation among all Christians vividly demonstrates their existing connections, and it also more clearly reveals the face of Christ as a servant... through this cooperation, all people who believe in Christ can understand and respect each other more deeply, and pave the way for the unity of Christians.", https://www.vatican.va/chinese/concilio/vat-ii_unitatis-redintegratio_zh -t.pdf, retrieved on 5 June 2020. (The decree of the Second Vatican Ecumenical Council "Ecumenism")

1841

1874

1931

1945

1969

1981

2000

Chapter 7
Pilgrimage and Conservation Period
(1981-2000)

In 1981, Sai Kung Sacred Heart Church celebrated its centenary, and for the first time the history of Sai Kung missionaries was addressed under the name of the parish. Books were published and historical photos were compiled, including anecdotes about Rev. Fraccaro and Rev. Lambertoni, such as their services for the fishermen community, dealing with the government and contacting the rural committee etc. These were all pieces of preaching life outside the parish remit, reminded people of the missionaries' deeds and the hopes for continuing the missionary passion.

In the early 1980s, the priests from the Immaculate Heart of Mary Church, Tai Po, visited various chapels to conduct special Masses. However, for most of the rest of time, the chapels in Sai Kung Peninsula were abandoned. The Catholic Scout Guild was entrusted by the Catholic Diocese of Hong Kong to manage the chapels located in Pak Tam Chung, Wong Mo Ying, and Pak Sha O, for scout training or holiday camps. Until the end of the 1990s, there were also individual enthusiasts, villagers or priests taking care of the old chapels. The sacred place becames a place of pilgrimage and spiritual gathering. In the millennium, St. Joseph's Chapel in Yim Tin Tsz was rebuilt, which once again aroused the interest of the parishioners in these historical chapels. Some parishes organised pilgrims to visit the chapels, re-experiencing the footprints of missionaries, and savoring rural life.

The 1980s was the beginning of Hong Kong's future problems. In 1984, China and Britain signed the *Sino-British Joint Declaration*, which formally agreed that Hong Kong would return to China on 1 July 1997. In addition, as urban construction and transportation became more developed and convenient, and Hong Kong's industrial development was becoming more and more prosperous, more and more villagers choose to emigrate to the urban areas or even to other countries, in order to seek better work and life quality, resulting in a sparse population of villagers in the New Territories. The villages that were once prosperous in the past were now empty, and the sacred place that filled with liveliness was now overgrown with weeds and left abandoned. Fortunately, some of the abandoned chapels were restored and functioned again with the support and promotion of enthusiastic church members.

The Catholic Scout Guild and Rehabilitation of the Church

In the early 1970s, under the leadership of the captain, a group of Catholic scouts were looking for camping places in Sai Kung, and in the meantime they found some abandoned chapels. They expressed their pity over the situation when they saw these chapels were overgrown with weeds and left unattended. On Easter 1974, The Catholic Scout Guild invited Rev. Fraccaro to preside over a spiritual meeting. Rev. Fraccaro shook his head and sighed during the homily, lamenting that many chapels in the countryside were in great need of repair and renovation, but no one would face this problem squarely and took action. The Catholic Scouts, who originally felt pity for the abandoned chapels in Sai Kung, started discussions after hearing Rev. Fraccaro's sigh, and came up with some plans for the restoration and revitalisation of these abandoned chapels. The Catholic Scout Guild submitted a letter to the Diocesan Procuration of the Catholic Diocese of Hong Kong in 1974, suggesting that these abandoned chapels should be rebuilt and used for other purposes in the Diocese, such as scout camps and retreats. In the end, their proposal was accepted by the Diocese. Three of those abandoned chapels were restored and converted to be the Catholic Scout Training Centre. They are the Rosary Mission Centre, Wong Mo Ying, Our Lady of the Seven Sorrows Chapel, Pak Tam Chung and Immaculate Heart of Mary Chapel, Pak Sha O.[1]

Wong Mo Ying Rosary Chapel

Since the 1960s, some of Wong Mo Ying's villagers have immigrated to the United Kingdom, while most of the rest who stayed in Wong Mo Ying would rather go to the Sacred Heart Church in Sai Kung to participate in Mass, and fewer and fewer Catholics went to the Rosary Chapel. From 1971 to 1974, Rev. Michele Pagani (PIME, 1920-2012) and some of the altar boys of the Cathedral would go to Wong Mo Ying to conduct Masses every Sunday.[2] Due to disrepair, the roof of the chapel was damaged, but no immediate repairs were made. During that time, the priest would still hold Masses for the villagers in the damaged chapel or the watch tower of the building. By

The activities conducted by Catholic Scouts in Wong Mo Ying Chapel. (Image Source: Paul Li)

the end of the 1970s, most of the parishioners in the village had moved out, the chapel was then abandoned.

Later, with the approval and support of the Diocese, the Scout leader of St. Vincent's Church, Wong Tai Sin decided to pay out of his own pocket and donate money to repair the chapel. The project started in 1976. In the following year, the chapel was rebuilt and became the activity and training centre of the Wong Tai Sin Scout 117 Brigade.[3] The opening ceremony of the centre was presided over by Vicar General Gabriel Lam, who was in charge of Catholic Scouts, and two priests from St. Vincent's Church, Wong Tai Sin and Sacred Heart Church, Sai Kung, as well as village representatives from Wong Mo Ying Village.

In 1983, the chapel became the Pioneer Engineering Centre of the Catholic Scout Guild, and received funding from Sir David Trench Fund Committee to purchase pioneer engineering supplies, such as long bamboos and ropes for the Catholic scouts to build facilities such as "monkey bridge", observation towers, and air corridors. In 2001, the Scouts of St. Vincent's Church again funded the repairment of the dilapidated chapel. However, due to the location of the Wong Mo Ying Activity Centre was relatively close to residential buildings, the Catholic Scout Guild has held fewer activities there since the millennium.[4]

In 2013, the Antiquities Advisory Board listed the Rosary Chapel as a Grade II historical building and affirmed its historical value. In 2019, the Catholic Scout Guild returned the chapel to the Diocese. The "Following Thy Way" working group is now planning to use the chapel to set up a memorial hall with the theme of Sai Kung chapels' history to promote the Catholic faith and Hakka culture to the general public.

Our Lady of the Seven Sorrows Chapel of Pak Tam Chung

Another chapel managed by the Catholic Scout Guild in 1980s was the Our Lady of the Seven Sorrows Chapel. In the 1950s, due to the destruction of the lime and brick kilns during the Japanese occupation, the establishment of Green Island Cement Co., Ltd. and the advancement of brick-making technology, the kiln industry of Sheung Yiu gradually declined, and the villagers could not make a living from it. They went out to work in the urban area of Kowloon or Hong Kong Island,[5] or even immigrated to a foreign country, leaving only a few villagers behind. The priests still visited several times a year to preach these villagers, and performed sacraments. According to the village representative, the priest would stay overnight in Sheung Yiu Village the night before in order to celebrate Mass in the next morning. Before the 1960s, if villagers from "Luk Heung" (literally means six villages, and it is a kind of territorial alliance formed by a number of villages) wanted to go out, they could choose to take the "Yung Pak Corridor" (the ancient road from Yung Shue O to Pak Tam Chung) to the shore of Kei Ling Ha where situated at the inner bay of Three Fathoms Cove, then take a boat to Tai Po. Villagers also could go to the jetty near Sheung Yiu, and took a wooden boat to Sai Kung Market. According to the village representative of Pak Tam Chung, his family used to build a house made with blue bricks at the entrance of "Yung Pak Corridor". It was located in a lush forest. In addition to living, it also operated a grocery store and even a village school. A covered corridor was opened in the living room of the house as a public passage for villagers in Sai Kung to pass through and to the "Yung Pak Corridor". The villagers would also shelter from the rain, took a rest and chatted in this passage, so it was named the "passing corridor".[6]

In the 1970s, Our Lady of the Seven Sorrows Chapel gradually stopped holding

Mr Paul Li, the leader of the 117th Scout Brigade posed in front of the Wong Mo Ying Rosary Chapel. (Image source: Paul Li)

The current interior of Wong Mo Ying Rosary Chapel. (Image source: Paul Li)

The main entrance of the Rosary Chapel today.

Masses. In 1979, the Diocese allocated funds for the Catholic Scout Guild to repair the chapel, the abandoned chapel was then restored to the original style of fusion of Hakka and Western architecture. The chapel was later used as a water sports centre for the scouts and continued to serve the community in other ways.

Similar to Pak Sha O, in Sheung Yiu, the Catholic faith and Hakka village life met and merged with each other. Architecturally, the Catholic chapel was hidden in a Hakka house, so its appearance was no different from an ordinary Hakka village house. Our Lady of the Seven Sorrows Chapel, which was located by the sea, was built on a high platform to prevent flooding, reflecting the Hakka people's architectural wisdom in response to the geographical situation. The chapel retains the structure of the Hakka village house and was converted into a church. In addition to the Hakka "hard mountain" style tile roof, the front door and the most upper part of the wall had a Spanish architectural style and was also similar to the roof of the Hakka door. The open area in front of the chapel was once used as a drying place for the Hakka people. With the addition of the door and western decoration inside, it forms a unique architectural style of Chinese and Western fusion.

In addition to the architectural style, an example that truly shows that the chapel was connected to the villagers was the cultural and spiritual life of the villagers in Sheung Yiu. When the villagers in Wong Nai Chau of Pak Tam Chung, and Sheung Yiu expressed their willingness to become the church members, they had to abandon the traditional religious beliefs in the past and participate in the rituals of Catholicism, such as giving up worshiping their ancestors, Tai Wong Yeh, Earth God and other popular deities. According to the memories of the elderly villagers in Wong Keng Tei, Pak Tam Chung celebrated the birthday of the Earth God twice a year, and each village in "Luk Heung" would send a villager to preside over the ceremonies of the birthday of the Earth God. Since the elders of Sheung Yiu Village were Catholics, they did not participate in this ceremony. At the same time, they also retained the traditional wedding customs such as wedding songs and other customary practice or rituals. The bridegroom's family conduct *qilin* dance while carrying the sedan chair to welcome the bride. At birthdays and wedding banquets, they would hold the feasts for three consecutive days and nights with the "six great dishes" together. On the other hand, Catholic priests also incorporated some Chinese traditions when performing ceremonies, such as celebrating Mass near Annual New Year Festival, and participating in the feast together with villagers outside chapel after the end of mass in feast days.

These all reflected the coexistence of Chinese tradition and Western Catholicism in an eclectic way, forming the unique community culture of the Hakka people.

The Leisure and Cultural Services Department has turned the abandoned Sheung Yiu Village into a folk museum, which displays various farming tools and rural furniture, hoping to show the public the Hakka rural life. This building has been listed as a monument, proving the long history of Sheung Yiu Village. However, the museum failed to fully display the appearance of the ancient village: the conversion of the village to Catholicism. If you want to understand Sheung Yiu more, studying its religious life is as important as farming activities. Not far from the museum, Our Lady of the Seven Sorrows Chapel reveals this little-known past and enriches the history of this Hakka village.

Following the completion of the restoration of the Wong Mo Ying Rosary Chapel, Our Lady of the Seven Sorrows Chapel in Pak Tam Chung also received Diocese funding for repair in 1979, and after the completion of the project, it was managed by the Catholic Scout Guild for the establishment of a water sports centre. The fund from the Sir David Trench Fund for Recreation sponsored the purchase of equipment such as

The folk museum has been established from the Hakka houses in Sheung Yiu in 1990s. (Image Source: Yuen Chi Wai)

The statue of Our Lady outside Our Lady of the Seven Sorrows Chapel today.

A bird's eye shot of Our Lady of the Seven Sorrows Chapel nowadays. | The Holy Cross and the picture of Our Lady in Our Lady of the Seven Sorrows Chapel today.

boats, canoes and motor boats for this sports centre in the next year.[7]

At present, the chapel was not only a water sports centre for Catholic Scouts, but also a place for pilgrims and public outings. At the same time, the public can also visit the Sheung Yiu Folk Museum and lime kiln near the chapel to learn about the Hakka architecture and lifestyle, as well as the history of the introduction of Catholicism to Pak Tam Chung.

Immaculate Heart of Mary Chapel of Pak Sha O

Immaculate Heart of Mary Chapel of Pak Sha O is the witness of the Catholic mission in Sai Kung in the early days of Hong Kong. In addition to the reflection of the village change before the lease of New Territories, Pak Sha O has also been a very important Catholic village. The Hakka people abandoned their traditional ancestor worship customs and other folk beliefs, and replaced the ancestral halls with churches which shouldered their traditional functions.

Before the 1980s, the highway from Sai Kung to Hoi Ha (Hoi Ha Road) had not existed. The external traffic of Pak Sha O must take the mountain path to Lai Chi Chong, and then from the waterway through the Tolo Strait and Tolo Harbour to the Tai Po Market. Since the old village's external traffic relied on the Tolo Harbour and Chek Mun Strait ferry to and from Tai Po Market, it was classified as a village of Sai Kung North in Tai Po District according to the division of administrative district of the Hong Kong government. From 1980 to 1998, Pak Sha O chapel still belonged to the Immaculate Heart of Mary Parish. Pak Sha O Village was surrounded by rivers and streams that flow into Hoi Ha Wan. The lowland at the north of the village was used as farmland. The rivers and streams beside it are favorable for farming and irrigation. The east, west and south of the village has mountains as barriers, making it an ideal place for farming. In 1980, Pak Sha O Village was nearly abandoned. The population of the village was only about 50 people. Only a few of the 17 houses in the village were still inhabited.[8]

The Immaculate Heart of Mary Chapel in Pak Sha O has ceased to be used in the 1970s, and no Sunday Mass was held by then.[9] Therefore, the inner part of the chapel has not been changed with the reform announced by the Second Ecumenical Council of the Vatican, and the traditional style of the past has been preserved.[10]

In 1980, the Diocese of Hong Kong agreed to fund the renovation of Immaculate Heart of Mary Chapel in Pak Sha O at a cost of about HK$180,000. After the renovation of the church was completed, it was handed over to the Catholic Scout Guild in March 1982, and the opening ceremony took place on 1 July of the same year. The chapel originally had an area of 638 square meters, but after the reconstruction, it was divided into various parts: the chapel, dormitories, kitchens, toilets and bathrooms. In addition, the chapel, like the two previous chapels that were converted into Scout Activity Centres, have also received funding from the David Trench Fund to purchase camping equipment.[11] At present, the chapel and activity centre can be used for camping, vacation, retreat, prayer and other activities. At the same time, it will also be used to arrange pilgrimage excursions for scouts and girl guides, parishes, associations and the public, and leading them to visit the chapels in the area of Sai Kung.[12]

On 13 March 2016, the Catholic Scout Guild held a Mass in the chapel to celebrate the 135th anniversary of the establishment of the Pak Sha O Chapel. The Mass was presided over by Cardinal Joseph Zen, and priests of the PIME, who used to dominate the evangelization work in Sai Kung, also attended the Mass. Although the weather was very cold that day, there were as many as 300 people attending the Mass, including dozens of scouts from the East Kowloon District. Due to insufficient seats in the chapel, some parishioners even stood or sat on the lawn outside the chapel, which shows their religious enthusiasm. After the Mass, the Catholic Scout Guild planted an olive tree in front of the Virgin of Mary Shrine outside the chapel, as a memorial to the patriarchs of Pak Sha O's mission. It also means that the Guild was willing to follow the example of the missionaries and hold out olive branches to people, and welcome them to pray and make a pilgrimage to the Pak Sha O Chapel.

It seemed that the three chapels which had already entered the dying year, became full of vitality again, due to the energetic Catholic Scouts Guild. Thanks to the efforts of the scouts and the Diocese, the three long-standing chapels have been properly preserved to this day.

The Immaculate Heart of Mary Chapel in Pak Sha O in the 1970s.

The Immaculate Heart of Mary Chapel nowadays in Pak Sha O. (Image source: Yuen Chi Wai)

Chapel Renovation: From Catholic School, Camp to Pilgrimage Site

Other chapels in the Sai Kung Peninsula, such as Epiphany of Our Lord Chapel in Sham Chung, Holy Family Chapel in Chek Keng, and Immaculate Conception Chapel in Tai Long, have also become gradually dilapidated due to the fact that most Catholics have moved to urban areas or foreign countries. They were deserted and the priests serving the district would only visit these chapels irregularly.

From 1962 to 1987, Rev. Narciso Santinon (PIME, 1916-1995) was the parish priest of the Immaculate Heart of Mary Church in Tai Po Market (then also known as the "Catholic Church in Tai Po Market", established in 1922 and rebuilt in 1961), and was also responsible for the management of four chapels (abandoned nowadays) in Sai Kung North, including: Cheung Sheung Mission Centre, Kow Low Wan Mission Centre, Our Lady Mediatrix of All Graces Chapel in Shiu Tong New Village, and Sacred Heart of Jesus Chapel in Ping Chau Tai Tong Village.[13] Therefore, Rev. Santinon has also visited these chapels. According to the memories of the Catholics of the Cheung Sheung Mass Centre, at that time, Rev. Santinon would go ashore from Sham Chung Pier. He would first visited Sham Chung Village, and then walked through Yung Shue O Village to climb up the stone steps commonly known as "Sky Ladder" to reach Cheung Sheung on the mountain plateau. The handbag he carried contained ritual utensils and vestments for Mass celebrations.[14] According to the villagers, in the 1970s, although there were only a few parishioners left, the priest still insisted on coming to the chapel once a week to celebrate Mass and had meals with them, which influenced them a lot.

There were about 248 parishioners in Chek Keng in 1959. Until the 1960s, there were still many residents in the village. During the Lunar New Year, it was still seen that every household posted couplets on their front doors. The content was related to Catholic teachings and Bible chapters. In view of the increasing population and the large number of school-age children, lack of the whole village school building and the primary school opened only in the lower floor of Chek Keng Chapel's priest dormitory, causing insufficient place for school-age children to study, the parish specially applied to Tai Po District Office to allocate more than 22,000 square feet of land on the hillside adjacent to the chapel for the expansion of four new classrooms and a small playground. The school was called "Ming Sun School".[15] It was originally a room on the lower

The chapels which belonged to the Immaculate Heart of Mary Church of Tai Po listed in the *Catholic Directory* in the 1960s.

floor of the priest's dormitory, with a table tennis room and a kitchen (canteen). Chek Keng Village had indigenous villagers and Ming Sun's headmaster was originally the indigenous people. After he retired, the post was taken over by a teacher from outside the village, who was Woo Chun Hoi.[16] The teacher and villager's children became very close. They farmed, chatted, played and even lived together, but the teacher also had requirements for the students: every student needed to recite five Tang poetries every semester. Therefore, they could memorise 60 poems by the time of graduation at the sixth year of school. If they failed to memorise them, the headmaster would not allow graduation and grant of the certificate. At that time, there was still no electricity and running water in the village, so the principal had to climb the mountain to carry firewood and fetch water. When students knew that he had no firewood, they would climb the mountain to help and cut vegetables for him to eat. The villagers sometimes even asked him to go to their house and use a large wooden barrel with hot water to bath. Even during the "1967 Riots", the relationship between teachers and students was not adversely affected.

At the time of the riot, whole village was covered with big-character posters. (Villagers) All believe in Catholicism, but 99% of them have leftist ideology, supporting the Communist Party, but not the Hong Kong government. The content of the poster was against British imperialism and semi-colonies. My school was on the hillslope, but my chapel and school were not posted with any posters. When I returned to school, I guessed the chapel should have been posted with all the posters. But I did find those posters up until the intersection of road as the upper part was within the scope of the church, and as the land belonged to the church. So I think it's weird. Why was so quiet without any posters on the above? It's found that the village representative was a reasonable guy.

However, by the 1990s, almost all the villagers in Chek Keng had moved away. Only three villagers still lived in the village. As the village became sparsely populated, the chapel became abandoned.[17] By the end of the 20th century, the chapel was not only overwhelmed by monkeys, but also damaged by the problem of illegal immigrants, and part of the roof collapsed. In May 2001, Mr. Chan Kwok On ("Ah Kok"), a resident of Tai Long Village, was responsible for repairing the chapel at a cost of HK$88,000.[18]

As for the Immaculate Conception Chapel in Tai Long, it was deactivated and became abandoned with moving out of the villagers.[19] Since the 1950s, Tai Long Wan had the highest population of 600 to 700 people. Rev. Lau Wing-Yiu Paul (1908-1986) and Rev. Paul Tsang Chi-Kwong were in charge of the Tai Long District. At first, Rev. Lau stayed in the priest dormitory of the Holy Family Chapel in Chek Keng. Later,

The New Year couplet on the portal of Tai Long Village, reflecting the fusion of Western religion and Chinese tradition.

Tan Ka Wan Sung Ming School still has a "Catholic Clubhouse" plaque.

Rev. Lau was transferred and Rev. Paul Tsang served in the church. He was living in the dormitory of Chek Keng Chapel. Sometimes he would go to Tai Long to live in the dormitory prepared by the faithful.[20] In 1979, the super typhoon "Hobe" struck Hong Kong, causing the clock tower of the chapel collapsed. The former village representative then tried to raise funds from the immigrant villagers of Tai Long Village in the UK. Unfortunately, it was not enough to cover the cost of reconstruction. The Diocese finally agreed to pay for part of the construction cost. The clock tower was demolished that year because it had fallen into disrepair. In 1981, Bishop John Wu came to Tai Long to preside over the opening ceremony of the reconstructed chapel. Since Catholic youths were in desperate need of an outdoor activity venue at that time, it was suggested that Tai Po assistant parish priest Rev. Paul Wan Yee Tseng should convert the abandoned rural chapel into a camp.[21] All the chapels in Tai Long, Chek Keng, and Sham Chung, as well as the old school sites attached to them, were converted into Catholic camps, while the Sung Ming school attached to St. Peter's Chapel in Tan Ka Wan was named "Catholic Clubhouse". The villages in which these chapels situated were reduced to less than 14 people resided in 1996. Fortunately, Rev. Wan was commissioned by Cardinal John Wu to visit these remote chapels at least once or twice a week. Tai Long, Chek Keng, Tan Ka Wan, Tung Ping Chau, Lai Chi Chong, Sham Chung and other places have been revitalised into Catholic camps then. Therefore, these ancient chapels could be renewed as ideal places for the parishioners to pray and conduct spiritual retreat together.[22] In the era of inconvenient transportation at that time, Rev. Wan's enthusiasm was indeed commendable, and this enthusiasm even affected many parishioners, and even non-Catholic believers.

Mr. Chan Kwok On, a retired resident living in Tai Long Village in 1997, used to see Rev. Wan, who was in charge of managing these chapels, took a ferry from Tai Po Kau to Chek Keng every week. Rev. Wan was also responsible for carrying the supplies on a forty-five minutes' walk to reach the Tai Long Village via Tai Long Gap. Chan Kwok On recalled:

> "He (Rev. Wan) often cleared the weeds in the chapel, and he and the parishioners even had carried three air-conditioners up the mountain. The villagers had a good relationship with Rev. Wan and often cooked for the priest, but the priest insisted on paying after meals and unwilling to let the villagers to spend. "

Chan Kwok On was deeply moved by Rev. Wan's serious attitude, so when he passed the nearby Chek Keng Holy Family Chapel one day, he couldn't bear to see that the main entrance of the chapel had been destroyed by the strong wind. Therefore, even if he was not a member of the church, he still took effort in repairing the chapel at his own expense, after he got the permission of the Immaculate Heart of Mary Church in Tai Po. After 70 days, the damaged part of the Holy Family Chapel was repaired. Afterwards, Rev. Wan invited him to continue to maintain the chapel. He then moved from Tai Long to the priest's dormitory of the chapel and has been living there for more than ten years. Although he has always believed that he should be baptised until he fully understands the grace of God, but under the guidance of the priest, he was actually no different from a Christian believer. In 2018, he unintentionally entered St. Joseph's Church in Kowloon Bay, where he met Rev. Wan, who he has not seen for many years, as the parish priest of the church. Later, he joined the church choir to serve the parish.[23]

After Rev. Wan took over these ancient chapels in Tai Long District and gradually developed into camps for retreat, to a large extent, the chapel was prevented from being reclaimed by the authorities on the grounds of being vacant. Thanks to their efforts, it has become a pilgrimage attraction for more people. Although Rev. Wan was transferred from the Tai Po parish to St. Joseph's Church in Kowloon Bay in 1997, the tradition of serving and retreating in remote chapels continues. Around 2010, Rev. Bonalumi Luigi (PIME) started to serve as the parish priest of the Immaculate Heart of Mary Church of Tai Po. Every year on the third day of the Lunar New Year, he would travel

The plaque of the "Catholic Camp" can still be seen in the Holy Family Chapel in Chek Keng.

to Tai Long with parishioners to celebrate Mass, so that more people would know about these chapels. Rev. Raja Duggimpudi (PIME), who took up the post of assistant parish priest of the Tai Po church in 2008, had also led the parishioners on a pilgrimage to the two chapels of Chek Keng and Tai Long. They even visited Chan Kwok On and the villagers, cleared weeds and cleaned the chapels, etc.[24] The villagers of Tai Long are

The old Tai Long Yuk Ying School: Bishop Bianchi visited Sai Kung in 1960 during his pastoral visit, and held the consecration when the reconstruction project was completed.

Bishop Bianchi was presented with salt-fish made by a parishioner. (Image source: Sai Kung Sacred Heart Church)

The parishioners followed Rev. Raja Duggimpudi to visit the Tai Long Immaculate Conception Chapel on a pilgrimage. (photo taken in 2018)

now introducing the history of Tai Long and there is a guide map of the chapel at the entrance of the village, so that visitors can better understand the relationship between the village and their beliefs.

As for the chapels along the coast of the Sai Kung Hoi, including Sha Tsui (which has sunk under the water), Sai Wan and Long Ke, in the past, priests used to go to these chapels mainly on foot and by boat. Before the construction of the High Island Reservoir, one of the ways to get to Sai Wan and Long Ke was to take a boat to Shui Keng Pier, and then walked ashore to Sha Tsui, Sai Wan and Long Ke (due to too strong wind and waves, it was rare to take a boat to Sai Wan and Long Ke). In the 1970s, with the construction of the High Island Reservoir, there was a road leading to the Man Yee Wan (formerly known as the "Lan Nai Wan"), and the traffic in and out of Sai Wan was more convenient than before. However, as the Kwun Mun Channel has converted into the High Island Reservoir, the original waterway leading to Long Ke and Sai Wan was blocked, and social and rural life began to transform. By the late 1970s, as the United Kingdom planned to tighten immigration laws, a large number of indigenous residents of the New Territories migrated to the United Kingdom. Many villagers in Sai Wan also migrated to the United Kingdom to make a living, and the population of the villagers has constantly decreased. Only a few female villagers remained behind, and the village was gradually abandoned. As the number of church members was dwindling, priests have also begun to reduce their visit to Sai Wan. By the end of the 1980s, the number of villagers was no more than ten, and there were only two students left. However, the priests of the Sacred Heart Church in Sai Kung still insisted on going to Sai Wan to celebrate Mass and visit the villagers once a month. In 1990, the chapel was renamed "Star of the Sea Mass Centre". According to the members of the Sai Kung parish, although there has not been a regular Mass since then, before 1997, Rev. Nevio Viganò (PIME) would also bring a group of altar boys to the Sai Wan Chapel to take care of the church every year.

Rehabilitation of St. Joseph's Chapel: the Conservation Road of Sai Kung Chapels

Like other villages in Sai Kung, the villagers of Yim Tin Tsai (now named "Yim Tin Tsz") gradually moved to the urban area or immigrated to the UK in the 1960s. The population of the island was declining. In 1997, the last resident moved out of the island, and Yim Tin Tsai officially then became an abandoned village. After more than ten years of desolation, the place where the villagers used to live had become forested, and many of the paths were also covered with weeds.[25]

Even though the island has long been uninhabited, Mr Colin Chan Chung Yin, the village representative of Yim Tin Tsai, took a boat from Sai Kung to Yim Tin Tsai almost every morning to clear the roads and repair the dilapidated village houses, hoping that this beautiful living environment can be preserved and will not be completely ruined.[26] His efforts alone may not have much effect, but things were so amazing that the core building on the island, St. Joseph's Chapel, made this abandoned island alive again.

St. Joseph's Chapel Restoration Project

Although Yim Tin Tsai has become a deserted village, every time when the feast day of St. Joseph's Chapel (St. Joseph Feast Day) was being held, villagers who have moved to the city or even immigrated to the UK would return to this small island to celebrate this important annual celebration.[27]

However, due to long-term lack of maintenance and care, the chapel gradually became dilapidated. The glass windows of the church were all broken, the walls were peeling and even water seeped, and the roof was broken to allow light to pass through, and weeds were overgrown. For safety reasons, the priest of the Sai Kung parish proposed in 2003 to cancel the annual Mass in St. Joseph's Chapel and instead conducted it in the Sai Kung Sacred Heart Church. However, this suggestion caused dissatisfaction among the villagers. Village representative Colin Chan wrote to Cardinal John Wu, Bishop of Hong Kong at the time, expressing his opposition to stopping Mass in Yim Tin Tsai. In view of this, Cardinal Wu appointed Rev. Dominic Chan Chi-Ming, who was also a indigenous villager of Yim Tin Tsai (then the Vicar General of the Diocese of Hong Kong) to deal with this issue. Rev. Chan suggested that he should be responsible for holding Mass for the villagers, but the premise was that the church must be restored to ensure the safety of everyone; at this time, another enthusiastic church member donated a sum of money to the Diocese, which could be used as a restoration project funds. Therefore, the restoration work of St. Joseph's Chapel officially started at the end of 2003. At that time, the architect Ann Kwong, who was in charge of the architectural development affairs of the Diocese, was appointed by Cardinal Joseph Zen as the supervisor of the project.[28]

As there was no building plan for the chapel, for the architectural details, the architect could only restore the original appearance of the church as much as possible, based on speculation. After the team's hard work, the restoration project was successfully completed on time in May 2004, and the villagers of Yim Tin Tsai were able to celebrate the Feast Day of that year as scheduled in the restored church.[29]

The dilapidated church has been renovated. In 2005, it won the Award of Merit of UNESCO Asia-Pacific Heritage Awards for Culture Heritage Conservation, the place was then recognised by international authorities, and attracted more tourists to visit Yim Tin Tsai.[30] This restoration project was indeed of special significance to the offshore village of Yim Tin Tsai, Sai Kung, and it was also an important milestone on the road of preservation of the Hong Kong churches.

The completion of the church restoration project did not mark the end of the conservation project. For the church and the villagers, there were still problems that needed to be considered and solved: the restored church needed to be maintained and taken care of on a regular basis, but who would undertake this work on this island? In addition, since the island was uninhabited, wouldn't it be a pity that the church was only used during St. Joseph's feast day? These problems prompted the villagers to reflect more on the current situation of the small island of Yim Tin Tsai, and at the same time gradually began to explore more possibilities.

The Yim Tin Tsai St. Joseph's Chapel Development Committee, with Rev. Dominic Chan as the convener, met every three months in Sai Kung Sacred Heart Church to discuss matters related to the work and development of Yim Tin Tsai. At first, everyone only concerned about the restoration work of St. Joseph's Chapel. Later, a plan to preserve and revitalise Yim Tin Tsai was gradually derived. The council formulated the Conservation and Revitalisation plan into four directions, namely religion, environment, culture and tourism, and considered various possibilities for the conservation of Yim Tin Tsai based on these four dimensions.[31]

Salt and Light Conservation Centre and Conservation of the Salt Field

As the restored St. Joseph's Chapel has attracted more people to visit and make pilgrimages after winning the prize, the village committee gradually felt pressure to receive tourists, and at the same time felt that it was difficult to undertake cultural restoration work on its own. They would prefer set up a fund, hoping to handle tourist affairs and future conservation work in a more organised manner. However, because the village committee was not legal entity, it was necessary for them to establish an independent statutory organization. They applied to the government in 2010 and obtained the qualification of being a charitable organization the following year and became a registered non-profit limited company. This newly established institution was renamed "Salt and Light Conservation Centre", and Mr. Nicholas Chan Tsz Leung, secretary of the village committee of Yim Tin Tsai Village, served as the chairman of the board of directors of the centre, and was responsible for leading the members to promote the conservation of Yim Tin Tsai. The name "Salt and Light" not only highlights its status as a conservation organisation for Yim Tin Tsai, but also reflects the common beliefs of the villagers in Yim Tin Tsai, expressing their response to the call of Christ and becoming "the salt on the earth, the light of the world" vision.[32]

Yim Tin Tsai, as the name suggests, is a salt-producing village. For Yim Tin Tsai, the production of salt can be said to be her unique mark. However, the original salt pans were deserted as early as the beginning of the 20th century, and no more salt was produced after the war. Today's villagers have never seen the old salt pans, nor do they know how their ancestors produced salt.[33] Nicholas Chan believed that in order to preserve Yim Tin Tsai, the first task is to make this village a salt-producing place again, and re-emerge the "salt flavor" of the past.[34] Therefore, the first job after the establishment of the Salt and Light Conservation Centre was to rehabilitate the salt field, which has been abandoned for many years.

In November 2011, Nicholas Chan and Salt Field Engineering Volunteer Consultant Rev. Deacon Faustus Lam led a group of construction contractors who were interested in participating in the salt field rehabilitation project to conduct a pre-bid site-visit to Yim Tin Tsai and explain to them the content of the plan. At first, the working group had only three million donated by enthusiasts as the funding for the project, but the bid price exceeded their expectations, which was about 23 to 200 million. This huge amount urged the working group to re-develop the content and scale of the plan in order to arrive at a lower-cost rehabilitation program. In addition, due to lack of experience and professional advice, the working group originally led by the villagers encountered many difficult problems in the process of implementing the plan. Therefore, the Diocese needed to coordinate and provide support.[35]

With the assistance of experts and volunteers, the Salt Field Rehabilitation Plan was ready to restart in August 2012. Anna Kwong, the architect who planned the restoration of St. Joseph's Chapel in the past, was invited to serve as a consultant for the restoration project and supervise the progress of the project. Based on financial considerations, the meeting decided to carry out the project in phases. It was hoped that the preliminary results of the project could encourage people to make further donations, and finally the entire restoration plan could be completed. In November of the same year, Anna Kwong led contractors interested in bidding to inspect the environment and then proceeded with the bidding work.[36] In March 2013, the ground-breaking ceremony of the salt field project was officially held, and the long-prepared restoration project finally started.[37]

In order to have a better understanding of the process of salt production and the details of formulating the restoration project, the engineering team went to the salt field in Shan Wei, Guangdong in April 2013 for a site-visit to learn more about their salt production methods.[38] For the rehabilitation team, the control of project expenditure was certainly the primary consideration, but the protection of mangroves and surrounding living creatures was also an important consideration. In formulating the details of the plan, the team tried to preserve the original ecological environment of the construction site, in order to strike a balance between function and environmental protection.[39] In addition, the geographical environment of Yim Tin Tsai has also increased the difficulty of the project: all construction equipment and materials needed to be transported to the island by boat, and the engineering team also needed to clear some trees and open a passage before the project could start.[40]

As the construction started off during summer, heavy rain made it difficult for workers to construct. Although the progress of the project was repeatedly delayed due to this, with the hard work of the team, the restoration project was finally completed in April 2014 and entered the acceptance process. On May 4th of the same year, Rev. Chan held a blessing ceremony for the newly restored salt field before St. Joseph Feast Day Mass, and he was pleased to present all the villagers and parishioners the work of the restoration team over the past few months.[41]

In May 2014, the salt field officially started operations and successfully produced the first batch of salt six months later. In September 2015, it won the Award of Excellence of UNESCO Asia-Pacific Heritage Awards for Culture Heritage Conservation.[42] Until now, Yim Tin Tsai still holds salt production workshops so that

St. Joseph's Chapel, Yim Tin Tsai after restoration. (Image source: Sai Kung Sacred Heart Church)

Old village house in Yim Tin Tsai.

the public can understand the process of salt production, and at the same time take part in salt production. However, for safety reasons, all salt produced will not be used for cooking, but will only be sold as souvenirs.[43]

St. Josef Freinademetz's Path to Canonisation

"The Path to Canonisation of Saint Joseph Freinademetz" was another spiritual project mainly coordinated by the church. It aimed to commemorate St. Josef Freinademetz, SVD, who had stayed in Yim Tin Tsai for preaching, and encourages the faithful to imitate him without fear of hardship and selflessness as an example of dedication.

Immediately after the Salt Field rehabilitation project entered the final stage, the construction of "The Footstep of a Saint" began, and the contractor in charge of the salt field project also undertook the project at the same time.[44] The engineering team cleared and restored the site of the old church of Yim Tin Tsai (also the former residence of St. Josef Freinademetz in Yim Tin Tsai), and kept the original appearance of the building as much as possible. The designer installed a Holy Cross made of steel on the stone wall on the site, and erected a statue of St. Joseph, carved from bluestone, for pilgrims to admire. In addition, on the road from the entrance to the ruins of the old church, there were also exhibition boards describing the life of the Saint, and at the same time as if following him on this path to God.

As a missionary who travelled from Austria to China to preach, St. Josef Freinademetz believes that love can overcome language barriers and touch the hearts of others. Because of this love for God and the Chinese, he worked tirelessly to preach and serve in China, and finally died of contracting typhoid fever.

An Episode of the Road to Canonisation Project: Unearthed Pottery Pieces in the Han Dynasty

During the construction of the "Road to Canonisation", a team of archaeological staff funded by the Hong Kong Archaeological Society entered the site and started excavations at the site of the old chapel. In fact, their purpose was only to confirm whether there are prehistoric human sites on the island, which has nothing to do with the project.[45]

After nearly a month of excavation, they accidentally unearthed some Han Dynasty pottery fragments, which was enough to prove that people had lived in Yim Tin Tsai since the Han Dynasty. In addition, the archaeological team also took the initiative to help excavate after knowing the plan of the "Road to Canonisation", and wanted to check whether there was direct evidence to support this place as the original site of the old church. Although the archaeological team finally failed to find clear evidence that the abandoned building was the site of the old church, with their help, the foundation and area of the buildings have been clearly revealed, bringing great convenience to the engineering team.[46]

The Retreat Home

"The Retreat Home" was a project funded and planned by Rev. Dominic Chan and his brothers and sisters. The Chan family worked together to restore a dilapidated village house on the island and arranged it into a house for spiritual practice and prayer.[47]

The furniture in the spiritual home was all delivered by Rev. Dominic Chan's brother Chan King-ming from the urban area and moved in one by one with bare hands. Although the layout project was affected by the heavy rain for several days, Rev. Dominic Chan still grasped the time and finally had time to complete the layout work before the feast of Saint Joseph.[48] On 5 May 2013, Rev. Chan held a blessing ceremony for the Spiritual Home before presiding over the feast of St. Joseph's Chapel, marking its official opening.[49]

Rev. Chan said that sharing the culture of Catholic faith and spirituality was an important feature of the village of Yim Tin Tsai. If there is no spiritual culture, Yim Tin Tsai will be no different from other villages. Although the chapel was a place of prayer and spiritual practice, the Retreat Home also provided a peaceful and comfortable environment for people to meditate. In such a fast-paced city, Rev. Chan hoped that this hub could be a place for urbanites to cleanse their hearts and spirit, and hoped that they can meet God here.[50]

The Outlook of St. Joseph's Chapel, Yim Tin Tsai (before renovation). (Image source: Catholic Diocese of Hong Kong)

The Outlook of St. Joseph's Chapel, Yim Tin Tsai (after renovation). (Image source: Catholic Diocese of Hong Kong)

Rev. Dominic Chan, Vicar General hosting the feast-day celebration in 2004. Next to him is Rev. Gianni Criveller. (Image source: Catholic Diocese of Hong Kong)

The Retreat Home.

Heritage Exhibition Centre (Tsing Boor School)

Tsing Boor School was a primary school founded by the Church in 1920 and located in Yim Tin Tsai. It provided education for villagers in Yim Tin Tsai and the other villages of Sai Kung. As the residents of the island started to move out, the number of students in Tsing Boor School gradually declined, and finally closed in 1997.[51] In 2004, when the church was rebuilt, the villagers of Yim Tin Tsai also took this opportunity to renovate the abandoned Tsing Boor School.[52]

In 2007, Professor Cheung Siu Woo of the Division Humanities of the Hong Kong University of Science and Technology (HKUST) discovered some household utensils used by the villagers and leftover items in some abandoned houses during his visit to Yim Tin Tsai. He believed that these items are ideal materials that can reflect the past lives of the villagers, so it is necessary to properly preserve them.[53]

In fact, the village committee members of Yim Tin Tsai Village had already collected some representative farming and daily utensils when the villagers moved out of Yim Tin Tsai, and stored them in a small room in Tsing Boor School. However, there were not many cultural relics preserved by the village committee, and these cultural relics did not cover the various areas of the villagers' past lives; at the same time, the paper materials left by the villagers in the past have not been properly organised and preserved.[54] In view of this, Prof. Cheung proposed a comprehensive collection of Yim Tin Tsai cultural relics, and believed that more historical materials reflecting the villagers' past lives can be unearthed.

After obtaining the consent of the village representative and the village committee, Prof. Cheung organized more than forty students to Yim Tin Tsai on Christmas Day in 2007, they sorted out different items from various dilapidated houses, and gathered them in one place.[55] However, due to lack of resources and experience, these cultural relics were gradually facing the danger of decay without special management. Therefore, the villagers needed to mobilise resources as soon as possible and formulate a complete plan to properly manage these cultural relics.

In 2013, with the consent of the church, the Salt and Light Conservation Centre planned to transform Tsing Boor School into a Hakka cultural relics exhibition hall, and established a heritage exhibition centre working group to deal with cultural relics management and exhibition work. In addition to Prof. Cheung who was the original person in charge of, the team also invited different experts to participate in, including

Prof. Lam Ip Keung, the former Lead Curator of the Art Museum, The Chinese University of Hong Kong (CUHK), to provide professional advice on the plan and made the entire heritage conservation work more perfect.[56]

In September 2013, Prof. Cheung once again led some students from the UST as volunteers to manually move the materials needed by the heritage exhibition centre to the island and clean the interior of the heritage exhibition centre. After that, other volunteers came to use the angle bars and wooden planks brought in by the students to build shelves, so that the cultural relics in the village can be systematically preserved. The students made an inventory of the cultural relics for three consecutive days, and carefully cataloged, photographed and archived the cultural relics in accordance with a museum's standard. Under the leadership of Prof. Cheung, the three-month student volunteer program organised thousands of cultural relics for the heritage exhibition centre.[57]

Rev. Franco Cumbo's certificate of registration as a manager of Tsing Boor School in 1979. (Image source: Sai Kung Sacred Heart Church)

Museum of rural farming tools.

Exhibits in the heritage exhibition centre.

Notes

1   "The new look of the Immaculate Heart of Mary Chapel in Pak Sha O managed by the Catholic Scout Guild", *Kung Kao Po*, 22 April 1983.

2   Rev. Sergio Ticozzi, "PIME's Evangelization in Sai Kung", unpublished.

3   "The Catholic Scout Guild assists the parish on the pilgrimage to Sai Kung", *Kung Kao Po*, 19 September 2004.

4   Ibid.

5   John Strickland (ed.), *Southern District Officer Reports – Islands and Villages in Rural Hong Kong, 1910-60* (Hong Kong: Hong Kong University Press, 2010), p. 266-267

6   Interview with Wong Shue Kei, Village Representative of Pak Tam Chung, 19 January 2019. Interviewers: Yuen Chi Wai, Anthony Yeung and Lam Suet Pik.

7   "The Catholic Scout Guild assists the parish on the pilgrimage to Sai Kung", *Kung Kao Po*, 19 September 2004.

8   "There are only 50 people left in the ten rooms and the abandonment of Pak Sha O Village, Sai Kung.", *The Kung Sheung Evening News*, 31 January 1980.

9   "Mass of the Catholic Scout Guild to Celebrate the 135th Anniversary of Pak Sha O Chapel", *Kung Kao Po*, 13 March 2016.

10 Anthony Yeung, *Pak Sha O: The Heritage of History, Culture and Belief* (Hong Kong: Catholic Scout Guild, 2014), p. 12.

11 "The new look of mmaculate Heart of Mary Chapel in Pak Sha O managed by the Catholic Scout Guild", *Kung Kao Po*, 22 April 1983.

12 "Catholic Scout Guild assists the parish on the pilgrimage to Sai Kung", *Kung Kao Po*, 19 September, 2004.

13 Catholic Directory of Hong Kong, Calendar for the year 1962 (Hong Kong: Hong Kong Catholic Diocese), pp. 132-133.

14 Interview with Hui Ngai Seng of Cheung Sheung, November 2020.

15 *Overseas Chinese Daily News*, 17 April 1963.

16 Wu Chun Hoi served as the principal and teacher of Ming Sun School from 1960 to 1972. See "Interview Records of Wu Chun Hoi's Oral History", The Collection of Hong Kong Oral History Collective Memory (Hong Kong: The University of Hong Kong, 2005), p. 28.

17 Han Youqi (ed.), *A Brief History of Father Paul Wan* (Furong: Shi Xiulan Foundation, publication date unknown), pp. 260-261.

18 Antiquities and Monuments Office: "Historic Architectural Record of the Chapel of the Holy Family in Chek Keng", the study was conducted from 2002 to 2004, identification number: AM04-2029.

19 According to the narration of the former head of Tai Long Village, Tsam Kuei Sing, the church in Tai Long Village was originally located in a place called "Yuen San Tsai" near Ham Tin Bay. Later, there were a large number of Catholics before it was rebuilt into the chapel that is seen today. All his family members are Catholics. His grandfather assisted the priest in preaching and taught and preached in Long Ke. See "Interview with Tsam Kuei Sing in Tai Long Village", 7 October 2018.

20 See "Interview with Tsam Kuei Sing in Tai Long Village", 7 October 2018. See also Cheung Siu Lan and Wong Yik Ching (eds.), "Guarding the Church, Expanding the Kingdom with the Holy Words: Father Paul Wan", *East and West: Oral History of the Catholic Church in Hong Kong* (Hong Kong: Centre for Catholic

Studies, The Chinese University of Hong Kong, 2019), pp. 189-196.

21   Han Youqi (ed.), *A Brief History of Father Paul Wan* (Furong: Shi Xiulan Foundation, publication date unknown), pp. 260-261.

22   Liu Shulian, Dou Jietian, and Liu Zhihang (eds.), *Fr. Paul Wan's ordination of the Diamond Jubilee 90th Birthday Commemoration Special* (Hong Kong: Editorial Team, 2020), pp. 38-39.

23   Interview with Chan Kwok On, 9 December 2017.

24   Interview with Rev. Raja Duggimpudi, 3 March 2018.

25   Rev. Dominic Chan Chi-Ming, "Previous Life. This Life - Yim Tin Tsz (1)" (Hong Kong: Catholic Diocese of Hong Kong, 2016), https://www.youtube.com/watch?v=9Rqrc7KDtqA&ab_channel=catholicvgoffice, retrieved on 15 September 2020.

26   Ibid.

27   Rev. Dominic Chan Chi-Ming: "Previous Life. This Life - Yim Tin Tsz (4)" (Hong Kong: Catholic Diocese of Hong Kong, 2016), https://www.youtube.com/watch?v=9Rqrc7KDtqA&ab_channel=catholicvgoffice, retrieved on 15 September 2020.

28   Rev. Dominic Chan Chi-Ming: "Previous Life. This Life - Yim Tin Tsz (2)" (Hong Kong: Catholic Diocese of Hong Kong, 2016), https://www.youtube.com/watch?v=9Rqrc7KDtqA&ab_channel=catholicvgoffice, retrieved on 15 September 2020.

29   Ibid.

30   Ibid.

31   Ibid.

32   Rev. Dominic Chan Chi-Ming, "Previous Life. This Life-Yim Tin Tsz (2)" (Hong Kong: Catholic Diocese of Hong Kong, 2016), https://www.youtube.com/watch?v=9Rqrc7KDtqA&ab_channel=catholicvgoffice, retrieved on 15 September 2020.

33   Rev. Dominic Chan Chi-Ming, "Previous Life. This Life-Yim Tin Tsz (1)" (Hong Kong: Catholic Diocese of Hong Kong, 2016), https://www.youtube.com/watch?v=9Rqrc7KDtqA&ab_channel=catholicvgoffice, retrieved on 15 September 2020.

34   Ibid.

35   Ibid.

36   Rev. Dominic Chan Chi-Ming: "Previous Life. This Life-Yim Tin Tsz (2)" (Hong Kong: Catholic Diocese of Hong Kong, 2016), https://www.youtube.com/watch?v=9Rqrc7KDtqA&ab_channel=catholicvgoffice retrieved on 15 September 2020.

37   Rev. Dominic Chan Chi-Ming, "Previous Life. This Life-Yim Tin Tsz (3)"(Hong Kong: Catholic Diocese of Hong Kong, 2016), https://www.youtube.com/watch?v=9Rqrc7KDtqA&ab_channel=catholicvgoffice, retrieved on 15 September 2020.

38   Ibid.

39   Rev. Dominic Chan Chi-Ming, "Previous Life. This Life-Yim Tin Tsz (2)"(Hong Kong: Catholic Diocese of Hong Kong, 2016), https://www.youtube.com/watch?v=9Rqrc7KDtqA&ab_channel=catholicvgoffice, retrieved on 15 September 2020.

40   Rev. Dominic Chan Chi-Ming, "Previous Life. This Life-Yim Tin Tsz (4)"(Hong Kong: Catholic Diocese

of Hong Kong, 2016), https://www.youtube.com/watch?v=9Rqrc7KDtqA&ab_channel=catholicvgoffice, retrieved on 15 September 2020.

41 Rev. Dominic Chan Chi-Ming, "Previous Life. This Life-Yim Tin Tsz (6)"(Hong Kong: Catholic Diocese of Hong Kong, 2016), https://www.youtube.com/watch?v=9Rqrc7KDtqA&ab_channel=catholicvgoffice, retrieved on 15 September 2020.

42 Ibid.

43 "The resurrection of the lost salt field for a hundred years, the rebirth of Sai Kung island", https://www.youtube.com/watch?v=SmMT49NOGvw&ab_channel=%E8%98%8B%E6%9E%9C%E5%8B%95%E6%96%B0%E8%81%9EHKAppleDaily, retrieved on 15 September 2020.

44 Rev. Dominic Chan Chi-Ming: "Previous Life. This Life-Yim Tin Tsz (4)"(Hong Kong: Catholic Diocese of Hong Kong, 2016), https://www.youtube.com/watch?v=9Rqrc7KDtqA&ab_channel=catholicvgoffice, retrieved on 15 September 2020.

45 Rev. Dominic Chan Chi-Ming, "Previous Life. This Life-Yim Tin Tsz (5)"(Hong Kong: Catholic Diocese of Hong Kong, 2016), https://www.youtube.com/watch?v=9Rqrc7KDtqA&ab_channel=catholicvgoffice, retrieved on 15 September 2020.

46 Ibid.

47 Rev. Dominic Chan Chi-Ming, "Previous Life. This Life-Yim Tin Tsz (3)" (Hong Kong: Catholic Diocese of Hong Kong, 2016), https://www.youtube.com/watch?v=9Rqrc7KDtqA&ab_channel=catholicvgoffice, retrieved on 15 September 2020.

48 Ibid.

49 Rev. Dominic Chan Chi-Ming, "Previous Life. This Life-Yim Tin Tsz (4)" (Hong Kong: Catholic Diocese of Hong Kong, 2016), https://www.youtube.com/watch?v=9Rqrc7KDtqA&ab_channel=catholicvgoffice, retrieved on 15 September 2020.

50 lbid.

51 Yim Tin Tsz Cultural Relics Showroom (Ching Bo School), https://www.yimtintsaiartsfestival.hk/Attractions.php?n=6&lang=tc, retrieved on 15 September 2020.

52 Rev. Dominic Chan Chi-Ming, "Previous Life. This Life-Yim Tin Tsz (4)"(Hong Kong: Catholic Diocese of Hong Kong, 2016), https://www.youtube.com/watch?v=9Rqrc7KDtqA&ab_channel=catholicvgoffice, retrieved on 15 September 2020.

53 Ibid.

54 Louis Ha Keloon (ed.), *The God as a Guest of Yim Tin Tsai: A Century Story of Yim Tin Tsai, Sai Kung, Hong Kong* (Hong Kong: Centre for Catholic Studies, The Chinese University of Hong Kong, 2010), p. 53.

55 Rev. Dominic Chan Chi-Ming: "Previous Life. This Life-Yim Tin Tsz (4)" (Hong Kong: Catholic Diocese of Hong Kong, 2016), https://www.youtube.com/watch?v=9Rqrc7KDtqA&ab_channel=catholicvgoffice, retrieved on 15 September 2020).

56 Ibid.

57 Rev. Dominic Chan Chi-Ming: "Previous Life. This Life-Yim Tin Tsz (5)"(Hong Kong: Catholic Diocese of Hong Kong, 2016), https://www.youtube.com/watch?v=9Rqrc7KDtqA&ab_channel=catholicvgoffice, retrieved on 15 September 2020.

Conclusion

The Missionary Footsteps and Religious Heritage

On 11 April 2015, Vigil of the Second Sunday of Easter (Divine Mercy Sunday), Pope Francis promulgated a Bull of Indiction "Misericordiæ Vultus" to proclaim an Extraordinary Jubilee of Mercy to be celebrated from 8 December 2015 (Solemnity of the Immaculate Conception) to 20 November 2016 (Solemnity of Christ the King). The central theme of the Jubilee was to encourage the Catholics to contemplate the merciful face of Jesus Christ, to have a personal experience of the Mystery of God's Mercy and to proclaim God's Mercy in words and deeds.[1] During the Jubilee of Mercy, the Diocese of Hong Kong has designated seven churches and chapels (including St. Joseph's Chapel, Yim Tin Tsai Village, Sai Kung) for Jubilee pilgrimages as an extraordinary moment of grace and spiritual renewal. In addition, the Diocese has also published the *Pilgrimage Guide Book Hong Kong*, which describes the history, architectural features and means of travelling of these seven churches or chapels for the sake of the faithful to make pilgrimages.

In Catholic faith, pilgrimages are sites connected with Jesus Christ as well as the journeys seeking to learn more about the heavenly Father. Believers seek God in the process of going to the Holy Land, so that their faith can be renewed; at the same time, it also means abandoning the secular world and sacrificing themselves as a kind of redemption. By being in the Holy Land, pilgrims can experience the presence of God more deeply, and at the same time they can feel communion with the Saints and the Church; by commemorating the deeds of the Saints of the past, pilgrims can be inspired to follow the example of the Saints so that they may become a more effective sign of the Father's action in their lives.

The history of the Catholic mission in Sai Kung narrated in this book is based on

---

1   Diocesan Ad Hoc Committee for Jubilee of Mercy, *Jubilee of Mercy Pilgrimage Guide Book Hong Kong* (Hong Kong: Diocesan Ad Hoc Committee for Jubilee of Mercy, 2015), pp. 2-7.

the ten historical chapels and their related villages. In addition to the historical value and architectural features of these chapels, they have also made a lot of contributions in terms of social functions. Although most of the believers, especially those who used to speak Hakka as the main language, have left their homeland, but the way they recited prayers in Hakka, reflected the integration of Chinese and Western cultures. There are still many historic chapels in Sai Kung district nowadays, that are currently vacant or in disrepair. The "Following Thy Way" team under the Catholic Diocese of Hong Kong, has been travelling along the mountain range and discovered the ten of them. They were scattered in Sham Chung, Pak Sha O, Tan Ka Wan, Chek Keng, Tai Long, Sai Wan, Long Ke, Leung Shuen Wan, Pak Tam Chung and Wong Mo Ying. These chapels have witnessed the development of Hong Kong's early traditional rural society to today's metropolis, but their history is rarely known to Hong Kong people. The mission of "Following Thy Way" is to reveal the contributions to the Chinese living in the countryside, by the missionaries who once served in these chapels. Looking back at the history of Catholicism in Sai Kung, we can make the following preliminary conclusions from the perspectives of Eastern and Western cultural exchanges, regional studies, rural beliefs and culture, and public resources.

First of all, from the Qing Dynasty to the post-war period, Sai Kung was a bridge between Hong Kong, Po On, Wai Yeung and other places in Guangdong. In fact, when the Roman Catholic Church in Hong Kong was established as Apostolic Prefecture of Hong Kong in 1841, missionaries in the Central District mainly served fellow missionaries in and out of the mainland, and also the local Westerners. However, they still wished to preach in the mainland, so they first set off to Sai Kung by boat, such as Yim Tin Tsai. As Sai Kung was still under the jurisdiction of San On County of the Qing government, so it could be regarded as the first training place for Western missionaries to get in touch with Chinese culture. They could also travel from Sai Kung to the villages of San On County along the Mirs Bay and went deep inland. This is the historical viewpoint initially established by this research.

In addition, the regional studies and the relationship between villages and chapels deserve more attention in Hong Kong history. Sai Kung was an area where Catholic villages were particularly densely formed: such as Pak Sha O, Tai Long and Chek Keng, etc. Previous studies in Sai Kung have basically ignored this aspect of research. For example, when some studies discussed about Sai Kung Market and the fishermen's community, they seldom mentioned the priests and the Catholic Social

Welfare Bureau not even the Catholic community, such as St. Peter's Village, Ming Shun Village and Tai Ping Village near Sai Kung Market. In addition, while mentioning the Hakka community, only very few of them would notice that some of the villages do not have any ancestral halls. Therefore, their bond was not only based on the lineage organizations valued by the historical anthropologists interested in the South China research, but rather the religious communities (such as Pak Sha O and Tai Long, etc.). When compared to Luk Yeuk and Shap Sze Heung areas, there is less research on the Sai Kung sub-district of Tung Hoi District.

The research in the rural religious communities in Sai Kung can truly reflect the problems encountered by Westerners in contact with the Chinese society. For instance, the difference between the murder cases of priests during and after the Second World War, the hindrance from local elites encountered by the priests when founding the chapels in local society, accusations of sabotaging *feng shui* etc. The crucial factors among these incidents have not yet been dealt with in detail in academia. Whereas this research could be an addendum for the history of minorities, in particular, the circumstances of the Italians in Hong Kong during the Japanese occupation are rarely touched by Hong Kong historical research. Since Italy was an ally of Japan, the precarious situations the Italian priests faced, the dilemma between the protection of the local people and the Catholics, and the practical need to maintain a delicate relationship with the Japanese army have not been given adequate attention. Moreover, they also had to face the situation that the East River Column regarded them as enemies. In the historical context of this dark period, the sacrifice of the missionaries is always memorable. In fact, the history of the Catholic Mission in Sai Kung reflects the connection established by the religious groups among the villagers through meaningful ritual activities, such as Masses, devotions, prayers and meditation.

The chapels within the field of this research are located in different corners of the Sai Kung Peninsula. Some of these chapels have been classified by the government as Grade II to Grade III historic buildings, but there are other chapels yet to be graded or under grading. Under the development of Sai Kung as the famous World Geopark and preservation area of other natural heritages, these chapels can be connected up meaningfully into the first religious heritage trail in Hong Kong. The establishment of such a heritage trail embedded with the cultural resources of Sai Kung District could help promote the cultural uniqueness of Hong Kong through cultural tourism developed with heritage of Catholic Mission as part of Hong Kong historical resources.

Inferred from visitation of the villages by missionaries in the past, the "Missionary Footsteps" could be well-established into three main historic routes:

(1) Sai Kung District route: starting from Wong Mo Ying, via Tai Mong Tsai to Pak Tam Chung and Leung Shuen Wan (including Sha Tsui and Pak A) with Long Ke and Sai Wan as the main destinations; a route running basically northwest-southeastward on Sai Kung Peninsula;

(2) Tai Long District route: taking path along the coastline through Tai Long, Tai Long Au, Ko Lau Wan, Tan Ka Wan and Chek Keng ; and

(3) Tai Po District route: taking Pak Sha O as the centre, passing through Nam Shan Tung to Lai Chi Tsong (Siu Tong), getting through She Shek Au to Sham Chung, then southward to Yung Shue O and climbing with the "Sky ladder" to Cheung Sheung, ending with stepping down to Ko Tong and returning to Pak Sha O.

The above three routes were not only the paths used by the early missionaries (except by boat), but also those often used by many parishioners in pilgrimage after the war. Therefore, the purpose of protecting these Catholic heritage is to preserve the rich history of Hong Kong and to convey the spirit of preserving the past to the public. A proficient use of public resources and cultural relics given by the God for planning a genuine "Camino de Santiago" (Routes of Santiago de Compostela) and preservation of religious heritage sites would be a significant challenge for the Hong Kong people and the Diocese of Hong Kong in the next decade.

Appendix

1841

1874

1931

1945

1969

1981

2000

Appendix I | Concise Biography of Missionaries and Priesthood in Sai Kung

St. Joseph Freinademetz, SVD, 1852 – 1908
聖福若瑟神父

Date of Birth	15 April 1852
Ordination	25 July 1875
Arrival in Hong Kong	20 April 1879
Service in Sai Kung	1879 – 1881
Date of Death	28 January 1908
Blessed on	19 October 1975
Beautified on	5 October 2003

Rev. St. Joseph was born in Tyrol, Italy, and grew up in a devout Catholic family. He was ordained as a priest at the age of 23, and two years later he joined Society of the Divine Word (SVD), a newly established missionary congregation. From August 1879 to April 1880, he was dispatched as the first batch of missionaries to preach in China. He was then first arrived in Hong Kong, and served in Sai Kung for two years.

During his service in Sai Kung, Rev. St. Joseph learnt Hakka, and first came into contact with the Chinese society, people and missionaries. He said that Hakka was difficult to digest, and this place were lack of abundant supply of food. He spent most of his time staying alone, which allowed him to concentrate on learning Chinese and Chinese culture, and to engage in missionary and pastoral work with the priests of the Milan Institute for Foreign Missions (MEM). St. Joseph and Rev. Luigi Maria Piazzoli once stationed on Lantau Island, later on they mainly served in Sai Kung, its coastal islands and villages, including Yim Tin Tsai and Pak Tam Chung, but Yim Tin Tsai was their major service area. The priests would stay there and baptize the villagers. Two Masses were held monthly for the local villagers, at that time there were around seventy of them whom have become believers.

At the end of 1881, he and Rev. John Baptist Anzer (1851-903) arrived in North China. When they began their missionary work in southern Shandong Province (Lunan) on 18 January of the following year, there were only 158 chunch members. He then worked in Shandong on behalf of the SVD for thirty years. His love for the Chinese and his spirit of hard work had been welcomed and highly esteemed by the locals. By the time when Rev. St. Joseph died of illness, the number of church members had already reached 46,000, 12 Chinese priests and 74 seminarians. During this period, he served as the acting Bishop and president of the SVD for six times, contributing to the cultivation of local preachers and priests in China. On 28 January 1908, he died at the age of 56 in Jining, Shandong province, after serving a typhoid fever patient.

Rev. St. Joseph had become a Saint in everyone's heart before his death. People of the Catholic Church in Lunan still call him "Father Fu" (Father of Fortune), and praise him as a living saint, as he had the great morality of the Confucius. He was beatified and blessed by Pope Paul VI on 19 October 1975, and was canonized by Pope John Paul II on 5 October 2003.

Rev. Burghignoli, Giuseppe, MEM, 1833 – 1892
穆神父

Date of Birth	21 May 1833
Ordination	17 May 1856
Arrival in Hong Kong	12 April 1860
Service in Sai Kung	1863
Date of Death	2 January 1892

Rev. Burghignoli born in Bologna, Italy in 1833. When he arrived in Hong Kong in 1860, he was once served in the Cathedral (the old site), as the Pro-Apostolle Prefect of the former Apostolic Prefecture of Hong Kong, and had led six Canossian sisters to Hong Kong, prompting the mission to develop children education and the work of raising orphans in Hong Kong. He assisted also in the establishment of Cathedral in Caine Road. He had contributed a lot in various aspects, especially the preaching in rural areas of Hong Kong. After that, he stationed in Tsuen Wan; and during his stay in Wun Yiu, Tai Po, he enjoyed staying with the villagers in simple village houses, and built schools for children. He also served in the British Army whom stationed in Hong Kong, and three years later he was dispatched to Tai Long, Sai Kung for missionary and pastoral work.

When the Apostolic Prefecture of Hong Kong was upgraded to the Procurator of Sacred Congregation for the Propagation of the Faith (abbrev. Propaganda Fide) Apostolic Vicariate in 1874, he was appointed as the responsible for transmitting to the several Mission of China, circulars and letters of every description, coming from the Sacred Congregation. He also served as the Procurator of the Italian Procuration in Pottinger Street, Central. On 8 December 1888, on the day of the Patriarch's feast, as Bishop Raimondi was still in the United States, the opening ceremony of the Cathedral was consecrated by Bishop Charles Arsene Bourdon, the apostolic vicar of Burma, who in transit in Hong Kong, and the celebration activities were carried out by Rev. Burghignoli. After he fell ill in the middle of 1891, he refused to return to Europe for medical treatment, but insisting on staying in Hong Kong to serve, and finally resting in 1892.

Bp. Raimondi, Giovanni Timoleone, MEM, 1827 – 1894
高主教

Date of Birth	5 May 1827
Ordination	25 May 1850
Arrival in Hong Kong	15 May 1858
Date of Death	27 September 1894

Bishop Raimondi was born in Milan, Italy in 1827, and was ordained in Milan in 1850, he then joined the Milan Institute for the Foreign Missions on 7 October of the same year. In 1858, according to the plan of the Sacred Congregation for the Propagation of the Faith (Latin: Propaganda Fide), the Apostolic Prefecture of Hong Kong was handed over to the Milan Institute for the Foreign Missions. Responsible for management, Rev. Raimondi arrived in Hong Kong with Br. Tacchini on 15 May. In June 1860, he was appointed as the Pro-Apostolic Prefect and Pro-Procurator to succeed Fr. Reina who returned to Italy. On 17 November 1867, he was appointed as the Apostolic Vicar, succeeding Msgr. Ambrosi, Luigi (1829-1867) who died earlier. In 1874, the Apostolic Prefecture of Hong Kong was promoted to Apostolic Vicariate, and Rev. Raimondi was then appointed on 22 November as the first Apostolic Vicar and Bishop of Acantho.

After becoming the first Vicar Apostolic of Hong Kong, Bishop Raimondi had been actively developing educational affairs, especially Catholic education. At the same time, he also planned establishing the new church—"Cathedral of the Immaculate Conception" in Caine Road, which was then completed in 1888.

Rev. Volonteri, Simeone, MEM, 1831 – 1904
和神父

Date of Birth	6 June 1831
Ordination	1857
Arrival in Hong Kong	7 February 1860
Service in Sai Kung	circa 1862 – 1869
Date of Death	21 December 1904

Rev. Volonteri was born in Milan, Italy in 1831. He entered the Milan Institute for the Foreign Missions in 1855 and was ordained in 1857. He was dispatched to Hong Kong for missionary work in 1860, and stationed in Aberdeen in the same year. In 1862, he transferred to Ting Kok district to establish a new mission station. He was one of the priests who first preached from Tsuen Wan, along the mountain road to Tai Po. The first mission station was in Wun Yiu Village, the south of Tai Po.

He later transferred to Yim Tin Tsai, Chek Keng, Tai Long in Sai Kung, and even Tam Shui in mainland for his mission. In 1869, he left Hong Kong and went to Henan to serve as a Vicarius Apostolicus, and was later installed as Bishop of Henan.

Rev. Leong, Chi-Hing Andreas, 1837 – 1920
梁子馨神父

Date of Birth	1837
Ordination	25 April 1862
Service in Continental District	1875 – 1877
Date of Death	15 May 1920

On behalf of the first batch of Hong Kong clergy, Rev. Leong Chi-Hing witnessed an important step in the development of the Hong Kong church—began to have a local clergy class. Rev. Leong was originally from Nanhai, Guangdong, and entered the Catholic Seminary in February 1850. He was ordained as a priest in Hong Kong in 1862 and started his preaching in San On County, Kwai Shin (Guishan) County, and Hong Kong. He and Rev. Volonteri went through field inspections and drew the "Map of The Sun-On-District (Kwangtung Province)". From 1868 to 1870, he served in Chek Keng and San On County (not called the "New Territories" at the time). In 1874, he was sent to work in Kwai Shin City. From 1875 to 1877, he accompanied Bishop Raimondi to visit the churches in mainland China, at the same time dealing with the debt problems of the Hong Kong missionary district. In 1877, he was sent to work in Wai Chow. From 1882 to 1890, he worked in the Chapel of the Immaculate Heart of Mary in Pak Sha O, until he returned to serve in the Cathedral at Caine Road in 1898. In 1912, he celebrated his Golden Jubilee of Ordination, and went to Rome to receive the honour of "Apostolic Missionary".

Rev. Leong was also the director and supervisor of the Hong Kong Catholic Chinese Union (1910-1918). He was fluent in Latin, Mandarin, and other Chinese dialects such as Cantonese, Hakka and Hoklo. He died in Hong Kong in 1920.

Bp. Piazzoli, Luigi Maria, MEM, 1845 – 1904
和主教

Date of Birth	12 May 1845
Ordination	1 November 1868
Arrival in Hong Kong	December 1869
Service in Continental District	1875 – 1877
Date of Death	26 December 1904

Bishop Piazzoli was the second Apostolic Vicar of Hong Kong. He was born in Bergamo, Italy in 1845. He entered the local seminary in 1864, and was ordained as a priest in 1868, belonging to the Milan Institute for the Foreign Missions. After a year of training, he set off for Hong Kong in 1869, and arrived in Hong Kong in December of the same year, then was dispatched to serve in Mainland China, before that, he mainly lived in Ting Kok, the first missionary station in Tai Po. He served from 1875 to 1877 as the missionary director of the mainland, he then returned to Hong Kong in 1891 because of poor health.

Bishop Piazzoli could speak six European languages and three Chinese dialects, he was a missionary with linguistic talents. In 1892, Bishop Piazzoli succeeded Rev. Burghignoli as the Procurator of the Propaganda Fide in Hong Kong. Two years later, due to the serious plague occurred in Hong Kong, a large number of people had left Hong Kong. Bishop Piazzoli and other priests and nuns went to the hospitals to visit patients. In 1895, he was appointed as the Apostolic Vicar of Hong Kong, and in the same year, he succeeded Bishop Raimondi. Under the leadership of Bishop Piazzoli, the Catholic missionary and pastoral work in the Kowloon Peninsula had made significant progress. He also concerned about the believers' life of faith, which he would stay in the Cathedral for their confessions, sometimes would last for three to four hours.

In 1904, Bishop Piazzoli returned to Italy to recuperate due to a worsening health condition, and died there in December of the same year.

Bp. Pozzoni, Domenico, MEM, 1861 – 1924
師多敏主教

Date of Birth	22 December 1861
Ordination	28 February 1885
Arrival in Hong Kong	19 December 1885
Date of Death	20 February 1924

Bishop Pozzoni was born in Como, Italy in 1861. He then joined the St. Petri M. of Diocese in Milan, later on he joined the Milan Institute for Foreign Missions in July 1882, and was ordained in 1885. After arriving in Hong Kong in 1885, he preached in Nam Tau of Po On, Wai Yeung, Hoi Fung and other places successively.

When Bishop Pozzoni left Milan to preach abroad, he was sent to work in the Mainland and spent several years in Hoi Fung and Wai Chow. He was very popular among the locals. He loved Wai Chow Mission District so much that he still visited Wai Chow every year after he was appointed as Titular Bishop of Tavia and Apostolic Vicar of Hong Kong. His care for the area was due to the establishment of a hospital and orphanage there years ago, and it was currently in charge by Rev. Kampa Grampa.

Bishop Pozzoni was also popular in Hong Kong, which he has actively promoted the social and other activities of Catholics. In addition to improving Catholic organizations, he also sponsored, attended and assisted in organizing various events. On 12 July 1905, he was appointed as the third Apostolic Vicar of Hong Kong, and was ordained as Bishop on 1 October of the same year. He passed away on 20 February 1924.

Bp. Valtorta, Enrico, PIME, 1883 – 1951
恩理覺主教

Date of Birth	14 May 1883
Ordination	30 March 1907
Arrival in Hong Kong	5 October 1907
Date of Death	3 September 1951

Bishop Valtorta was born on 14 May 1883 in the suburbs of Milan, Italy. He was ordained as a priest on 30 March 1907, and came to Hong Kong for preaching on 5 October of the same year. He used to preach in Hong Kong, Po On, Wai Yeung, and Hoi Fung. From May to June 1924, he participated in the First Conference of Chinese Catholic Churches held in Shanghai with Rev. J. M. Spada. On 8 March 1926, he was appointed as the fourth Apostolic Vicar of Hong Kong, and became the Bishop on 13 June of the same year. On 11 April 1946, the Holy Order of the Church was established in China; the Apostolic Vicariate of Hong Kong was promoted to Catholic Diocese of Hong Kong. On 31 October 1948, Rev. Valtorta was officially promoted as the first Bishop of the Diocese. He passed away on 3 September 1951.

For the past 25 years, Bishop Valtorta had established many social undertakings, such as the Precious Blood Hospital in Sham Shui Po, Ling Yuet Sin Infants' Home in Pokfulam Road, St. Teresa's Hospital in Kowloon Tong, and St. Paul's Hospital in Causeway Bay; he then handed over the Ruttonjee Pulmonary Disease Nursing Home to the Columban Sisters for taking care of the medical work. Regarding the education development, the important schools established during his presidency included: Wah Yan College in Hong Kong and Kowloon, La Salle College in Kowloon, Maryknoll

Girls' School in Hong Kong and Kowloon, Tak Sun Boys' School in Austin Kowloon, and Joan of Arc's English Evening School in Hong Kong, etc. Under his management, there were seven hospitals, nine clinics, three nurseries, two homes for the elderly, two homes for blind girls, and 151 primary and secondary schools were established. More than 20,000 boys and girls were admitted, and the number of church members was about 40,000 at that time. In 1949, Bishop Valtorta started the work of helping the people in need, by first setting up a centre in Tiu Keng Leng, which was assigned to the Congregation of Saint John the Baptist.

He also welcomed various religious congregations and missionary groups to come to Hong Kong, for example: Dominicans, Franciscans, Jesuits, The Salesians of Don Bosco, Society of the Divine Word, Missions étrangères de Paris, Maryknoll Fathers, Cistercians, Congregation of Saint John the Baptist, and the Institute of the Brothers of the Christian Schools (De La Salle Brothers), etc. As for the congregations of women, there are: Carmelite Monastery, Franciscan Missionaries of Mary, Congregation of Missionary Sisters of Our Lady of the Angels, Missionary Sisters of the Immaculate Conception, St. Columban Sisters, Missions étrangères de Paris, Salesian Sisters of St John Bosco, etc. He also founded the Regional Seminary for South China in Aberdeen, and the Holy Spirit Minor Seminary in Sai Kung. As for the Catholic Truth Society and Catholic Centre, they were also established in this period.

Rev. Situ, Teng-Chiu John, 1872 – 1947
司徒廷昭神父

Date of Birth	11 December 1872
Ordination	6 January 1902
Service in Sai Kung	1902 – 1914
Date of Death	9 August 1947

Born in Macau, later joined the Hong Kong Catholic Seminary, and was ordained as a priest, which started his first mission in Sai Kung in 1902. During the period, he also visited Kwai Shin (1908), To Yeung and Sha U Chung (1909-1912) to assist in ecclesiastical affairs. In 1914, he succeeded the late priest Rev. Joachim Leong and served as the Parish Priest of St. Francis Church in Wan Chai. In 1925, Rev. Situ served in the newly completed St. Margaret's Church in Happy Valley. In 1926, he was awarded the title of "Apostolic Missionary". In September 1929, he started working in Cathedral (Caine Road) and was responsible for the Chinese Congregation in the church. In June 1934, he served as the Rector of St. Peter's Chapel in Aberdeen until 1941.

Rev. Ferrario, Angelo, PIME, 1876 – 1933
羅奕安神父

Date of Birth	13 March 1876
Ordination	25 February 1899
Arrival in Hong Kong	15 October 1900
Service in Sai Kung	1900 – 1910 and 1913 – 1914
Date of Death	17 June 1933

Rev. Ferrario was born in Inzago of Milan, Italy in 1876. He entered the seminary on 17 August 1896, and was ordained in 1899. After Rev. Ferrario arrived Hong Kong, he was assigned to serve in Sai Kung until 1910, and started his preaching in Sha U Chung and To Yeung from 1911 to 1912. From 1898 to 1913, under the evangelization efforts of Rev. Pozzoni, Domenico (later appointed Bishop) and Rev. Ferrario, the ecclesiastical affairs of Sai Kung developed rapidly, and the churches of Lung Shuen Wan (1910) and Kei Ling Ha (1913) were built successively. In 1905, he applied to the government for exemption from paying the rent of more than ten Sai Kung chapels, but the government did not endorse his application. Rev. Ferrario left Hong Kong in 1914, and died on 17 June 1933 in Milan, Italy.

Rev. Teruzzi, Emilio, PIME, 1887 – 1942
丁味略神父

Date of Birth	17 August 1887
Ordination	29 June 1912
Arrival in Hong Kong	December 1912
Service in Sai Kung	1914 – 1927 and 1942
Date of Death	26 November 1942

Rev. Teruzzi was born in the town of Lesmo in Milan, Italy. He later joined the Milan Institute for the Foreign Missions, and was ordained as a priest on 29 June 1912. He arrived in Hong Kong in December of the same year and began his service in Sai Kung. He was guided by Rev. Ferrario, who was in charge of the New Territories at the time, for learning the local language and customs.

In November 1914, Rev. Ferrario had left Hong Kong due to serious illness. Rev. Teruzzi, who had only been ordained for more than two years, took the place of the management for the New Territories. Under his jurisdiction, there were 15 churches and chapels at that time. Rev. Teruzzi had visited various villages to preach, including Sai Kung, Yuen Long, Pat Heung, and Tai Po. He also held Masses for the villages, repaired their damaged churches, and built new churches in Long Ke, Tan Ka Wan, and Wong Mo Ying. Rev. Teruzzi's service was not limited to the scope of the church. He also negotiated with the home affairs department to defend the interests of the villagers, and also established the Sung Tsun School in Sai Kung Market.

During his work in Sai Kung, he faced tremendous economic pressure, and that he resigned in 1927 and transferred to the Diocesan Curia as Chancellor, Archivist, and Master of Ceremonies. He was later appointed as the Chaplain of Victoria Goal, and briefly served as the Rectors of the Cathedral, and St. Margaret's Church in Happy Valley. He enthusiastically encouraged the parishioners to set up Catholic Action Association and promoted the Catholic Scouts Movement. From 1937 to 1940, Rev. Teruzzi left Hong Kong to serve in Italy and England. However, he was deeply concerned about Hong Kong, and later returned to service under the strong invitation of Bishop Valtorta, and once again assumed the post in the Diocesan Curia before leaving Hong Kong.

By August 1942, Hong Kong had been occupied by Japanese troops, and Rev. Kwok King-wan, who was serving in Sai Kung, was abducted and killed. Rev. Teruzzi nominated himself to replace him. He then returned to Sai Kung in October, and insisted to continue visiting the parishioners in various villages, hoping to relieve them and bring encouragement. Unfortunately, he was abducted by armed guerrillas at his home in Tai Tung Village on 25 November. About a week later, his floating body was found in the Sham Chung beach and thus Rev. Teruzzi was martyr for his belief.

Rev. Lo, Lee-tsung Philip, DHK, 1889 – 1970
盧履中神父

Date of Birth	15 June 1889
Ordination	2 June 1917
Arrival in Hong Kong	December 1912
Service in Sai Kung	1917 – 1923
Date of Death	6 May 1970

Rev. Lo was born in Shunde, Guangdong. After he was ordained, he was sent to Sai Kung to serve as the Co-adjutor (assistant), and as Rev. Teruzzi's assistant. He and Rev. Teruzzi constantly visited every village and held Mass for the parishioners. It also attracted new catechumens, and he would stay longer when necessary. During their visits, they increased their contact with parishioners of places such as Yuen Long, Pat Heung, Tai Po, and even as far as Lung Kwu Tan in Tuen Mun. Rev. Lo guided the villagers to be baptized, and because of his sincerity and helpfulness, he won the love and esteem of everyone.

Bp. Bianchi, Lorenzo, PIME, 1899 – 1983
白英奇主教

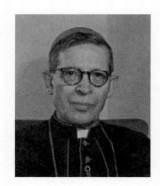

Date of Birth	1 April 1889
Ordination	23 September 1922
Arrival in Hong Kong	13 September 1923
Date of Death	13 February 1983

Born in Godano, Italy in 1899, Bishop Bianchi entered the local minor seminary in 1911, and was ordained in 1922. He was the member of the Pontifical Institute for Foreign Missions. Bishop Bianchi came to Hong Kong in 1923 and started preaching in Wai Chow and Hoi Fung. In 1949, he was appointed Bishop Coadjutor of the Diocese of Hong Kong. Although the political situation in mainland was uncertain, he still had no fear of returning to Wai Chow to preach.

In 1950, Bishop Bianchi and several Italian missionaries were detained in Hoi

Fung. By the death of Bishop Enrico Valtorta in 1951, Bishop Bianchi was still unable to return to Hong Kong to handle the religious affairs. He was not released until 1952, and became the second Bishop of the Catholic Diocese of Hong Kong.

In the 1950's, a large number of new immigrants from mainland came to Hong Kong. Bishop Bianchi devoted himself to the relief of refugees and established the Hong Kong Catholic Welfare Association; he also promoted education and charity work.

During the tenure of Bishop Bianchi, the number of local Catholics increased from about 24,000 to 250,000; he assembled local groups of church members to form the Hong Kong Diocesan Council For The Lay Apostolate (the predecessor of the HK Central Council of Catholic Laity in 1959, encouraging Christian evangelization. After returning to Hong Kong after attending the Second Ecumenical Council of the Vatican, he was committed to implementing the church's reformation, promoting the unity of Christians, and the reform of liturgy. During his tenure, he had visited Catholic villages in the New Territories many times, especially in remote villages. He also visited the Sacred Heart Church in Sai Kung and the Ping Chau Chapel, which was located very close to the mainland.

Bishop Bianchi was humble, always care about the poor and weak, and had a deep affection of the Chinese church throughout his life. He strived to advance the management of the Hong Kong Diocese by Chinese priest–Bishop Francis Hsu was ordained in 1967 as the Auxiliary Bishop, who was the first Chinese Bishop of the local church.

After Bishop Bianchi laid the foundation for the Hong Kong church, he resigned in 1968. He returned to Italy the following year. After returning home, he still missed China and continue to pray for Hong Kong, Hoi Fung and Wai Chow at Mass every day. On 13 February 1983, he rested in peace at the age of eighty-three.

Rev. Famiglietti, Giuseppe, PIME, 1916 – 2004
范慕琦神父

Date of Birth	17 December 1916
Ordination	29 June 1940
Arrival in Hong Kong	6 October 1947
Service in Sai Kung	1949 – 1964
Date of Death	3 January 2004

Rev. Famiglietti was born in southern Italy in 1916. He was ordained as a priest in Milan in 1940, and then started teaching mathematics at the Pontifical Institute for Foreign Missions. In 1947, he was sent to Hong Kong and served as Co-adjutor (assistant) of the Sai Kung District from 1949 to 1955, assisting the evangelisation of Rev. Caruso, Giorgio (1908-2004). His preaching was until he was called back to Italy to teach mathematics.

After returning to Hong Kong in 1960, he served as the Rector of Sacred Heart Church, Sai Kung from 1961 to 1964. He also served as the manager of the Sacred Heart School in Sha Tsui Village, Sai Kung in the 1950s. From 1965 to 1990, he served as the Rector priest of Rosary Church, Hung Shui Kiu in Yuen Long.

Rev. De Ascaniis, Quirino, PIME, 1908 – 2009
江志堅神父

Date of Birth	5 August 1908
Ordination	24 September 1932
Arrival in Hong Kong	August 1933
Service in Sai Kung	1956 – 1961
Date of Death	11 January 2009

Rev. Ascaniis was born in Italy on 5 August 1908. He joined the Pontifical Institute for Foreign Missions in 1929. He was ordained as a priest in 1932 and was sent to Hong Kong to study Chinese in August 1933. He later went to serve in Po On and Wai Yeung in southern China until 1941, when his service was suspended due to war. After returning to Hong Kong, Rev. Ascaniis took up the post of the Rosary Church Assistant and was transferred to Macau in 1944.

Rev. Ascaniis went to Wai Yeung again in 1945 to preach, and helped the local Christians regain their church life after the war. In 1950, he was sent to Wai Chow under house arrest along with his fellow Bishop Bianchi and others. He was released in October 1951 and returned to Hong Kong. After his returning, Rev. Ascaniis served as the Rectory of the Holy Spirit Seminary in Sai Kung. He served in the local district from 1955 to 1961, and also participated in the establishment of the Sacred Heart Church, Sai Kung. From 1961 to 1965, he served as the Vice Co-operator of St.

Teresa's Church; from 1966 to 1993, he served as the Assistant of Rosary Church, and participated in the pastoral work of the Elizabeth Hospital.

Rev. Ascaniis retired in 1993, and moved to Sheung Shui at the St. Joseph's Home for the Elderly, which was originally set up in Ngau Chi Wan by the Little Sisters of the Poor. In April 2008, when the Pontifical Institute for Foreign Missions celebrated the 150th anniversary of its service in Hong Kong, it celebrated Rev. Ascaniis's 100th birthday as well. Rev. Ascaniis has written 17 volumes of missionary and spiritual notes during his lifetime.

Rev. Fraccaro, Valeriano, PIME, 1913 – 1974
范賚亮神父

Date of Birth	15 March 1913
Ordination	4 April 1937
Arrival in Hong Kong	1952
Service in Sai Kung	1966 – 1974
Date of Death	28 October 1974

Rev. Fraccaro was born in Veneto, Treviso, Italy. After he was ordained, he was sent to Shaanxi, China for missionary work, and arrived in Hanzhong in the same year. At the time when Japan invaded China, the missionary work was extremely dangerous. Rev. Fraccaro escaped the Japanese airstrike, but was imprisoned in a concentration camp. In 1949, when the Chinese Communist Party came to power, Rev. Fraccaro was detained again, and was later deported permanently by the government. He then arrived Hong Kong in 1952.

He served in the parishes of Aberdeen, Sha Tin and Castle Peak, and was appointed as the Rector of Sai Kung Sacred Heart Church in 1966. Rev. Fraccaro was obese and short, an amiable smile was always on his face. He was kind and was very popular among Sai Kung villagers. He liked getting along with the residents of Sai Kung. Apart from visiting the villagers house by house and preaching the gospel, he also visited fishermen and held Masses for them on small fishing boats. In addition, Rev. Fraccaro, whose family ran a bread business, was fond of delivering bread he baked to the villagers every morning, sharing his love to Catholics and non-Catholics. This showed that Rev. Fraccaro not only nourished the villagers' souls by teaching God's principles, but also presented bread to satisfy their physical needs. Rev. Fraccaro also served as the supervisor of Sung Tsun School (Sai Kung). He admitted children who lacked self-confidence, and taught them bread-making skills so that they might earn a living by it.

On 28 October 1974, Rev. Fraccaro was killed in the dormitory of the church. He was lying naked in a pool of blood. Throughout his lifetime, he had worked tirelessly to serve the Sai Kung villagers. He was lovable, and had never incurred hatred with others. The reason for his murder is still a mystery at present.

Rev. Lambertoni, Adelio, PIME, 1939 – 2006
林伯棟神父

Date of Birth	20 September 1939
Ordination	30 March 1963
Arrival in Hong Kong	September 1965
Service in Sai Kung	1967 – 1974
Date of Death	7 July 2006

Rev. Lambertoni was a Regular Priest of the Pontifical Institute for Foreign Missions. He was born in Velate of Milan, Italy, and was ordained as a priest on 30 March 1963. He was later promoted to the priesthood by Cardinal Montigny, who became Pope Paul VI. He arrived in Hong Kong only two years after being ordained, and temporarily resided in the Tai Po church for learning Cantonese. Since 1967, he had been appointed as the Vice Co-Operator of Sai Kung District.

Rev. Lambertoni believed that missionaries should actively care about social issues, and his service in Sai Kung implemented this belief. During his tenure, he often drove a motorcycle to visit various villages, to know more about the life and needs of the villagers and fishermen. His services included also applying the children's home for orphans, and even adopted eight children whom had different family issues and raised them as adults. He also organized various summer activities for children, held trainings for young parishioners to obtain leadership and social responsibilities, and introduced the Legion of Mary group therefore Sai Kung parishioners would have the chance to serve the community, etc. But the most delighted talk-about was his contribution to the establishment of Tai Ping Village and Ming Shun Village, improving the living environment of Sai Kung fishermen.

As Rev. Fraccaro was killed in 1974, Rev. Lambertoni was transferred in short from Hong Kong to Thailand and Italy. He returned to Hong Kong in 1978 and continued serving in the parishes of Wong Tai Sin, Kwai Fong, and Shek Lei. During this period, he led the social concern group of the PIME, petitioning for the residents, hawkers, and boat people in the area, and concerned on various kinds of social issues in Hong Kong, including the Ma Chai Hang disaster incident, Yau Ma Tei boat household incident, Kowloon Bay temporary housing area incident, the Vietnamese boat people problem, etc. At the same time, he also served the Society for Community Organization – a social organization dedicated to improving local marginal groups and poverty issues.

Rev. Lambertoni was diagnosed with lymphoma in 1995 but continued to work and serve in the community until two months before his death. The local government of Rev. Lambertoni's hometown named a trail after him, and awarded him the "Highest Citizen Honor Award" in recognition of his contribution to the needy.

Rev. Paul Wan Yee Tseng
溫以政神父

Date of Birth	24 March 1930
Ordination	2 July 1960
Arrival in Hong Kong	September 1949
Service in Sai Kung	1977 – 1997

Rev. Wan was born in Xiaopoyang Village, Jiexi Diocese of Swatow, Guangdong Province. He entered St. Peter's Minor Seminary in Jieyang at the age of 16 and a half in September 1946. Later, due to the war, he entered the Holy Spirit Seminary in Sai Kung in September 1949, and then the Regional Seminary for South China (now Holy Spirit Seminary, Aberdeen).

Rev. Wan was ordained by Bishop Bianchi on 2 July 1960. In the same year, he went to Kuala Lumpur to serve the local Chinese, and stayed for 15 years. During this period, he vigorously developed the Legion of Mary group and expanded the local praesidia, from two to eleven. In addition to managing the parish, Rev. Wan also served the leprosy hospital, often attending dinners with the patients and holding Masses for them.

He returned to Hong Kong in May 1975 and first served as the Co-operator of Cheung Sha Wan Christ the King Church, and then transferred to the Immaculate Heart of Mary Church in Tai Po in 1977 as Assistant, where he served until 1997. At that time, the Tai Po Parish also managed several Sai Kung chapels near Tolo Harbour, namely the Sham Chung Epiphany of Our Lord Chapel, Chek Keng Holy Family Chapel, Tai Long Immaculate Conception Chapel, and Tan Ka Wan St. Peter's Chapel. He was also responsible for the Chapel of the Sacred Heart of Jesus in Tung Ping Chau. Rev. Wan was entrusted by Cardinal Wu Cheng-chung to keep these chapels intact, or they would be taken back by the government due to abandonment. Rev. Wan then worked with a group of young church members to repair them into pilgrimage sites, Catholic campsite, and so on.

In addition, he established the "Holy Words Life Association" in 1989. One of its purposes was to establish a faith group in harmony with the Chinese church through pilgrimage to the country. The association served as a bridge between the Hong Kong Diocese and the Chinese church, promoted the integration of different groups within the Chinese church, and helped the Chinese church train seminarians and nuns. The association was moving towards small groups, in 52 Hong Kong local parishes. In 2010, these groups assembled and formed a federation, collectively referred to as the "Yee Tseng Association of Sacred Words and Life".

Rev. Narciso Santinon, PIME, 1916 – 1995
桑得嵐神父

Date of Birth	23 January 1916
Ordination	6 August 1939
Arrival in Hong Kong	2 April 1952
Service in Sai Kung	1960s – 1980s
Date of Death	18 May 1995

Rev. Santinon was born in 1916 in a devout Christian family in Barcon di Vedelago, Treviso, Italy. He entered the minor seminary of the PIME of Treviso at the age of 11. He has been serving as a teacher, vocation promoter and vice-president of the minor seminary for seven years after he was ordained.

In 1947, Rev. Santinon went to preach to Hanzhong, Henan, China. After the liberation of the mainland in 1949, he and his assistants have been arrested, imprisoned, and labored. When he was released and arrived in Hong Kong in 1952, he was in the midst of a wave of refugees. As he was fluent in Mandarin, he was appointed by Bishop Bianchi to take care of the faith and needs of the refugees. He worked in the Cathedral and the refugee centre in Chuk Yuen until 1957.

Rev. Santinon returned to Hong Kong in 1961, which was four years after returning to Italy as the Rector of the PIME Minor Seminary at Treviso. On 11 June 1961, Bishop Bianchi of the Diocese of Hong Kong presided over the consecration of the Immaculate Heart of Mary Church in Tai Po, and Rev. Santinon was the first Rector. In 1962, he was appointed as the parish priest of the Tai Po and Tai Long area. He had occasionally held Masses at Sham Chung and Cheung Sheung. The briefcase he carried was kept by parishioners as a memorial, and the Pok Oi Public School, the centre in which he had celebrated Mass before is still existent now in Cheung Sheung Village until 1988. During his pastoral work, he founded the Sacred Heart of Mary Primary School and the Valtorta College.

From 1988 to 1991, he served as the Assistant of Ss. Peter and Paul's Church in Yuen Long, and was appointed as the Home Chaplain of St. Joseph's Home for the Aged in Ngau Chi Wan on September 1991. In 1995, he resigned from the nursing home due to illness and lived in his convent.

Rev. Caruso, Giorgio, PIME, 1908 – 2004
文明德神父

Date of Birth	11 January 1908
Ordination	19 September 1931
Arrival in Hong Kong	30 September 1932
Service in Sai Kung	1936 – 1953; 1962 – 1966
Date of Death	6 December 2004

Rev. Caruso was born in Naples, Italy on 8 January 1908, and entered the minor seminary in 1918, after that he joined the PIME in 1927, and made a permanent vow in March 1931. He was ordained in September of the same year. Rev. Caruso arrived in Hong Kong on 30 September 1932 and studied Cantonese at the St. Margaret's Church. In the 1930s, he served in Cheung Chau, Lantau Island and Sai Kung successively. During the Japanese colonial period, he began serving the Rosary Church (Kowloon) in April 1940. In September, he went to the Macau seminary to assist the pastoral work. He later returned to Sai Kung in 1941, and then returned to Macau to serve the local Hong Kong refugees in 1949.

After the war, Rev. Caruso again returned to serve in Sai Kung in 1946. In 1952, he was appointed as the priest of the seminary. He has been a diocesan consultor from 1953 to 1961 and served in St. Jude's Church of North Point in 1953 and became ill during this period. Then from 1955 he was transferred to Cheung Chau for teaching Cantonese. In 1961, he was seriously ill and had to suspend his duties. He returned to the former site of the Sai Kung seminary. After restoring his health, he went to St. Teresa's Church in Kowloon as an Assistant in 1965 until his retirement in the church in 1990.

Since his arrival in Hong Kong in 1932, Rev. Caruso has never returned to his hometown Italy. He has been enthusiastic about church work in Hong Kong.

Rev. Galbiati, Pietro, PIME
嘉畢主神父

Date of Birth	14 December 1930
Ordination	28 June 1957
Arrival in Hong Kong	26 October 1961
Service in Sai Kung	1987 – 1990

Rev. Galbiati was born in Monza, near Milan, Italy in 1930. After graduating from the Fifth Form in 1948, he joined the PIME and studied theology in Milan. He was ordained as a priest in 1957 and consecrated by Pope Paul VI. After being ordained, Rev. Galbiati taught in the seminary of the Milan Congregation and was responsible for seminary affairs for four years. He was sent to Hong Kong in 1961, where he initially lived in Cheung Chau and learnt Cantonese and English there. In 1962, he was appointed by the then Bishop Bianchi to serve as Assistant parish priest at Rosary Church in Tsim Sha Tsui. On 23 December 1969, the Diocese formally established St.

Paul's parish in Yau Ma Tei, Kowloon, and Rev. Galbiati was transferred to the church as Assistant. From 1977 to 1981, he served as the Rector of Ss. Peter and St. Paul Church in Yuen Long Parish.

In July 1981, the superior of PIME transferred him back to Italy and he devoted himself to cultivate his brothers in the seminary. Three years later, he served as the superior of another seminary. He first served as the Rector at the Sacred Heart Church in Sai Kung after he came back to Hong Kong in 1986. During this period, he visited many villages, including St. Peter's Village, Wo Mei Village, Sai Wan Village and Wong Mo Ying Village. Although there was no church, he would occasionally visit the homes of old parishioners in Kei Ling Ha Village. He also registered the household for the parishioners in the villages. Because of the remoteness, he had to travel by car in Yuen Long and Sai Kung, and by bicycle in Sha Tin. From September 1990 to January 1999, he was the Rector of St. Alfred's Church, Tai Wai, Sha Tin. In December 1999, he was deployed to the Cathedral as an Assistant and he acted as the spiritual directors of many church associations. He also visited the sick at the Canossa Hospital every week.

Rev. Chan, Chi Yan, Philip, 1925 – 2018
陳子殷神父

Date of Birth	1 May 1925
Ordination	6 July 1957
Service in Sai Kung	1957 – 1960
Date of Death	13 July 2018

Rev. Chan was born in Guangzhou in 1925, and his family later moved to Hong Kong and Macau. In 1938, when he was 13 years old, he entered the St. Joseph's Seminary in Macau, and later enrolled in the Regional Seminary of South China (later the Holy Spirit Seminary) in Hong Kong. In 1957, he was ordained by Bishop Bianchi in Hong Kong. Then he served in Sai Kung Sacred Heart Church in 1957, the parishes of Yuen Long and Kam Tin in the 1960s, and went to Italy for further studies in 1967.

Rev. Chan had an unforgettable experience with the indigenous residents: Rev. Chan was once sent to Sai Kung to serve as the Assistant when he was first ordained. Rev. Quirino De Ascaniis would send him to different villages to celebrate Masses every weekend. On one occasion, Rev. Chan was appointed to the fishing village of Tan Ka Wan to officiate a marriage Mass for a couple, so he went with his servants and food. On the day of the wedding, the couple had not shown up for quite a while, so Rev. Chan was prepared to leave. At this moment, not far from the shore, a boat was heading to the direction of him. The new couple, with barefoot and sweating, got out of the boat and walked towards Rev. Chan–they were fishing at sea all night. Rev. Chan also took off his shoes when he saw this scenario, and walked into the chapel with them in barefoot to celebrate the Mass.

Rev. Chan once served in Pokfulam Church of Our Lady of Lourdes in 1972, the Church of Our Lady of Rosary in Western District from 1973 to 1976, St. Paul's Church in Yau Ma Tei in 1977, and transferred to St. Lawrence's Church in Cheung Sha Wan from 1988 to 1993. After that he worked as a researcher at the Holy Spirit Study Centre from 1994 to 1997.

In his later years, Rev. Chan has been listening to confessions in Caine Road Cathedral for a long time, and sometimes served the parish and led overseas pilgrims. He passed away on 13 July 2018.

Rev. McAsey, Joseph, SJ, 1913 – 1992
張光導神父

Date of Birth	10 March 1913
Ordination	19 May 1945
Service in Sai Kung	1969 – mid-1970s
Date of Death	1 March 1992

Rev. McAsey was born in Ireland on 10 March 1913. He entered the Jesuit seminary on 7 September 1931, and was ordained as a priest in China in 1945. From 1969 to the mid-1970s, Rev. McAsey, who was a Jesuit priest, served the Tai Long district as the Assistant of the Tai Po District. He went to Tai Long district every Friday to Sunday to preach. Starting from Friday evening, he would arrive at Chek Keng, held Mass after dinner, and arrived at Pak Sha O and Sham Chung at noon on Saturday, and held Mass and Eucharist at the Epiphany of Our Lord Chapel. Finally, Mass was held at Chek Keng, Tai Long and Sai Wan on Sunday. According to the *Catholic Directory*, every Saturday at 12 noon was the time for Mass to be held in Sham Chung Chapel in the 1970s. It was during this time that Rev. McAsey went to Sham Chung Chapel to hold Mass.

Rev. McAsey died in Dublin on 1 March 1992.

Rev. Kerklaan, Gerard, SDB, 1921 – 2005
顧達明神父

Date of Birth	18 November 1921
Ordination	29 June 1949
Arrival in Hong Kong	1949
Date of Death	11 October 2005

Rev. Kerklaan was born in Rotterdam, the Netherlands in 1921, and made a vow in Ugchelen, the Netherlands on 16 August 1943. He had been devoting his life to priesthood and education. After he came to Hong Kong in 1949, he served in the school under the Bosco Charity Association and was ordained as a priest in the same year. Rev. Kerklaan had also served in the Hong Kong Scout Movement for a long time. He served as the brigade commander of the 16th Hong Kong Brigade (St. Louis Secondary School) and founded the 35th Hong Kong Brigade (Hong Kong Tang King Po College). He also served as the leader of the brigade and the priest of the general association. He also accepted and completed the formal and rigorous training of the Scout Leader Wooden Medal. To commend Rev. Kerklaan for his outstanding service in the Scouting Movement, the Association awarded him the Cross of Merit and Honor in 1984.

Rev. Kerklaan prioritised the work of scout pastoral work, and never shirked when the brigade invited him to the camp to host the mass. The most unforgettable event was that he, alone riding a motorcycle, and wearing a neat uniform, went to the camp in the deep mountains of Ting Kok, Tai Po, and the Shek Hang camp in Sai Kung, where he would hold a Mass for the scouts who were camping there at the time, and he had to walk from the trail to the camp, which took about 45 minutes. He did not mind the long journey to the camp to hold Mass for the Catholic Scouts, including the Rosary Chapel in Wong Mo Ying Village. There was still a picture of Rev. Kerklaan in the chapel as a commemoration. After his retirement in 1990, Rev. Kerklaan returned to his hometown in the Netherlands. Although he was not in good health, he still supported the Scout activities. In 2002, he visited Vancouver, Canada from the Netherlands in a wheelchair to join the gatherings with Hong Kong Scouts and members from Salesians of Don Bosco Hong Kong and Macau.

Rev. Kerklaan died on 11 October 2005 in Scheidam, the Netherlands.

Rev. Ruggiero, Nicola, PIME, 1925 – 2012
陸之樂神父

Date of Birth	27 February 1925
Ordination	26 June 1949
Arrival in Hong Kong	14 January 1951
Service in Sai Kung	1976
Date of Death	13 July 2012

Rev. Ruggiero has been serving the Hong Kong Church for 38 years and shepherded Hong Kong immigrants in Canada. He was born in Perugia, Italy on 27 February 1925, and was the fourth among the six brothers and sisters. He was nurtured in the seminary of the PIME, and came to Hong Kong to serve in 1951, when he was 25 years old. After learning Cantonese and English, he was first assigned to the Precious Blood Church in Sham Shui Po (later merged into St. Francis Church) as an assistant parish priest. He served Cheung Chau, Peng Chau and Lantau Island from 1952 to 1963, during the time he established Our Lady of Fatima Church in Cheung Chau. He served in Sham Shui Po St. Francis Church from 1964 to 1969. Since 1969, he has been transferred to the Ss. Cosmas and Damian Church in Tsuen Wan. In 1975, he served in Sai Kung Sacred Heart Church again. He also served as the Supervisor of Catholic schools in Cheung Chau, Sai Kung and Kowloon.

Rev. Ruggiero had an approachable personality and was very popular among parishioners. He had a number of public positions, including a member of the Sai Kung Rural Committee, a consultant to the Home Affairs Department, and supervising a government-sponsored recreational organization. From 1980 to 1985, Rev. Ruggiero served as the Regional Superior of the PIME in Hong Kong, and together with missionaries, they had faced new challenges in the society. He was able to balance different opinions, had a sense of humor, and treated each of his friends sincerely. In 1989, Rev. Ruggiero was sent to Toronto, Canada to pastor the local Chinese immigrants. He served the Chinese Martyrs' True Blessing Church and St. Cao Guiying Church successively, and prepared pastoral facilities for Hong Kong people who immigrated to Canada. Rev. Ruggiero retired due to health problems. In 1998, he was admitted to the nursing home of the PIME in Lecco, Italy. In his later years, he needed a wheelchair to travel. In 1999, he celebrated the golden jubilee of ordination with local bishops, priests and friends in his hometown of Perugia.

Rev. Ruggiero was put to rest in Italy on 13 July 2012, at the age of 87.

Rev. Morlacchi, Paolo, PIME, 1936 – 2016
莫保祿神父

Date of Birth	26 August 1936
Ordination	1961
Arrival in Hong Kong	14 November 1971
Service in Sai Kung	1980 – 1987
Date of Death	24 August 2016

Rev. Morlacchi has been preaching in Hong Kong for 41 years. He was born in Azzano S. Paolo in Bergamo, northern Italy on 26 August 1936, and was ordained as a priest of the Diocese of Bergamo in 1961. After the ordination, he first served in different Italian dioceses, while some of them were in lack of clergymen. He joined the PIME in 1970 and arrived in Hong Kong for the first time on 14 November 1971. He had always said that he wanted to spend his days in the land he loved. In here he had served in the parishes of Sai Kung, Yuen Long, Ho Man Tin, Tsim Sha Tsui and Sha Tin. He was diligent in visiting patients in hospitals. Rev. Morlacchi had a serious traffic accident in 1973 and 1997. These long hospitalization experiences made him more concerned about the plight of the sick.

Rev. Morlacchi passed away on 24 August 2016 at St. Joseph's Home for the Aged in Sheung Shui.

Appendix II | Chronology of Events in Chapels of Sai Kung

Wong Mo Ying Rosary Chapel

1750 -1840	Hakka people settling in Wong Mo Ying.
1870	Evangelisation extended to Wong Mo Ying.
1923	Consecration of Wong Mo Ying Chapel.
1939	Completion of expansion works of Wong Mo Ying Chapel (Rosary Chapel). The Inauguration Ceremony and Mass was held by Bishop Valtorta.
1941	The East River Column's Anti-Japanese Guerrillas stationed as a stronghold in Wong Mo Ying Village.
1942	The guerrillas set up the East River Column Hong Kong and Kowloon Independent Brigade in the chapel.
1944	The village was besieged by Japanese troops. Some villagers were martyred in the chapel.
1970's	The Chapel was gradually abandoned.
1974	Wong Mo Ying Road (later renamed as "Mo Ying Road") opened.
1976	The chapel became a Scouts Activity Centre campsite after being repaired.
2013	The Antiquities Advisory Board of the Hong Kong Special Administrative Region listed the Rosary Chapel as a Grade II historic building.
2018	The Rosary Chapel was returned to the Catholic Diocese of Hong Kong for management.

Sai Wan Star of the Sea Chapel

17th Century	The Lais whose ancestors came from Jiangxi began to settle in Sai Wan.
1910s	Villagers in Sai Wan expressed their wish to become Catholics.
Early 1940s	The villagers of Sai Wan went to the mainland to escape from the war. After the war, they returned to Sai Wan.
Late 1940s	Missionary work extended to Sai Wan.
1949	The first batch of catechumens were baptised in Sai Wan after the war.
1953	Star of the Sea Chapel and School were established in Sai Wan village.
1962	Villagers in Sai Wan suffered heavy losses due to typhoon "Wanda", and the chapel was also seriously destroyed.
1963	Reconstruction of the chapel.
1970s	Most of the villagers in Sai Wan migrated to live and work outside the village.

(cont.)

1990	Star of the Sea Chapel renamed to "Star of the Sea Mass Centre".
1992	Star of the Sea Primary School Closed.

Chek Keng Holy Family Chapel

19th Century	Chek Keng Village was already recorded in the *San On County Chronicles* which was compiled in 1819, Jiaqing period of the Qing Dynasty.
1866	Missionary activities in Chek Keng were started by Rev. Burghignoli.
1867	Chek Keng Holy Family Chapel was established.
1874	Due to typhoon damage, the Holy Family Chapel was rebuilt into a larger chapel.
1879	Apostolic Vicar Bishop Raimondi went to Chek Keng for pastoral visit.
1942	The Holy Family Chapel became the guerrilla base of the East River Column Hong Kong and Kowloon Independent Brigade.
1953	Bishop Bianchi went to Chek Keng for the villagers' confirmation.
1954	Holy Family Chapel was served by the clergy stationed at Tai Po Market Church and under the jurisdiction of Tai Long District.
1980	The Holy Family Chapel was under the jurisdiction of The Immaculate Heart of Mary Church, Tai Po.
1990s	There were only a few residents left in Chek Keng Village. The Holy Family Chapel was developed into a Catholic campsite, and was gradually abandoned afterwards.

Tai Long Immaculate Conception Chapel

1867	The chapel in Tai Long Village was completed, which was the predecessor of the Immaculate Conception Church. Rev. Burghignoli baptised the first batch of believers.
1906	The chapel was damaged by the 1906 typhoon.
1931	Tai Long District was established, and managed by Rev. Francis Wong.
1932	With funding from Bishop Valtorta, Tai Long Chapel was rebuilt. In December, Rev. Francis Wong held the first Mass in the new chapel, and celebrated the feast of Immaculate Conception.
1942	Rev. Francis Wong was murdered.
1954	The Chapel was managed by the priests of the Holy Family Chapel in Chek Keng, and was renamed the "Chapel of the Immaculate Conception".
1957	Reconstruction project of Yuk Ying School was completed.
1960	Bishop Bianchi went to Sai Kung for a pastoral visit, and performed the sacrament of confirmation for Tai Long villagers.

(cont.)

1979	The chapel was damaged during the Typhoon "Hobe", and was rebuilt by the Diocese.
1980	The Tai Long District was abolished, and the chapel was officially transferred to the Tai Po parish.
1981	Bishop John Wu went to Tai Long to preside over the opening ceremony of the restored Chapel of the Immaculate Conception.

Tan Ka Wan St. Peter's Chapel

1865	Rev. Simeone Volonteri and Rev. Gaetano Origo proceeded to various villages in Sai Kung, passing by Tan Ka Wan.
1872	During the visit to Sai Kung villages, Mgr. Raimondi arrived at Tan Ka Wan and established new mission station. At that time, twelve villagers became Catholics.
1873	Tan Ka Wan St. Peter's Chapel was established.
1874	Hong Kong was struck by several typhoon disasters, and the entire Sai Kung including the Tan Ka Wan chapel was damaged.
1875	Bishop Raimondi visited Tan Ka Wan, and pointed out that the roof of the new chapel was blown away by the typhoon.
1880	Another chapel in Tan Ka Wan was built.
1895	Bishop Piazzoli visited Tan Ka Wan during his pastoral visit to Sai Kung.
1908	The Catholic Church signed an agreement with the government to acquire land for building the St. Peter's.
1931	Tai Long District was established. From 1931 to 1941, St. Peter's Chapel in Tan Ka Wan was supervised by Rev. Francis Wong. He held Masses in Tan Ka Wan chapel regularly.
1954	St. Peter's Chapel was under the management of the priest of the Holy Family Chapel in Chek Keng.
1960	Tan Ka Wan Chapel was managed by the priest of Sai Kung District.
1962 -1970	Tan Ka Wan Chapel was managed by the Tai Po District.
1967	Shung Ming School was closed.
1997	The Finnish Mission of the Christian Lutheran Church leased St. Peter's Chapel as Ling Oi Drug Rehabilitation Centre.

Sham Chung Epiphany of Our Lord Chapel

| 1705 | The Lee clan, originally from Po On County, moved to Sham Chung during the Kangxi period. |

(cont.)

1872	Bishop Raimondi visited Sai Kung, accompanied by Rev. Volonteri, Bros Antonius Tam and Fu. One of the stops was Sham Chung.
1874	When Rev. Tam was travelling on a sampan from Ting Kok to Sham Chung, there was a strong wind making he fell into the sea and drowned.
1875	Bishop Raimondi visited Sham Chung on the boat "Star of the Sea".
1879	The old Epiphany of Our Lord Chapel was established. Bishop Raimondi revisited this place.
1892	All villagers of Sham Chung became Catholic.
1908	The land of the chapel was held by Rev. Ferrario as the trustee.
1930	The land of the chapel was held by Rev. Teruzzi as the trustee.
1931	The chapel was under the jurisdiction of Tai Long District.
1942	Rev. Teruzzi was kidnapped by gunmen during his preaching in Tai Tung Village on the opposite bank of Kei Ling Ha Hoi, and was killed and martyred in the sea near Sham Chung.
1946	Rev. Lau Wing Yiu was sent to the Tai Long District to preach, and he was in charge of repairing the chapel.
1948	The government rebuilt the gate embankment and erected the Bridge Gate Stele.
1954	The chapel was managed by the priest of the Holy Family Chapel in Chek Keng, New Territories, which belonged to the Tai Long District.
1956	Reconstruction of the chapel and establishment of Kung Man School.
1958	Villagers such as Lee Yau-yan set up another school, Sham Chung Public School.
1959	The Department of Education and the Catholic Church reached a consensus to establish Sham Chung School.
1960	The chapel was managed by the priest of the Sai Kung parish in the New Territories.
1962	The chapel was managed by the Tai Po District; the Sham Chung Pier was completed. Rev. Santinon began to visit chapels in the Tai Long district, including Sham Chung, Cheung Sheung Mass Centre, etc.
1980	The chapel was under the jurisdiction of the parish of the Immaculate Heart of Mary Church of Tai Po.

Pak Tam Chung Our Lady of the Seven Sorrows Chapel

1830	Wong Fat Sing of Huangcaoling Village, Tam Shui, Wai Chow, Guangdong Province, settled in the village of Sheung Yiu.
1900	Our Lady of the Seven Sorrows Chapel was established.

(cont.)

1905	The government issued the Block Crown Lease, and the owner of the chapel was registered as "Lo Ma Tong".
1908	The owner of the chapel was transferred from "Lo Ma Tong" to the "Apostolic Vicar of the Roman Catholic Church of Hong Kong". Rev. Ferrario was then the trustee of the chapel.
1930	Rev. Teruzzi became the trustee of the chapel on behalf of the Catholic Church of Hong Kong.
1954 & 1956	The chapel was managed by the priest of Sacred Heart Church, Sai Kung, under the Tai Long district.
1955 & 1957 -1979	The chapel belonged to Sai Kung District.
1960s	Rev. Famglietti visited the chapel to celebrate Masses several times a year.
1966 -1974	Rev. Fraccaro and Rev. Lambertoni went to the Our Lady of the Seven Sorrows Chapel to celebrate Masses.
1980	The Chapel was managed by the Sacred Heart Parish Sai Kung. Later it was handed over to the management of the Catholic Scouts of the 117th Brigade of East Kowloon (St. Vincent's Chapel in Wong Tai Sin).

Pak Sha O Immaculate Heart of Mary Chapel

1872	The first batch of the Third Order of the Canossian Daughters of Charity (predecessor of Sisters of the Precious Blood) was sent to Sai Kung villages, including Sham Chung, Pak Sha O, and other villages for a few weeks of preaching.
1880	The Pak Sha O chapel was established.
1882 -1890	Rev. Leong was based in Pak Sha O, and was responsible for missionary work in this area.
1895	Bishop Piazzoli's pastoral visit in Sai Kung areas, including Sham Chung, Pak Sha O, Chek Keng and Tai Long.
1915 -1927	Rev. Teruzzi went to Pak Sha O every few months on foot to visit the villagers and celebrate Masses.
1916	The Immaculate Heart of Mary Chapel in Pak Sha O was established. Bishop Pozzoni officiated at Pak Sha O.
1931	Originally under the jurisdiction of Sai Kung District, the chapels of Sham Chung, Pak Sha O, Chek Keng, and Tai Long were subsumed under Tai Long District.
1931 -1941	The chapel was managed by Rev. Francis Wong. During the period, he visited the villages in the district and celebrated masses in the chapel.

(cont.)

1954	It was named the Holy Spirit Chapel, managed by the priest of the Holy Family Chapel in Chek Keng, New Territories, and under the Tai Long District.
1956	Renamed to the Sacred Heart of Our Lady Chapel, it was still managed by the priest of the Holy Family Chapel in Chek Keng, New Territories.
1960	Renamed again to the Immaculate Heart of Mary Chapel, and was then managed by the priests of the Catholic Church in Tai Po Market.
1980 -1998	Belonged to the parish of the Immaculate Heart of Mary Church of Tai Po.

Long Ke Nativity of Our Lady Chapel

1918	The chapel was established.
1954 & 1956	Managed by the priest of Sai Kung Sacred Heart Church, and was under Tai Long District.
1955 & 1957-1966	Managed by Sai Kung Sacred Heart Church, and was under Sai Kung Sacred Heart District.
1968	The Operation Dawn applied to the government to acquire the chapel in Long Ke as its venue, and Pastor Paul Chan established here the first evangelical drug rehabilitation village in Hong Kong.
1976	The Operation Dawn has been allocated by the government the Town Island, as the permanent base. The site of Long Ke and the chapel have been abandoned again.
1980	The Pastor who founded the Christian Mutual Love Centre proposed to Sai Kung District Office to establish the Wu Oi Drug Rehabilitation Village (now renamed as the Male Adult Training Centre) at the chapel premises.

Leung Shuen Wan Lung Shuen Wan Chapel

1910	Lung Shuen Wan Chapel was established, under Tai Long District.
1954 & 1956	Managed by the priest of Sacred Heart Church, Sai Kung.
1955 & 1957-1979	Renamed as Lung Shun Wan Mission Centre, under the Sai Kung District.
1980	Managed by Sacred Heart Church, Sai Kung, and belonged to the Sacred Heart Church, Sai Kung Parish.

Epilogue and Acknowledgements

"Follow the Missionary Footsteps with an Evangelising Heart" was the advice given to pilgrims by Cardinal John Tong Hon, Bishop Emeritus of the Diocese of Hong Kong, when the Catholic Diocese of Hong Kong Diocesan Working Committee for "Following Thy Way" was established. On the path of the pioneering missionaries, we would find abandoned stones on the road or abandoned by their owners. Have we ever thought about what Jesus had said:

"The stone that the builders rejected has become the cornerstone; this was the Lord's doing, and it is amazing in our eyes"

— Matthew 21:42

Why does "the stone that the builders reject" became "the cornerstone"? According to the Teaching of St. Paul, the Church is "built upon the foundation of the apostles and prophets, with Jesus Christ himself as the cornerstone" (Ephesians 2:20), so Jesus established the Holy Church for those who believe in Him as the cornerstone. We should take good care of this huge building, so that when pilgrims enter the sanctuary, sing praises of the Goodness and Mercy of the Lord, and thank the Lord for helping the weak and restraining the strong.

We hope that we can gain strength in the process of evangelizing the footprints of the pioneering missionaries, and work together to move towards a bright future for Hong Kong.

In the process of writing this book, "Following Thy Way Historical Research Group" received valuable assistance, support and encouragement of many priests, sisters, men and women religious congregations, organsations, educational institutions, professors and friends from all walks of life. We would especially want to thank two PIME spiritual directors, one is Rev. Mario Marazzi and the other is Rev. Raja Duggimpudi. Rev. Mario Marazzi, who just celebrated 60 years of missionary priesthood in 2020, is our tutor in foreign languages, in particular, Italian and Latin. He has assisted us in the translation of a considerable number of PIME and diocesan documents, and has also enabled us to find useful materials in the library and archives of PIME. The information not only gave us an in-depth understanding of the aspects of the missionaries in Sai Kung, but also allowed us to understand the importance of their history; Rev. Raja Duggimpudi showed us a lot of the archives, letters and school records of the Sacred Heart Church in Sai Kung, especially the historical photos of Rev. Fraccaro and Rev. Lambertoni from the 1960s and 1970s which brought us much closer to the life and feelings of the priests and villagers at that time. In addition, I would like to thank the Hong Kong Catholic Diocesan Archives for allowing us to use and reproduce the historical archives and photos of the Sai Kung Mission and chapels for publication purposes, which will further our work in the conservation of the history of the Sai Kung Catholic Mission. Immaculate Heart of Mary Church in Tai Po also lent out various old photos and photos of pilgrims visiting the historic chapels around the millennium, so that we can better understand the conditions of the chapel at that time. I would also like to express my sincere thanks to the following organisations (in alphabetical order):

Antiquities and Monuments Office
Basel Mission Archives
Catholic Asian News (UCAN)
Catholic Centre
Catholic Truth Society of Hong Kong
Caritas Hong Kong
Centre for Catholic Studies, The Chinese University of Hong Kong
Church of St. Benedict, Sha Tin
Fat Kee Store
Heung Yee Kuk N. T.
Holy Spirit Seminary College of Theology & Philosophy
Hong Kong Catholic Diocesan Archives
Hong Kong Central Library
Hong Kong Museum of History
Hung On-To Memorial Library, The University of Hong Kong
Immaculate Heart of Mary Church, Tai Po

Information Service Department

Kung Kao Po

Legion of Mary, Our Lady of China Church, Tai Kok Tsui

Operation Dawn

PIME Asia News

Pontifical Institute for Foreign Missions (P.I.M.E)

Public Records Office, Government Records Service

Sacred Heart Church, Sai Kung

Sai Kung North Rural Committee

Sai Kung Sung Tsun Catholic School (Secondary Section)

Shum Chung Manor

Sisters of the Precious Blood

St. Paul Media Centre

Talentum Bookshop

Tao Fong Shan Christian Centre

The Hong Kong Institute of Asia-Pacific Studies, The Chinese University of Hong Kong

University Library, The Chinese University of Hong Kong

Valtorta College

Wu Oi Christian Centre ELCHK, Ling Oi Centre

Last but not the least, the editorial committee is most grateful for the following priests, nuns, teachers and friends in the assistance of writing and translation of the book:

Rev. Chan Kwok-fai, David

Mr. Chan Kwok-on

Ms. Sally Chan

Ms. Eddith Chin

Rev. Raja Duggimpudi

Rev. Ip Po-lam, Martin

Prof. Kwok Siu-tong

Ms. Rosa Lai

VR. Lai Yan

VR. Lai Yuk-yue

Prof. Lau Yee-cheung

Mr. Lam

Ms. Celine Lam

Ms. Maria Lam

Ms. Lam Tsun

VR. Lee Chun-fai

VR. Lee Kwok-on

Mr. Lee Wai-kwong

Ms. Agnes Leung

Mr. Leung King-wai, John

Ms. Li Yun Tsung

Sr. Luigia Mindassi

Ms. Ng Siu-han, Constance

Rev. Noh Hyun-chul, Isaac

Ms. Pauline Poon

VR. Sit Bo

Ms. Susanna Siu

Rev. Sergio Ticozzi

Mr. Herman Tsang

Mr. Wong Hon-chung, John

Mr. Wong Koon Lun

VR. Wong Shue-kei

Sr. Yu Suk Ching

Dr. Yuen Mee-yin, Mary

Bibliography

Catholic Archives

Archives of Sisters of the Precious Blood.

Archives of the Sacred Congregation of Propaganda Fide, Rome.

Hong Kong Catholic Diocesan Archives.

PIME, *Hong Kong Regional Archives.*

PIME, *Le Missioni Cattoliche* (Vol. II,IV,VII,XV,XVI,XVIII,XX,XXI,XXIII,XXIV,XXVII,XXIX) (1895,1896,1913 – 1916).

Register of Baptisms, Vicar General's Office, Catholic Diocese of Hong Kong.

Repertoire des members de la societe des Missions Etrangeres 1659 – 2004, Archives de Missions Etrangeres (Paris, 2004).

Catholic Publications

Catholic Diocese of Hong Kong — Annual Report (Hong Kong: Catholic Diocese of Hong Kong).

Monita and Missionarios Vicariatus Hongkonensis (Hong Kong: Typis Reformatorii S. Aloysii, 1877).

Government Archives

政府檔案處。《銘新學校，新界赤徑》。原檔案編號：NT913/60C。現存檔案編號：HKRS 943-2-95。

政府檔案處。西貢（北）區宗族歷史。原檔案編號：N.T.6/442/56。現存檔案編號：HKRS 634-1-9。

地政總署測繪處。丈量約份 297 號，年份：自 1905 年起。區域：大埔。

AMO, Record of Historical Buildings/Historic Building Appraisal: Pak Tam Chung, Long Ke, Sai Wan, Tan Ka Wan, High Island/Leung Shuen Wan.

Return of the Number of Churches, Chapels: 1910,1917,1920,1930,1939.

Hong Kong Cadastral Survey Record.

Hong Kong Gazette Plan.

Hong Kong Government Gazette.

Hong Kong Government Rates Book.

The Land Registry, Government Lease.

Schedule of Crown Lessees: Kei Ling Ha, Wo Mei, Siu Tong San Tsuen, Cheung Sheung, Pak A, Tai Long, Chek Keng, Pak Sha O, Wong Mo Ying, Pak Tam Chung, Long Ke, Tan Ka Wan, High Island/Leung Shuen Wan, Ko/Kau Lau Wan.

Hong Kong Sessional Papers.